The Novel and The Novelist
An Insider's Guide to the Craft

TOM MORRISEY

◢Blue Corner
Belle Isle, Florida

Copyright

Blue Corner Creations, Inc.
Belle Isle, FL 32812-3706

First printing: January, 2014

ISBN-13: 978-0615960340 (Blue Corner)
ISBN-10: 0615960340

# # #

Grateful acknowledgement is made to **Bethany House Publishers**, a division of Baker Publishing Group, for rights to reprint previously published material:

In High Places, by Tom Morrisey, © copyright 2007 by Blue Corner Creations, Inc. Used by permission.

Pirate Hunter, by Tom Morrisey, © copyright 2009 by Blue Corner Creations, Inc. Used by permission.

Wind River, by Tom Morrisey, © copyright 2008 by Blue Corner Creations, Inc. Used by permission.

# # #

Author represented by the literary agency of
Alive Communications, Inc.
7680 Goddard Street (Suite 200)
Colorado Springs, Colorado 80920
http://www.alivecommunications.com

Visit Tom Morrisey's website at
www.tommorrisey.com

Interact at:
http://novelandnovelist.blogspot.com/
www.twitter.com/MorriseyWriting
Facebook: Tom Morrisey Novelists

Dedication

Right about the time that I first considered the need for a book such as this, I received word that my longtime literary agent—and, more importantly, my very good friend—had been diagnosed with a grade IV glioblastoma: a highly malignant form of brain tumor.

He underwent an aggressive surgery that involved the removal of a significant portion of his frontal cortex and, two years later, gave every indication of having recovered completely. Even with only part of a brain, he remained smarter, more articulate and funnier than me, and he even resumed a favorite annual tradition: climbing Pike's Peak, the beautiful mountain that fills the horizon from his family-room window.

Then, just as I was completing this work, he wrote to tell me that his cancer had returned. Its progress was rapid, and he passed away three months later.

As I refer to him in the present tense several times in this book, I opened my manuscript to make the necessary revisions ... and found that I could not bring myself to do it; I could not speak of him in the past tense. So I left things as they were.

And perhaps this is more appropriate. After all, I know in my heart of hearts that he still lives.

This book, then, is for Lee Hough. I miss you every day, buddy, and I'll see you when the trumpet sounds. — TM

Contents

If there's a book you

really want to read

but it hasn't

been written yet,

then you

must write it.

TONI MORRISON

| Before We Begin...

APPEARANCES ASIDE, the phrase, "unselfish novelist" is not, and should not be, an oxymoron.

I don't know what it was that caused J.D. Salinger to publish *The Catcher in the Rye* and then bury himself in Cornish, New Hampshire for the rest of his life, surfacing only to file lawsuits. I only know that when I feel reticent about discussing my work, self-consciousness lies at the root. Reading a novel takes several hours—hours that my readers will never get back—and I wonder ... was what I put on paper really worthy of their investment?

They could, after all, have spent that tiny yet irreplaceable fraction of their lives doing so many other worthwhile things.

They could have taken a nap.

But enough people have written to me about my books to keep me writing more of them. And my ability to keep writing is due in large part to the investment made in me by others along the way.

There was Gwendolyn Brooks; she visited when I was at The University of Toledo, read her work and said it was time to hear from the audience. No other hands went up, so I stood and shared a poem that I was working on, reciting it from memory, and as I did, her eyes sparkled and she clapped the heels of her hands together, as if I had just presented her with the most marvelous and thoughtful gift possible.

It was the first time I shared my work in public, and that experience convinced me it is not literature until it is shared.

I interviewed the poet and novelist Howard McCord for the PBS radio affiliate in Toledo, Ohio, and afterward he told me I needed to apply to a writing program, and invited me to try his. That brought me to Bowling Green State University, where Phillip F. O'Connor was my thesis advisor and my friend, willing to discuss fiction either in his office in the afternoons, or long into the night, over the ruins of a dinner.

While I was at Bowling Green, James Baldwin was there as well, first as a writer in residence and later as a visiting professor in the Department of Ethnic Studies.

He wasn't even in my department, and the two of us could not have been more different: he a giant of late twentieth-century literature, New-York smart, African-American-hip and wise with years; I a white rube from the Midwest, still wet behind the ears.

Yet he treated me as an equal, and told me that his first name was not "Doctor" or "Professor" or even "sir"—it was "Jimmy." He read my work, commented on it, and we talked about writing, rambling conversations that would begin on-campus and end at a pizza place downtown.

It was Baldwin who taught me that storytelling was an oral tradition, that until work sounded right to the ears it was not ready for life on paper, and that time at the keyboard—a typewriter keyboard back then—should be an act of recollection, and not an act of creation.

The list goes on.

Michael Mott taught me to think, even when writing prose, with a poet's economy. I only met Gary Snyder twice, nearly three decades before he won the Pulitzer Prize, but those two meetings were enough to remind me that the background from whence I had sprung was only a narrow and relatively recent slice of the world's great cultural feast.

Jim Harrison sent me some notes that convinced me to write what I love (as well as teaching me that the better of the Jamaican Pickapeppa sauces was absolutely the red one).

And Albert Lee—a nonfiction writer with a fiction-writer's heart—convinced me that good artists should never starve, and I owed it to myself to at very least make a living from the words I set on paper.

So I laid my foundation with the help of entire legions of writers.

These days, I stay in touch (and oftentimes correspond daily) with a wide circle of novelists and others who collectively have forgotten more about writing than I could ever hope to learn in several lifetimes. And I am constantly running, however briefly, into others—the novelist Peter Ho Davies and playwright David Henry Hwang are two recent examples—happy to talk craft and help me keep the work-lights burning.

I feel, then, that I owe a debt.

In an attempt to discharge it, I've gone to book festivals and writing conferences, teaching workshops over the years, operating on the principle that, if I can at least spare someone else the mistakes I made—for, despite all my mentors, the mistakes were many—then maybe I can help them arrive at the good part of writing, the productive part, and spare them having to go through at least some of the preliminaries and angst.

Early on, I taught mostly workshops on elements that were of the most pressing interest to me at the moment—things such as writing realistic dialogue, or how to work with a copy editor.

Some of the writers in my classes appreciated these, and I like to think that most did. After all, that was how the sessions were advertised and, by delivering, I felt I was upholding my end of the deal.

But in every class, there was at least one writer, and sometimes several, who listened with a level of disengagement that bordered on pleading. And when I look back on those earlier workshops now, I understand where that came from.

These were writers who had a vision. They could picture books: novels with their names on the covers. They wanted to know how to make that dream a reality.

And the silent message they'd been sending me was, "Dialogue is nice, and I'd like to get one day to a point where interaction with a copywriter is necessary, but for right now what I really want to know is … How do I *do* this? What goes into it and how do I start? How do I *write a novel*?"

To those who have been writing publishable book-length fiction, the answer to those questions might seem obvious. After all, it's right there on the pages of our books.

But reading a novel and writing one are two very different things. Just because you can drive a car doesn't mean that you have the background and the insight to design one.

And I understand where those writers are coming from, because years ago—nearer, it seems, than the calendar may indicate—I was one of them.

So how does one make the leap?

"There are three rules for the writing of a novel," Somerset Maugham supposedly once said. "Unfortunately, no one knows what they are."

That statement rings true because the novel is a category, and not a specific form. What works well for literary fiction may not even make it to the starting blocks for popular romance. There is even a great gulf of difference between such seeming cousins as mysteries, thrillers, suspense and crime novels. And the novel is continually morphing and changing as new novelists come onto the scene and breathe into it elements and possibilities that were never there before.

Still, there are some generalities that will hold true from one book to the next, and what differences there are can be examined and explained. If even a chink of that sort of light can be admitted onto the subject, it is certainly better than fumbling about in the dark. And heaven knows, when I was first starting out in this, I spent more than my share of hours in that darkness.

This, then, is the book I wish someone had written for me back in the day. If you are wondering where one begins, and how, and what one should consider with each fresh element, then this is the book for you. You'll learn enough to think constructively, and you'll know enough to ask good questions, and it is shorter than my typical novel, so it won't take that long to read. I have kept it that way because I am still conscious of the time you are investing as a reader, and the fact that, even though this particular book is about the novel, and not a novel itself, you're still missing that nap.

Book One of this work—"The Novel"—is a nuts-and-bolts journey into how a piece of book-length fiction comes together. Because the journey from theory to application can sometimes seem diffuse, I have also included in Book One, where applicable, case studies based upon one particular novel that I wrote a few years ago. And while I'll use other examples as well, I'll come back to that one book frequently, so you can see how the bits all went together.

I'll admit I had some hesitance about doing this. In his interview with *The Paris Review*, Ernest Hemingway said:

"In company with people of your own trade you ordinarily speak of other writers' books. The better the writers the less they will speak about what they have written themselves."

Like much of what Hemingway said to interviewers, there is a lot of baloney in this. Hemingway frequently spoke about what he had written. You can go online today and find a carefully prepared audio recording of him describing the writing of his play, "The Fifth Column."

Still, baloney or not, it carries a hint of truth. Talking about one's own work feels a lot like pulling out the baby pictures. But I think there are places where it is fine to talk something you have written. The workshop is one of them, and a work such as this is another. So, with that demon expelled, let me tell you about that one particular book.

It is a novel called *In High Places*, written within the last decade. I've selected it as my case-in-point because, although it was published and well reviewed and even a finalist for an international award, I originally wrote it without a contract or a deadline hanging over it. I wrote it for the joy of writing it and, as it was a work of the heart and not of the assembly line, I remember each piece well—what I was thinking at the time, the challenges and the opportunities posed in the process, and how I approached each one.

This is not to say that you must read *In High Places* to make sense of what you're reading here. You don't; in the few cases where an excerpt is necessary to illustrate something, I've included it.

But if you'd care to read that novel nonetheless, another reason I've selected *In High Places* is because it is available and should remain indefinitely so on all the major e-book platforms, it is still sold in either hardcover or paperback in many bookstores, and it appears to be carried by any number of libraries, so it's not that hard to find.

And, of course, the corollary to all of this is that, if you *do* intend to read *In High Places* sometime, and you'd rather not have the novel utterly and completely spoiled beforehand, then you'd probably better set this book aside right now, and go read that one first.

Book Two of this work—"The Novelist"—looks at the habits, care and feeding of the person doing the work. Writing book-length fiction is an endurance sport; if you don't want to blow up in the first half-mile, you have to train for it. Doing that will help you avoid the mistakes that seem obvious and elementary in retrospect.

It's important enough that I was tempted to make it Book One, but I know writers well enough to understand the hunger for the nuts and bolts, so I'll satisfy that first.

Once again—and out of deference to my publishers, who are playing along with this madness and have granted permission for an obscene number of pull-quotes—if you want the experience of reading my novel, *In High Places*, without stepping into the backstage regions and having the ending and several other elements spoiled, now is the time. Close this book now, and go read it.

Still here?

That's settled, then; let's get started.

Book One

The Novel

| ONE: Time, Place and Focus

Don't tell me the moon is shining; show me the glint of light on broken glass. — ANTON CHEKOV

IT ALL BEGAN at 7-Eleven.

This was back in the summer of 2000. My daughter was nine years old then—nine going very quickly on ten—and she was collecting the state quarters, which is to say that, actually, *I* was the one collecting the quarters. When I found one she needed, I would set it aside, give it to her when I got home, and that evening we would press it into a collector's book made of thick gray cardboard covered with faux blue leather.

I cannot remember whether the stop at 7-Eleven was for gas or junk food, although I suspect it was the latter, because I paid with cash and was sorting through my change on the short walk back to the truck, when I found it—not any of the state quarters we were looking for, but a Bicentennial quarter, from 1976.

You know the one I'm talking about: the quarter with a Revolutionary War drummer on the back. Everybody called him the "drummer boy," although when I look at one of the quarters now—I have one next to the keyboard as I write this—I see that the drummer is a grown man with arms the size of Arnold Schwarzenegger's in his prime.

They must have minted those quarters by the boatload that year, because I still see them in my change every so often.

But at the time I hadn't seen one in quite a while, and discovering that coin was a trip back in time.

For me, 1976 was a seminal year: the year I graduated from college, and the year I had my first successes as a freelance writer.

I had no novels back then, but I was beginning to break into the magazines, writing several feature stories for local titles and the occasional shorter piece for a national publication. It was a year of victories, a year of great beginnings.

For the nation, the feeling was oddly similar. The Bicentennial celebrated the two-hundredth birthday of America, but somehow the event made us all feel brand-new ... younger. From tall-ship pageantry to the movement to restore Ellis Island and the Statue of Liberty, it was as if an entire society was catching its collective breath and starting over.

Businesses celebrated by making everything red-white-and-blue. And if memory serves me correctly, at least half of those re-white-and-blue things also smelled like lemons; lemon was the marketing fragrance of that year.

So: 1975 or 1977? Not much comes to mind when I think back to them. But 1976? I remember it clearly, especially the summer after my college graduation. And the more I inspected that quarter and thought about it, the more I thought about writing a novel that would be set mostly during that summer of 'Seventy-Six.

Going Back

In 1976, I was living in Toledo, Ohio, in a big, white Italianate house in a section of town known as the Old West End. It was favored by university people—teachers, students and shoestring-budget artsy types—although, because of details such as stained-glass sidelights and parquet floors, the old homes were slowly being reclaimed by the gentry.

I was not one of the gentry.

I also did not spend a lot of time at home that year. I had a new passion—rock climbing—and had been researching what would become my first book: a nonfiction travelogue of American mountaineering. I was doing it on a student's budget, so my research involved a lot of vagabonding, bumming rides and sharing a rickety old VW Alpine microbus with friends, heading off to all the places I wanted to feature in the book.

One place I kept coming back to was Seneca Rocks.

Seneca is in West Virginia, about a nine-hour drive from where I lived back then. I could always find two or three friends who wanted to head there for a few days, and it was a good place to keep my climbing skills sharp and relax a bit before beginning graduate school in the fall.

More than that, 1976 was Seneca's moment.

The early to mid 'Seventies were the culmination of a golden age of rock climbing, an era when climbers all over North America were pushing the envelope, and a time when the sport was—and I realize this seems like an odd word to describe an outdoor pursuit—*pure*. There were no climbing gyms to speak of in those days; climbers climbed on rock. And climbers then operated according to a code of ethics that virtually amounted to a religion. Rock climbing was a close-knit community, and those who deviated from its standards were shunned.

Seneca itself was different in 1976.

The giant rock formation had a distinctive thirty-foot pinnacle in its center—the Gendarme—that has long since fallen away. The town at its base was later altered forever by a flood that literally scoured away several landmarks.

And even the name of that small town has changed: today, it is called "Seneca Rocks," but in 1976 it was called "Mouth of Seneca," named for Seneca Creek, which had its terminus (or "mouth") at the spot where the tiny village was built.

Thirty years removed from these memories, I kept that quarter, looked at it over the next few days, and pondered all those things.

The time and the texture were compelling, and I gradually decided I was going to write a novel that would take place principally at Seneca Rocks during the summer of 1976, and would revolve around the world of rock climbing. I did not have a character, a purpose or a plot, but I had time and place and focus, and that was enough to get me started.

Starting with Setting

Time, place and focus (or area of activity) constitute the setting for a book, and I believe that most, if not all, novelists find the genesis for their work in a setting—at least the time and place elements.

I know I'll get argument on this point. There are authors who insist that they begin with character, or plot, but the fact is that characters and plot don't play well in a vacuum; they require a stage. While it may be subliminal, writers concoct some semblance of that stage before they begin to people it with characters and saturate it with story. Setting may not be the most pivotal element of a novel, but it is almost always the part that comes first.

By choosing Seneca and the golden age of climbing, I did something I often do—I decided to give my book an exotic setting.

By "exotic," I don't necessarily mean far-off or culturally oblique. I simply mean that most readers will not be familiar with it. After all, most people have never climbed a rock and never will. Many have never been to West Virginia, and among those who have, a significant number have never been to Seneca Rocks—far from the interstates and so well off the beaten path.

The Unfamiliar

There is an issue to using a setting that will be unfamiliar to most readers; the writer has to invest more into setting it up. If I say "Washington, D.C.," a specific image probably pops into your head. But when I say, "Seneca Rocks," you may very well draw a blank, even though Seneca lies less than 160 road-miles from Washington.

So when I tell you about Seneca, I have to place you there, and to do that, I must describe it for you.

This can be a blessing, rather than a curse. By starting with a relatively blank slate, I can concentrate on those details that heighten my story, and leave out all the distractions. When I describe Seneca Rocks, I can paint a picture: a castle-like, mist-shrouded rock formation smudged with the occasional dots of bushes and trees … a place with all the beauty of a classical Japanese painting. I can paint that picture, and you will see it.

From atop the rock, I can show you row after row of lush, forested hills, fading to the blue mist of distance, and you will feel the beauty of the image.

Just Enough

Now, back to ... shortly after I found that quarter.

As I thought about where all this was heading, I knew that even setting the novel within a sport as esoteric as rock climbing could also be an asset, rather than a liability, provided I did not go overboard and try to turn my novel into a textbook. People like to learn new things, as long as it doesn't feel like school.

And I knew where the boundaries of "overboard" were.

A few years before I started work on my Seneca story, I wrote a novel called *Turn Four*, set within the world of NASCAR auto racing. My editor on that book was a good friend, Dave Lambert, and, as was my custom, I sent him the first chapter, which took place from the point of view of a driver doing his warm-up laps and then starting a race.

I'd done my homework. I had read a lot about NASCAR. I'd gone behind the scenes at the races and watched teams in the pits. I'd even visited some of the shops where the racecars were fabricated, and talked with the people who built them. So I knew my subject inside and out, and I was proud of that accomplishment. I poured everything I knew into that initial chapter, right down to describing the interior and exterior diameters of the roll-cage tubing.

And Dave, after reading that chapter, wrote me an email that said, "Tom, your readers only have to understand that it's a racecar; they're never going to be called upon to actually build one."

Which was Dave's very diplomatic way of telling me that, if I kept on the way I was going, I was going to bore my readers to death.

The process of giving readers the background information about a story and its setting is known as "exposition." The beginning of every story will contain a certain amount of exposition—it's the opening element in the rising and dropping storyline that writers refer to as the "narrative arc." But the key is to deliver it in a natural and unobtrusive manner.

Dave reminded me that, when you're working within an exotic environment, the trick is to provide your readers with just enough information to see and feel the setting and move the story forward—and no more.

And the key is that, if you reach a point where you ask yourself, "Am I providing too much background?" ... then, almost certainly, you are.

Dreams

Another advantage of an exotic setting is that many of them are aspirational. By this, I mean that they are the sorts of places that people dream about visiting—the sorts of places they will read about and save for years in order to visit for a week. So by setting a novel in one of those places, I give those readers a free (or nearly free) trip to a place that they have been dreaming about ... I figure the exotic setting makes the book more desirable.

Operating on this premise, I have set novels, or significant portions of novels, in the Bahamas, on the Yucatan Peninsula, in Bermuda and the British Virgin Islands. I've put my characters in London and Washington, DC. I've described them driving A-1A along the Intracoastal Waterway in Florida, and Highway 1 down the California coast.

There is a caveat here, and that is, if you choose to set your novel someplace exotic, it still needs to ring true with those readers who have either been there or otherwise have great familiarity with the setting. So you will be miles ahead of the game if you physically go to the place where your book is set, and experience it yourself.

I proved the value of this when I was working on my fourth novel, a book called *Dark Fathom*, much of which was going to be set on Bermuda. When I began the novel, I hadn't been to Bermuda yet, but I'd read a few articles—enough to get the lay of the land. And when my character arrived on Bermuda, I had him travel from his airport to the hotel the same way that I would normally get around in a new place: I had him rent a car.

I even described the novelty of driving a car from the right-hand side, something I'd experienced personally only a few months before in the Cayman Islands. I thought it was a clever detail.

Then I got to Bermuda and discovered that there are no rental cars there. None. Not at the airport and not in the entire country.

Bermuda, it turns out, has extremely restrictive laws concerning automobiles.

To keep the small nation's roads from becoming a gridlocked nightmare, even residents are limited to one car per household, regardless of how many people there are in the family. Tourists get around using motor scooters, taxis, or a remarkably easy-to-understand bus system (if the bus stop has a pink pole, the bus is headed toward Hamilton—the capitol—and if the bus stop has a blue pole, the bus is headed away from Hamilton and toward the sea).

This means that, if I put my character in a rental car, I would have had him getting around Bermuda in a mode of transportation that did not exist.

Reasonable Suspension of Disbelief

This may not seem like that big a deal. A novel is a work of fiction, not a guidebook, and novelists have, by definition, license to make things up.

But when the novel is set in a location that actually exists, that license has limitations.

In nonfiction and specifically in the essay, there exists something called "the contract with the reader." Essentially, this says that the reader has the right to believe that everything the essayist says is true.

Fiction, in general, contains no such contract. So, if you are J.R.R. Tolkien and you choose to set your novel in a place called "Middle Earth," and populate it with hobbits, you are absolutely free to do so. It doesn't matter that the setting does not exist.

But if you decide to set your novel in a place called "Columbus, Ohio," and if your novel takes place in the same world that the reader lives in, and not in some parallel universe … then the Columbus you describe had better sound passingly familiar to anyone who's ever been there.

I say this because of another principle closely related to "the contract with the reader"—a principle called "reasonable suspension of disbelief."

Under reasonable suspension of disbelief, the reader agrees to enter into the world of the novel and live there a while, as long as the writer does nothing to jar the reader out of that place. And for a reader who has been to Bermuda, or knows something about it, a character renting a car is an action that would jar them. It creates a "this writer doesn't know what he/she is talking about" sort of speed bump, and it might be enough of a bump to convince the reader to set the novel down and never come back. Then, in this Internet-connected world, that reader may also register an opinion with a few hundred friends.

Time Machines

The issues are compounded when the exotic setting that you are working with no longer exists.

I've run into this a couple of times. For my novel *Deep Blue*, I had a backstory set in Civil-War-era Florida—very different from contemporary settings in the rest of the Deep South—and I had to do a fair amount of reading to get the texture right.

For another novel, *Pirate Hunter*, I set my contemporary story in modern-day Key West (easy to research—I've been there more times than I can count), told against a historical story that takes place on and around pirate ships in the British Virgin Islands of the eigthteenth century, as well as the Outer Banks of what is now North Carolina.

Now, the eigthteenth century is not someplace I can visit. And most of what we "know" about pirate ships from popular culture is wrong; they were not the galleon-like ships captained by Johnny Depp in the movies—for the most part, they were small, fast, highly maneuverable sloops.

So I interviewed British Virgin Island historians and then visited historic sites in the islands, looking at harbors and shorelines and imagining what they looked like long before any of the area was developed. I visited the Crystal Coast of North Carolina and spent a few days with the leading living authority on the pirate Blackbeard, and I accompanied a university team in research dives on the wreck of the *Queen Anne's Revenge* (Blackbeard's pirate ship).

And I read history after regional history of both areas and the times; it's safe to assume that, for every word I wrote about those places, I read several hundred.

Suddenly, working in the genre of science fiction or fantasy sounds extremely attractive, doesn't it?

But the truth is that, even in speculative fiction, writers need to adhere to any ground rules they establish earlier in the work. If the atmosphere of the world in your book doesn't have oxygen, but a character stranded at night decides to start a fire—which requires oxygen to burn—that's going to bother some people.

The opposite of the exotic setting is the familiar setting, and this, too, comes in two flavors.

The Stock Event

One type of familiar setting is a setting that most of us have experienced at some time in our lives. High school, a company office, the passenger compartment of an airliner—we've all been there, done that, and can relate. Just the barest amount of description can take us well into the setting and keep us there.

Some specific events come with their own expectations as far as settings go. Graduations, births, deaths, weddings... all of these have major impact on our lives, but are so ubiquitous that the writers-workshop expression for such a thing is a "stock event"— everybody has them, and because of that, it doesn't take much at all to set the stage and progress into story.

This is probably why there are so many movies set around weddings, or funerals... or both.

Icons

The other general type of familiar setting is that which we have become so accustomed to through news media, films, television shows or popular stories that we can immediately "fill in the blanks" when presented with it.

Here's an example: a California diner catering to high school students in the 'Fifties.

You may never have lived in California and you may not have even been born when the 'Fifties rolled around, but this setting has been presented so often in popular media that, just thinking about it, you can see the booths and vinyl-topped stools, the crew cuts and poodle skirts, the cuffed-up blue jeans and tough guys with their pompadours and black leather jackets. You hear the rock-and-roll coming from the jukebox, and smell the burgers cooking on the grill.

A Midwestern farm: you can see the red barn and the green tractor, smell the fresh air, hear the breeze rustling the rows of corn, even if you grew up in the Bronx.

And never mind that most farms don't have barns anymore; in the mind's eye, they all do.

One issue with these sorts of settings is that we have seen them so often in popular culture that they all too easily become a pastiche of themselves. But they do have the merit of allowing you to move quickly into the story.

The Historic

Another type of setting that allows you to move quickly into the story is the setting that points to a specific time and place in history. Pearl Harbor on December 7, 1941 does that, as does Philadelphia on July 4, 1776. So does New York City on September 11, 2001.

When James Cameron pitched his film *Titanic* to Fox Pictures executives, all he had to do was open a book and show them a painting of the great ocean liner sinking, every light ablaze, and they immediately "got it" as far as setting was concerned.

But as Celine Dion is rumored to have said when she was approached to sing the theme song for *Titanic*, "How can they make a movie out of it? Everyone knows the ship sinks."

And that's the thing with these moment-in-history settings. The reader already knows the outcome of the overarching historical event, so your job as a writer is to create a story that is a counterpoint to that outcome, and possibly use the reader's foreknowledge of outcome to create a deeper emotional sense, be it light or dark.

For instance, in *Dark Fathom*, I have a character trapped in a stairwell in one of the towers of the World Trade Center on September 11, 2001. Firemen are struggling to reach her, and the tension is heightened by the reader's certain knowledge that, within minutes, the tower is going to collapse. The question that keeps the reader turning the page is whether the character is going to be rescued before the tower falls.

This timeless device is called "anticipation." It worked in *Macbeth*, it works when someone you love is due to arrive on the next plane, and it worked every Christmas morning when you were small.

Better still, it is not bound in by culture; everybody in the world understands it and can relate.

The Atmospheric

Similar to the moment-in-history setting are settings that place the reader at an event that does not have a definitive outcome. Chicago during the Columbian Exposition of 1892 is one example of this—it was a world's fair sort of event that ushered in a changing of the technological guard, making lavish use of electrical lighting at a time when many homes were still illuminated by oil lamps, and highlighting mechanical power at a time when the average person traveled by horse. That, plus the otherworldly appearance of the event—it made lavish use of epic architecture and building materials that were white in color—made this a historical event with a profound sense of time and place, and several very good novels, prize-worthy novels, have been set in Chicago during the exposition.

Place as Personality

James A. Michener was a novelist who took setting to new heights, positioning place as the one consistent element in his books and making readers think about location the way they usually think about characters. In novels such as *Hawaii* and *The Source*, no character present at the beginning of the story is still alive at the end of it, and this is a hallmark of the modern-day American saga—it tells stories not over a span of seasons or lifetimes, but of generations.

Years ago, I was fortunate enough to spend an entire day with Michener in Austin, Texas, interviewing him for a magazine piece. As a young writer just beginning to work with character-based stories, my mind reeled at the thought of writing novels in which the narrative arc of the novel would be completed by the descendants of the people who started the story out, so I asked him why he wrote that way.

"I don't think of myself as a novelist,' Michener told me. "I think of myself as an educator, and I use the stories to teach."

That, then, may be a question you want to consider as you consider potential settings for your novel: what resonant element do you want to leave readers with once they've reached the conclusion of your novel?

Do you want them to have greater understanding of something they may have thought they understood at the outset? Do you want them to have empathy for a character, to understanding something about that character that they did not understand when they began the book? Or are you looking for a bit of both?

The setting you select will have an influence on all of these things.

And the setting can be another reason for the reader to fall head-over-heels for your book. Some settings can do that. Some places—Paris is one of them—have the ability to make you fall in love again, even if you go there by yourself.

That's powerful. And you can use that.

Putting Things in Perspective

Be careful, though. In setting, as with every other element of your novel, a good thing to remember is this: until you have reached

THE NOVEL & THE NOVELIST

the conclusion of your story, your level of investment, as the writer, will always be greater than that of your reader.

This is a polite way of saying that, at the outset, the reader does not care. And the reason the reader does not care is because you have not yet given the reader a reason to care.

Perhaps this overstates the case a bit. Certainly the reader cares a little; otherwise he or she would never have started your book in the first place.

But it's a precarious relationship. If you still hope to have the reader there with you on Page Two—or Page Three, or Page Three Hundred—you need to bear in mind that the most burning question in the reader's mind is not, "What happens next?" but "Why should I *care* what happens next?" To do that, everything you write has to move the story forward. And that includes everything you write about setting.

Knight to Rook 4

Think of writing as a chess game. As the author, you are the grand master; you can see with perfect clarity things that are going to happen five, ten or twenty-five moves into the game. The reader does not share this insight, and you run the risk of losing his or her interest unless, with each detail you deliver, you also provide a reason for having that detail there.

I mention this because, as writers, it is natural to think of our settings as a great, grand stage, and to want to give the reader every detail of that stage before commencing into action.

But the difference between theater and the novel is that, in theater, that great, grand panoply of detail is conveyed in an instant. To provide the same detail in a novel takes time, and in a novel, time passed without action equals boredom.

For novelists, this is one of the most difficult lessons to learn regarding setting. When it is pointed out to us, our very human reaction is to argue: "But it's important for the reader to understand what this place looks like, sounds like ... the atmosphere in which the action is going to take place."

Why?

When we have that very human reaction, the question we should be asking ourselves is, "Why?"

Let's say, for instance, that our novel opens on a pirate ship in the Caribbean in 1735. Because we have done our homework, we know that this pirate ship will probably not be the great, three-masted sailing ship of the movies, but rather a smaller, two-masted vessel, usually of a type known as a "Jamaica-built sloop."

Fine. So we open our novel in the close quarters of such a sailing ship. It's perfectly okay to do that.

But then, having spent hours in the library researching Jamaica-built sloops, we begin to describe ours in great detail. We provide length, width, the type of timber it is made from, and the way it was constructed, using pegs instead of nails, and exactly how the planking was caulked to make it watertight, and pretty soon our readers are tapping their feet, wondering when this exquisitely described ship is going to *do* something.

Our fascination is not yet their fascination, and they become bored.

Or maybe we're smart enough to realize that the reader is going to be looking for the reason they are getting all this detail. We know they are asking, "Why?"

So we tell them. We tell them that the pirates of this period desired this sort of vessel for two reasons: because it is more maneuverable than the cargo ships they prey upon, and because the shallower draft of the sloop allows it to escape pursuit by fleeing into shallow water—water in which a deeper-draft vessel, such as a man of war, cannot sail. And the problem with doing this is that we are now telling, rather than showing (you knew I'd get around to that eventually, did you not?).

We're spending too much time in exposition.

Worse than that, we are telling supporting detail, rather than telling a story. And all the while some of our readers are still tapping their feet and thinking, "Isn't this a pirate story? And if it is, then when is all the *pirating* going to start?"

The solution to all of this is to dispense your setting in easily digestible pieces, each bit conveyed as it is necessary.

Telling by Showing

So rather than explaining why our pirates chose such a small vessel, we show how, by rapidly sailing in close to their quarry, they are able to quickly reach a point where shots fired back at them pass harmlessly overhead.

We show how the maneuverability of the sloop lets it literally sail circles around the vessel it is attempting to capture, seeming to attack it from all sides at once.

Then, when the navy shows up to pursue them, our pirates sail for shallow water, leaving the larger naval vessels frustratingly out of gun range. We have still conveyed all the information we needed to convey, but we have satisfied the "Why?" by showing it— through action.

Easy Does It

That, to me, is the crux of conveying setting in a compelling manner—resisting the urge to over-describe, and resisting the urge to tell the reader about details, rather than showing the reader the details through compelling action.

Over-description is easily rectified. The last of Elmore Leonard's ten rules of writing is, "Try to leave out the part that readers tend to skip."

Detailed setting description is one such part. So when you have written a first draft, set it aside, let it cool, and come back to it a week or a month later, pretend you don't know what happens next, and see which parts you find yourself skimming over. Then use the "delete" key for the purpose for which it was intended.

You will kill a lot of writing this way. I used to find myself deleting half of what I'd written. But eventually you'll pare yourself down to essence in the first drafts. It is a long process (I still delete huge chunks of my initial drafts), but what you end up with will move the story along.

And that takes us through the undergraduate course of study in setting.

Five Senses

The graduate school comes, to me, in our choice of how we show these details.

For most twenty-first century novels, the authors choose to *show* literally—to select *visual* details.

I blame television and the movies for this. They are primarily visual media, and they have accustomed us to think of the world in visual terms. But most human beings are born with four other senses, and these get underplayed in much of our writing today.

Back to our pirate ship ... the little sloop would pitch and heel as it maneuvered. Most pirates of the day would be bare-footed, and the decks would be gritty with sand spread to provide traction on surfaces that would soon be wet with salt spray and blood. When the pirates climbed rigging and handled lines, the ropes would be slick and wet, yet still rough to the touch.

All of these are tactile observations: the sense of touch. And they add a dimension that cannot be conveyed by simply showing the reader a picture.

Sound ... the hiss of water rushing past the hull. The mast creaking against the strain of the wind. The oddly two-dimensional sound of a cannon's report when there is nothing to throw back an echo. And pirates of the day would accompany their attacks with hellish music that they called "vapors," to strike terror in the hearts of their victims.

Sound adds elements mere visual description cannot approach. I remember well one windy evening when I left the balcony door open on my hotel room, next to a marina in the British Virgin Islands. The rigging of the sailboats moored below turned into gigantic stringed instruments, floating Aeolian harps that created a low and plaintive moan: music fit to accompany the returning dead.

Taste is another vital sense. Men believing they are about to die will have a stale and cottony taste in their mouths. Men in the act of dying will taste the copper and iron of their own blood.

And scent.

I am constantly amazed at how underused this sense is in most novels (although I do recall one amazing novel—*Perfume*, written by the German author Patrick Süskind, and published in 1985—in which the sense of smell predominated).

After all, of all the senses, smell is the one that most quickly and completely will transport a person back to a time and a location, no matter how long ago that memory took place.

Our pirate ship would have been filled with scents—the acrid smell of the pitch-covered vests that the boarding party would wear to turn a knife, the hellish sulfur of burning black powder, the stench of sweating men in close quarters, and the brine of the ocean wind.

Application

Knowing all of this, I looked at that quarter I found in my change and thought about how I would convey my West Virginia setting to my readers.

Because I understood the importance of leading with action, I decided to open on a climb.

And because I was opening on a climb, I decided to lead with a feeling—the "think I'm going to fall" sensation of vertigo. I remembered the clean scent of pine trees mixed with the fear-tainted smell of a person's own sweat, the stale taste of cotton-mouth, the sound of wind soughing over a ridge.

I remembered all of this. But I could not present it as my—the author's—memory. I needed to present it from the viewpoint of a character.

So next, I needed to decide just who that character would be.

| TWO: People and Relationships

When writing a novel a writer should create living people; people not characters. A character is a caricature.
— ERNEST HEMINGWAY

IN THE BIBLICAL story of Genesis, God spends six days creating a setting: a universe with light and darkness, land and water, grasses and trees to keep the land from being barren, day and night to mark the passage of time, birds and fish and beasts to populate the air and the sea and the land, and a garden at the center of that world, verdant, good and full of life.

It is a setting—in every sense of the term, it is the original setting—but it is not yet a story.

We get nearer to a true Genesis story when God creates a character: Adam, the first man.

And almost immediately after that (twelve sentences later in most English translations) God creates a second character: the first woman, whom Adam calls "Eve."

With that second character in place, the narrative is able to progress and become a story.

It Takes Two

It is difficult, although not impossible, to create a story that contains but a single character. They do exist; Jack London's "To Build a Fire" is one example. In it, a man is attempting to avoid freezing to death in sub-zero wilderness. And an interesting bit of trivia about this story is that there are two different versions of it.

In the first version, published in 1902 in a magazine called *The Youth's Companion*, a young man named Tom Vincent succeeds after multiple attempts in creating a fire to warm himself, and emerges a wiser person for the ordeal.

This version of the story is remembered only in London biographies and literary criticism because, properly speaking, it is not a story at all.

Technically, it is more of a treatment—a vignette. It reads like a chapter from a longer and more complete work.

London must have realized this because, six years later, he revisited and rewrote the story. In the considerably longer revised version, published in 1908 in *The Twentieth Century Magazine*, London subtracted the main character's name (he is now simply "the man") and added a new element, the man's dog (referred to simply as "the dog").

In the 1908 version of "To Build a Fire" (just as in the 1902 story) the potentially life-saving fire is extinguished by snow dropping from a bough above it. And without warmth, the man is in danger of freezing to death.

But here the story changes. Desperate, the man attempts to kill the dog so he can put his hands in the carcass and warm them, but he makes the attempt too late; his hands are useless and he cannot unsheathe his knife. The man dies and the dog trots away up the trail. He is going, in London's words, "where were the other food-providers and fire-providers."

Although not human, the dog nearly becomes a second character. I say "nearly," because while we get the narrator's assumptions about what the dog is thinking, we never get those from the dog himself, and the creature remains an animate but mute object, no more a genuine character than the volleyball, "Wilson," in the motion picture, *Castaway*.

Still, the dog is a being for the man to interact with: the element with which Jack London completes the arc of the story.

To re-state the obvious: it is very, very difficult to write a story that has only a single character.

It is even more difficult to write a book that has only one character.

Ernest Hemingway set out to do it in *The Old Man and the Sea*. This piece was undertaken originally as "On the Blue Water," a story for *Esquire* magazine, and was revised and published as a book in 1952, the final significant work of fiction published during that author's lifetime. This is a book that, with its one straightforward plot and length of just 26,560 words, is technically a novella, although it is often referred to as a novel; even the *New York Times* has called it that.

The *Old Man and the Sea* is the story of Santiago, an old Cuban fisherman considered by his peers to be unlucky, a has-been at his craft. In the book, he succeeds after a long ordeal in catching a giant marlin, but the fish is too large to pull into the boat, so much of it is devoured by sharks.

In a letter to Maxwell Perkins, his editor, Hemingway summarized it as:

"Everything he does and everything he thinks in all that long fight with the boat out of sight of all the other boats all alone on the sea. It's a great story if I can get it right."

He got it right.

Like "To Build a Fire," *The Old Man and the Sea* is a classic tale of man versus nature. And like "To Build a Fire," Hemingway's book requires additional elements—the marlin, certainly, is one.

In fact, purists will point out that there are several characters in the work, in addition to old Santiago.

There is a boy, "Manolin," whom Hemingway uses as a second point of view and the other side of the two sections of dialogue that set the story up and conclude it. A chorus of fishermen measures the ruins of the marlin and admires Santiago's skill. There is a proprietor of a seaside café who talks to the boy. And a passing group of tourists wonder about the remains of the fish and then accepts the café owner's explanation that it was nothing but a shark.

But throughout the core of the book, Santiago is the sole character. And the considerable talent and skill necessary to accomplish such a feat were sufficient to earn Ernest Hemingway a Pulitzer in 1952 and, two years later, the Nobel Prize in literature.

The point here is that, unless you simply want to do it for the extraordinarily formidable inherent challenge, you should probably avoid trying to create a story that contains only one character.

Human beings are social animals. We shun loneliness, seek companionship and are naturally interested in narratives that have to do with the interactions of other human beings ... plural.

So readers gravitate to stories that have to do with relationships. It is how we are wired.

Situations containing at least two characters are situations that pique our interest.

And to capture and hold that interest through a work the length of a novel, or even the shorter length of a novella, usually requires more than two characters.

The Major Characters

The world of fiction writing lacks accord on what we should call all the people running around in our novels.

Some writers refer to them in the language of film, or the stage—two media in which scripts always have to be discussed and rewritten, and there needs to be a general understanding and agreement regarding who's who.

Bestselling suspense writer James Scott Bell is one who uses the language of film.

He writes legal thrillers and is himself a successful attorney, but he studied as an actor before that (and then, upon marrying an actress, "decided that one of us should have a way of making a living"). Bell—whose work on craft has appeared frequently in *Writers Digest*—calls his central character "the lead," and refers to "main characters" and "supporting characters."

Others have their own vocabularies. I always smile when Veronica Heley, a wonderful English mystery writer, refers to one of her sinister characters as "the baddie." It's quaint, it's British, and when she says it, I know exactly who she is talking about.

In talking with other working novelists, I've found that virtually everyone lumps the characters into two large groups: those without whom the story could not proceed, and those who supplement the story but are not essential to it. But I wasn't finding the phrase or term that would describe that former group.

Finally, novelist Jill Stengl and publisher Jeff Gerke both asked me exactly the same thing: "Why don't you just refer to them as 'the major characters?'"

Duh. So that's what I'll call them here. And here's who they are, starting with the one at the center of it all…

The Protagonist

The main, or lead, character is the one who, in literature classes, would be referred to as a "protagonist." The word is Greek in origin and made up from two Greek roots: *proto* (meaning "first") and *agonistes* (meaning "one who strives."). The similarity in roots between *agonistes* and "agony" is no coincidence, and tells volumes about what the ancient Greeks expected of their drama: for them, the protagonist was literally "the first to agonize." And for us, the protagonist is at very least the central figure in the journey of the novel.

As to what the character is striving for, many genres of fiction, especially genres such as suspense and mysteries, have what writers refer to as a "MacGuffin." This is a term from filmmaking, and a master of that medium, Alfred Hitchcock, is cited in the *Oxford English Dictionary* as explaining it this way:

> **"It is the mechanical element that usually crops up in any story. In crook stories it is almost always the necklace, and in spy stories it is most always the papers."**

To that I would add that a MacGuffin can be anything pursued by your character or characters. It could be buried treasure. It could be a date for the prom. The point is that it is pursued and, if your story has a MacGuffin, the protagonist is the one who's struggling to reach or find it.

No Rules

There are, properly speaking, no rules when it comes to creating the character at the center of your novel. More than a century ago,

Anna Sewell's *Black Beauty* and Jack London's *White Fang* established that the character doesn't even have to be human: Sewell's lead character was a horse, and London's was another dog (this one endowed with the gift of narrative and a point of view).

And Audrey Niffenegger's *Her Fearful Symmetry* proved that the main character doesn't even have to be alive. Nor is this even remotely a spoiler; Niffenegger's main character, Elspeth, is dead within the first two words of that novel.

If this begins to make it sound as if anything goes when creating your main character … well, that is pretty much the case.

That said, there are some guidelines that can be of great help as one creates the main character.

Make Them Human

One mistake newer novelists make is understandable in the extreme. We think of our main characters as heroes. And because of that, we tend to make them … well, *heroic*.

By "heroic," I mean that we make them perfect. First-time novelists are often tempted to create characters that have straight teeth, clear skin, hair with plenty of volume and no split ends, and the sorts of bodies rarely seen without the benefit of Photoshop.

They are strong, smart, always know what to do and are able to do it. And that doesn't work very well.

After all, Christian charity aside, don't you absolutely hate—hate and want hurtful things to happen to—the sort of person I just described? And even if you don't hate those types of characters, do you find it even remotely possible to identify with them?

Nor do I. Nor does anyone.

You, I and every single human being you or I know, have known, or will ever know, have one thing in common; we all have flaws.

And another thing most of us have in common is that we tend to fix upon, and magnify, our own flaws. We think they are more apparent than they actually are, and as a result we view ourselves as damaged goods.

So, to strike the readers as realistic, and to give the readers someone they can relate to, the main character needs to have, and be to some degree burdened by, his or her own flaws.

I say "flaws" (plural) because that describes most of us. But as the character is introduced, it works better for both the writer and reader if we focus this a bit: a single flaw, maybe two.

Sometimes the opening flaw is physical. Christopher Snow, the lead character in Dean R. Koontz's "Moonlight Bay" Trilogy, is afflicted with *xeroderma pigmentosum*, a rare but real adverse reaction to ultraviolet light (including that part of the ultraviolet spectrum present in daylight). This makes him of necessity a creature of the night, and so challenged in his ability to interact socially with most people.

When we first meet Smithy Ide, the hero of Ron McLarty's debut novel, *The Memory of Running*, Smithy is obese—maybe not worthy of thirty minutes on The Discovery Channel, but certainly far too heavy for his own good.

Sometimes—and usually—the flaw is internal or psychological. In Stephen King's novel, *11/22/63*, the lead character is Jake Eppling, an English teacher whose wife has left and divorced him for another man (whom she met at her Alcoholics Anonymous meeting). *In Gone with the Wind*, Margaret Mitchell's Scarlett O'Hara's precociousness masks her central characteristic—her internal insecurity. Don Quixote is convinced he is a knight on a heroic quest; indeed, it is this delusion that is central to his charm as a character.

And certainly the main character's flaw can be both physical and psychological: the wounded war hero who does not think he will ever return to a normal life, or the athlete who finds her life without purpose when an injury keeps her from competing.

So that's where fiction differs from most other forms of art. Sculptors begin with unflawed marble, and painters start with a perfectly prepared canvas, but if you want your novel to work, you will find your work easier if you open your work with a character who has flaws.

Make Them Grow

Years ago—so long ago that he was not yet a member of The Rolling Stones—Ronnie Wood co-wrote and sang a rock song, "Ooh La La," that had this refrain:

"I wish that I knew what I know now, when I was younger."

In a novel, an essential part of the main character's journey is earning that precious knowledge.

And when we say "knowledge," we don't necessarily mean the crux of what the book is, ostensibly, about. Chase the MacGuffin if you want—in some genres, you absolutely must—but remember that character growth is a separate element.

This knowledge won by the character is something far more intimate: something in addition to the plot element. The main character gains knowledge that results in something beyond an answer to a mystery: personal growth. The character emerges at the end an older, but wiser, man (or woman ... or dog ... or horse, as the case may be).

In fact, a very effective device can be for the main character to grow in direct opposition to what that character is seeking in the book. For instance, in F. Scott Fitzgerald's *The Great Gatsby*, narrator Nick Carraway declares that, after World War I:

Instead of being the warm center of the world, the Middle West now seemed like the ragged edge of the universe—so I decided to go East and learn the bond business.

Yet by the end of the book Nick, having experienced the sordid side of the lives of the wealthy and nouveau riche, is only too happy to flee back to the honest and familiar territory of the Midwest.

Sometimes, and particularly in shorter works of fiction such as the short story and the novella, a character's room for growth is apparent from the very beginning of the narrative. In Charles Dickens' classic, *A Christmas Carol*, Ebenezer Scrooge appears at the opening of the story as a dour, stingy and thoroughly reprehensible old man. At the end of that story, Scrooge is generous, personable and filled with the Christmas spirit.

Evolving a character in this fashion is interesting and dramatic, but it does pose a couple of problems.

The first problem has to do with keeping readers engaged even though they dislike the main character. One way to do this is to introduce some sympathetic secondary characters; in *A Christmas Carol*, the reader is encouraged to continue the story out of concern for Scrooge's clerk, Bob Cratchit, and because of the cheerfulness and good nature of Scrooge's nephew, Fred.

Another hurdle posed by using an obviously broken character such as Scrooge is that story direction becomes pretty obvious; the character has no place to go but "up." This wasn't much of a hurdle for the readers of Dickens' serialized stories in their day.

Nor is it that much of an issue in our day. *A Christmas Carol* and *Oliver Twist* have been absorbed into popular culture, so most modern readers have a good idea of how everything is going to pan out before they so much as open the book.

But your fiction, and my fiction, is not nearly as ubiquitous as that of Charles Dickens. We're usually better off keeping our cards a bit closer to the chest.

Still, as the story progresses, we need to see the shortcomings. The main character's growth cannot happen in a vacuum. It's best if the reader sees, feels and otherwise experiences the situations that nudge the character toward growth.

Protagonist(s)?

Just as it is very difficult to write a novel that has only one character, it is usually difficult to write a novel that has more than one protagonist.

There are exceptions. In romance, it is common for both would-be lovers to take on virtually all of the characteristics of a protagonist. Novelist Angela Hunt shared with me a term she's heard used to describe this: "contagonists."

And in epic literature, including such relatively recent epics as the sweeping novels of James Michener, entire cultures may serve as protagonists.

But that mainstay of modern-day cinema—the ensemble cast, in which a group of characters are all on more or less equal footing, each the protagonist in his or her own small story—is difficult to pull off successfully in writing.

I think part of the reason for this is that, unless inserted as a voice-over device, cinema has, properly speaking, no narrator.

In effect, the camera is the narrator and, as the camera has no soul, it is the hopes, struggles and failings of the characters that come through.

Try this in a novel, even with a distant and omniscient narrator, and what's being said about each character will color the impressions being conveyed.

In order to rectify this, some writers tell the same story from multiple points of view. That can be an interesting writing exercise, but not so interesting to read unless the segments are written in a dispensational fashion—i.e., the reader gains new insight with each segment and the story reaches its climax with the final segment.

But this places extra emphasis on the final character's point of view, so—inevitably—the characters in the ensemble will not be equal in that regard.

In my own writing, I've found that characters who rise to contagonist status usually do so naturally, as the work progresses, and are not planned that way. In fact, these days, that ascendancy is one of the few things that I do not plan out, beforehand, as I write a novel.

Starting out, I usually think of a book as having only a single protagonist. And I concentrate on creating my story with that one main character, plus one more: the character that is impeding my protagonist in his or her quest.

The Antagonist

In fiction, as in life, if you are after something and it is something worth pursuing, then there is probably someone who is either competing with you or trying to keep you from achieving it.

In fiction, that person is known as an "antagonist." Like "protagonist," this is a word with Greek roots, and it literally means "the one who works against the one who strives."

Want a shorter definition? Ask most people to give you a one-word definition for a literary antagonist and chances are they'll say "villain." Ask for two words, and you'll probably hear, "bad guy."

But not all antagonists are villains. Not all are bad. Antagonists are adversaries, and there are certainly such things as benign adversaries.

If, for instance, your protagonist is a minor who wants to join the military, and her father will not sign the consent form because he is worried that she will wind up in combat, then that protective father is—in this situation, at least—an antagonist. The reader may understand his point of view and may even side with him, but as viewed by the main character, this character is the force preventing her from reaching her goal.

Antagonists, then, can be good as well as bad. In fact, if you do decide to create an evil antagonist, it doesn't hurt to endow him/her/it with some redeeming value, however small. Just as heroes work best when flawed, villains work best when you add some perspective that, without justifying their actions, at least explains why they act the way they do.

I had an evil antagonist in *Yucatan Deep*, my first published novel. I even gave him a deliberately evil name: Viktor Bellum. But within the space of a few sentences, it became apparent to me that I was creating a caricature, rather than a believable person.

So I began thinking about what had made him bad.

Now, true, some people seem to be born without the chromosome for goodness within them. History is full of seemingly good and loving homes that produced heartless dictators and serial killers.

But more often, if you search within the past of people gone bad, you will find the catalyst that made them go that way.

I decided to give Bellum such a catalyst.

I made him the son of a missionary, a missionary who dedicated his life to reaching an obscure tribe of Mayans in the jungles of tropical Mexico. And I had Bellum try and fail to attract an equal measure of his father's love. That wound—being unloved by the most important person in his young life—sets the young Viktor Bellum on the path toward villainy.

Bad, good, distant, approachable—the only hard and fast rule for an antagonist is that they need to be the fly in the protagonist's ointment. The antagonist is the character that presents an obstacle to the protagonist reaching his or her goal, and that's important because, if it's smooth sailing all the way, with no obstacles to overcome, then you probably don't have a story.

Other Major Characters

Most novels have more than two characters—more than a protagonist and an antagonist. And oftentimes these additional characters are key to the story's success.

If the novel is not a classic romance, yet it contains a love story, then certainly the love interest is one of these essential characters. And if another character has a day-to-day say over the comings and goings of the main character (a commanding officer in a military story, a warden in a prison story, a parent in a young-adult novel, etc.), that character is also essential. Those characters may even have their own personal arcs within the larger narrative.

My rule of thumb is that, if a character is important enough to have a point of view in the work, or to express a point of view through extensive dialogue, then that character can be treated as a "main character lite," with empathy-inducing flaws and growth throughout the course of the novel.

And certain of these other major characters can nearly become main characters themselves. *The Great Gatsby* is, ostensibly, about Gatsby, and he certainly does figure mightily in the book—you will, in fact, get arguments among readers as to whether the protagonist there is Gatsby or Nick Carraway (or both).

This is not simply because Nick is the first-person narrator here.

Dr. Watson is the first-person narrator of the Sherlock Holmes mysteries, and I've never heard anyone argue for protagonist status for Watson; he has neither the sympathetic flaws nor the potential for growth that Holmes has.

In fact, part of the charm of Watson as a narrator is that, while he is observant and intelligent throughout the Holmes canon, he remains stuck resolutely at Square One—always a bit mystified by, and astounded at, his Baker Street flat-mate.

But Nick Carraway and Gatsby both have room for growth a-plenty. Nick is, nonetheless, the foremost of the main characters because the reader is far nearer to his growth and struggle.

Approachability

We observed a moment ago how, in *A Christmas Carol*, it helped to have a likeable Bob Cratchit who can balance out the stingy and contemptible Ebenezer Scrooge. And even if your novel's main character is nowhere near as nasty as Scrooge, you will do well, if the main character initially appears unlikable, or even distant or aloof, to have a second character who is the opposite of all these things.

You want this because the reader is going to be looking for someone with whom he or she can identify.

It's in our nature. Did you ever, as a child, change schools? Or if not, can you remember the first day at college, or the first day on a new job? Remember walking into the lunchroom or cafeteria? What's the first thing you did?

Very probably, you looked for a friendly face.

Human beings are social creatures, and readers are human beings.

When we read, we treat novel worlds as real worlds, so, as we "walk in" to the first chapter, we are looking for someone we can identify with.

As authors, we help both the readers and ourselves if we provide that friendly face (or at very least, someone with whom the reader can identify). That is the connection that invites the reader to stay and, as writers, we want them to stay.

These other major characters are a pretty adaptable species. They can be who the book is, ostensibly, about (Jay Gatsby in Fitzgerald's *The Great Gatsby* or Owen Meany in John Irving's *A Prayer for Owen Meany*), narrators (Dr. Watson in the Sherlock Holmes novels), love interests (Dejah Thoris in Edgar Rice Burroughs' *A Princess of Mars*), sidekicks (Dr. Watson, again), catalysts (the character M in Ian Fleming's James Bond novels), somewhat distant bad guys (Goldfinger, Dr. No and a host of others in the James Bond books, or Professor Moriarty in the Sherlock Holmes books), a foil inserted to draft a contrast with the main character (the brothers in Jim Harrison's *Legends of the Fall*) and a hundred other things. These other main characters are the Swiss Army Knife of novel-length fiction.

Other Characters

If the ancillary main character is the Swiss Army Knife of the novel, then the secondary character is a hammer, useful for accomplishing brief, swiftly performed tasks. Secondary characters are important enough to be named, but not so central to the story that they need to grow over the course of the book (although they may). And below secondary characters are all the tertiary rest: the minions and extras of the novel.

Some of these will still get names. As a reader, I expect that if a character is important enough to be named by my narrator—"Miss Moneypenny," as opposed to "M's secretary"—then that character is someone I need to remember because I am going to see, hear from, or hear of them again later in the book.

And as a writer I am conscious of this; in the back of my head, I may have already decided that the doorman is named "Fred," but unless he's going to show up again later—and show up to the extent that it would be passing odd for him not to be named—I don't share that information with the reader. In this respect, as with so many other areas in the novel, I don't need to tell the reader everything I know; I only need to share enough to tell my story and accomplish the purpose of the book.

The thing that separates them, in my mind, is that we are absolutely *not* going to be growing these characters. Scotland Yard's Detective Lestrade, while not the incompetent dullard that we see in the movies, in nonetheless going to be a step or three behind Sherlock Holmes in the stories and is never, never, ever going to catch up. Queequeg, the harpooner who is best friends with Ishmael in *Moby-Dick*, is half-savage and half civilized at the opening of the story, and remains resolutely imprisoned within that state; he is mostly there as the device that gets Ishmael signed onto Ahab's crew. In *Tom Sawyer*, Aunt Polly remains the same mothering reformer throughout the work; she has to, because solid rocks don't change.

I am deliberately sparing with my named characters. Put too many of them in there, and your work starts looking like a phone book, rather than a novel.

Human beings are ten-fingered creatures, and ten is about as many named characters as we can approach in a story without them all beginning to run together. So if you go beyond that number in your book—and none of them are going to die off, move away or otherwise fall by the wayside in the course of the story—be forewarned and proceed with caution.

That, in general, takes care of *who* the characters are in our work. And the next order of business is to consider *what* they are.

Description

One thing that novelists often wonder about is to what extent, and when, a character should be described. And it's not just newer novelists who wonder this.

The reason for the fogginess on this subject is that the levels of character description expected by the reader will vary from genre to genre, and even from book to book.

In popular romance, for instance, detailed description is fairly common. It's so common that publishers often depict the principal characters of a romance on the cover of the book. This makes sense: people tend to dwell on the objects of their infatuation, so especially if the story is being told from the point of view of one of the parties to the romance, it would be odd not to get some idea of what their love interest looked like.

On the other hand, in general contemporary literature and particularly in literary fiction, it's more common to have little in the way of character description.

The classic example of this is Ernest Hemingway's "Hills Like White Elephants," published in his 1927 short-story collection, *Men Without Women*.

There are two principal characters in this story, identified by the narrator only as "the American and the girl with him." And the first paragraph of dialogue looks like this:

"What should we drink?" the girl asked. She had taken off her hat and put it on the table.

That is worth noting because it contains the only bit of character description in the entire story: the fact that the girl has a hat … a hat that she is no longer wearing.

Many people who are just passingly familiar with "Hills like White Elephants" are surprised to hear this, because they come away from the story with a fairly clear idea of what the characters look like. But they are getting this idea entirely from their own imaginations—which is not at all a bad place for it to come from.

A certain level of reader imagination is necessary in any work of fiction. When we watch the opening shot of the movie, all the details are there in front of us, but to convey that same depth of detail in words would require page after (boring) page of verbiage. So, as authors, we depend on the readers to fill in the blanks, and they do.

And the same principle applies to character description; if the author doesn't paint an image, not to worry: the reader will.

When to Show and Tell

There are times, of course, when the story itself requires character description.

Smithy Ide is a middle-age guy who loses weight throughout Ron McLarty's *The Memory of Running*; he has to be heavy at the beginning of the book, and the reader has to know this. This book was originally written as an audiobook (McLarty is a veteran voice actor), and his audio rendition of Smithy is even performed in the slightly breathless style of a man who has carried too many pounds throughout most of his life.

But even without that audio help, we need to know that Smithy needs to lose weight as he sets off on a cross-country bicycle trip to claim the body of his dead sister. The book needs that detail to work, every bit as much as *The Hunchback of Notre Dame* requires … well, a hunchback.

A middle-ground approach is to provide just a few details concerning your characters: hair color, eye color, and perhaps the briefest description of body type. I've often done this, even though, for better or worse, some readers will leap to their own conclusions about blondes, or redheads, or blue eyes.

When I was writing my novel, *Pirate Hunter*, a review came out of a previous book in which the critic took me to task for my predilection toward green-eyed heroines. Partly as a snide response to that, and partly because I had just seen a film starring the actress Kate Bosworth, I gave Sheila, the lead female character in one of the two stories that comprise *Pirate Hunter*, the same condition as Kate Bosworth: *heterochromia iridum*, in which the eyes are of two different colors (most commonly brown and blue). And this condition was often commented on by my readers, who seemed to uniformly like it.

Defaults

If you choose not to describe your characters at all, you can safely assume that the reader will leap to one of several conclusions.

If the character has an ethnic name (say, "Yukio Nakamura" or

"Hector Rodriquez"), the reader will assume an ethnic type associated with that name. If you, as an author, are well known, the reader may assume an ethnic type similar to your own. And absent any of these clues, readers will very probably assume character ethnicity similar to their own.

So if none of these are the case, and the detail is important, you probably want to convey that early on.

In his novel, *The Great Leader*, Jim Harrison has a character named "Kowalski" who is ethnically Hispanic. We need to know that detail, because otherwise we would not understand how he blends so seamlessly into the deeply *macho* drug-cartel-influenced setting of an Arizona border town.

In that same novel, by the way, Harrison waits until we are roughly halfway through the book before telling us that Sunderson, his main character, looks like the actor, Robert Duvall—in fact, he looks so much like him that he is frequently mistaken for him.

This jarred me. Not enough that I threw down the book and walked away, mind you, but certainly enough that I was startled out of Harrison's world and aware that I was sitting on my pool deck in Florida, reading a book.

The main reason I was startled was because I have met Jim Harrison, have corresponded with him a couple of times, and between that and times when I have seen him in magazines and on TV, I have enough of an idea of his appearance that I'd assumed Sunderson looked, approximately, like him: possibly bigger and more athletic (Sunderson is described as being very strong), certainly younger (in the book, Sunderson has just hit retirement age, and Harrison is past that) and with two good eyes (Jim Harrison is blind is his left eye, and looks it).

Still, while Robert Duvall may not look like Jim Harrison, the two are close enough that I have no doubt Duvall could play Harrison in a movie. So I was able to make the adjustment and move on, and when I read the book a second time, I did not stumble when I hit the comparison.

That's not always the case. If, left to her own devices, your reader decides your main character has shoulder-length, wavy black hair, and you wait until Chapter Three to let her know he actually has sandy hair and a crew cut, the dissimilarity may strike sufficient discord to keep her from continuing with the book.

That's why, if you are going to describe a character, you'll make things easier for the reader if you do that when the character is introduced, or shortly thereafter.

This doesn't mean that you should heap on the adjectives immediately before or after first mentioning the character's name. That may be the way some writers do it, but I think (and sincerely hope you'll agree) that's a bit too blunt of an instrument for an art as fine as storytelling.

Subtlety works better. And while I may not always hit it, it's what I strive for in my work.

For instance, in one of the two stories in *Pirate Hunter*, there is a main character, Bold Ted, who is no longer a boy, but not yet a full-grown man, and who is African, recently rescued from a slave ship. Just before Ted's first line of dialogue, I describe him from the point of view of the pirate captain who rescued him. Here's the paragraph:

> **The pirate gazed down his nose at the barefoot and bare-chested fifteen-year-old on the other side of the table. The younger man's skin was a deep chocolate brown, almost as dark as his jet-black hair, a fact that made his eyes appear larger than they were, giving him the appearance of an innocent.**

My aim here was to describe Bold Ted while remaining fully and naturally within my narrative. And I like to think, or at least hope, that this passage does that.

Lifestyle, Religion and Politics

Like most working writers, I read voraciously. And as a rule of thumb, I read one contemporary or fairly contemporary novel a week, on the theory that, as I am writing for twenty-first century readers, I should be at least moderately aware of what else they are reading.

My own reading falls into two broad categories: literary fiction (to give me a standard of quality to shoot for), and well-written popular fiction (to remind me that one niggling but important purpose of the exercise is to move books through bookstores).

As I write this chapter, one book on my nightstand (okay, it's actually a book on my Kindle, but the Kindle lives on the nightstand) is *The Trinity Game*, a thriller by Sean Chercover.

Chercover is a good writer, and *The Trinity Game* is engaging.

Yet, a little shy of halfway through the book, Chercover introduces a secondary character, Special Agent Steve Hillborn of the FBI Chicago Division, and adds this comment:

Hillborn didn't usually mind being called in on a Sunday, but he'd promised to meet Fred at five o'clock at the Lakeview Athletic Club's climbing wall. They'd only been dating a couple months, and Hillborn had been putting a lot of hours in at the Bureau lately, and he didn't think Fred would enjoy being stood up … again. But that's the life of a cop's boyfriend, he thought as he stepped into the elevator, and if Fred couldn't accept it, the relationship wasn't gonna last anyway. Better to find out now.

Now, I read as a writer—it is an inescapable occupational hazard—and this paragraph jumped out at, and intrigued, me.

Sometime in the future, maybe forty or fifty years from now, it might be possible to read right past that paragraph with no takeaway other than that Special Agent Steve Hillborn is a very busy and dedicated guy, and law enforcement takes a certain toll on those who dedicate their lives to it.

But in the here and now, it strikes me that, to ninety-nine percent of today's readers, this paragraph is going to evoke one of three possible reactions.

One is the reader who hits this paragraph, brightens up at the mention of the relationship, sees this as a cultural indication that alternative lifestyles have reached a high degree of acceptance in today's society, applauds this as the new normal and reads on with this filter in place.

Another is the reader who gets to this paragraph, is appalled at the casual reference to Hillborn's homosexuality, draws a conclusion then and there regarding the author and his agenda with this work, and either continues with a chip on his or her shoulder, or sets the book down in disgust.

And the third group—which I suspect is the vast majority of readers—will read the paragraph two or three times to make sure they aren't missing something. Then they'll wonder how likely it is that an FBI field agent would be openly gay.

They might—as I did—set the book aside long enough to go to the FBI website and research the subject (for the record, the FBI has agents who are gay, agents who are lesbian and agents who are bisexual, and it *might* have agents who are transgender, although the website makes it sound as if they—and this, mind you, is the Federal Bureau of Investigation we're talking about—don't really know).

Members of this third group are almost certainly going to wonder: *At this point, I don't know how old Hillborn is, what his ethnic background is, or anything about what he looks like. I don't know if he's pudgy, slender, crew-cut or bald ... so why it is important that I know, and know from the get-go, that this FBI agent is gay?*

They may wonder if the author is giving us this information to provoke a reaction and, if so, what reaction he is after.

Either way, we have been jarred out of the narrative.

And it's not just lifestyle revelations that produce this sort of startled-from-the-literary-dream-state sort of speed bump. If, from the top, you introduce a character as a Tea Party Republican, a Blue Dog Democrat, a socialist, a Communist, a Nazi, a Mormon, a Shiite Muslim, a skyclad Wiccan, an orthodox Jew, a PETA activist, an NRA member or an anarchist, you do the same thing: you initiate a subconscious call for a vote among your readers, and interrupt suspension of disbelief.

So ... does this mean you should adopt a "don't ask, don't tell" philosophy with respect to the political leanings, religious persuasion and sexual orientation of every character in your novel?

Of course not: not unless your goal is to write a drab and uninteresting clinker of a book.

Some characters *have to* possess one or more polarizing characteristics. Lisbeth Salander, the title character in Stieg Larrson's *The Girl with the Dragon Tattoo*, is bisexual, and promiscuously so. She is also a tattooed and pierced goth, a loner, an Asperger's-like genius with an eidetic memory, and a professional computer hacker.

Not your everyday heroine.

In the only interview he ever gave on the subject (with Lasse Winkler, later published in both Sweden's *Svensk Bokhandel* and the UK's *Telegraph*), Larrson said this:

"I considered Pippi Longstocking. What would she be like today? What would she be like as an adult? What would you call a person like that, a sociopath? Hyperactive? Wrong. She simply sees society in a different light. I'll make her twenty-five years old and an outcast. She has no friends and is deficient in social skills. That was my original thought."

Lisbeth is "fringe" in every sense of the word. But an important part of the journey in that book is the readers' own journey, in which we develop sympathy for Lisbeth, and finally look upon her as we would a wayward niece.

We may not approve of the choices she has made, but we feel protective toward her, nonetheless.

Larrson did this by showing us glimpses of Lisbeth's heart early in the work. She is an adult under the care of a guardianship, and she is fond of her guardian, but when he suffers a stroke, her new guardian rapes her. This is presented, not as a mitigating factor in her sexuality—Lisbeth is already counter-culture in more ways than you can count—but to bring to the surface the fact that she is a young person who has been repeatedly injured throughout her life.

And it works; Lisbeth may be everything most people hope their family members will never become, but they cannot help but view her with an avuncular fondness.

Characters such as Lisbeth are where the art of the novel intersects with the craft of it. Probably less than one-tenth of one percent of readers would identify with her (and those that would probably wouldn't read Scandinavian crime fiction to begin with). But for his novel to work—and it does—Larrson had to get *all* of his readers to care deeply for Lisbeth.

The Character You Hate to Love

This is the sort of issue I face all the time, because every one of my novels to date has contained characters with evangelical Christian worldviews, certainly another of those love-it-or-hate-it propositions. And as a Christian myself, I often reach out to those inclined to hate it.

Which is an absolutely huge proportion of my readership.

Certainly I understand the sentiment. When two guys with short-sleeve dress shirts, clip-on neckties, gospel tracts and Scofield Reference Bibles show up on my front porch, I hide behind the curtains and refuse to answer the door, just like everybody else.

Part of the reason I do this is because I've read the Bible several times, and have yet to find the chapter and verse where Jesus shows up in a geeky Kmart dress shirt with a pocket full of gospel tracts.

And another part—the main part—is because so much of contemporary Christianity is so bull-headedly confrontational. The message may be "repent and be saved," but the thinly veiled subtext is "convert or be damned," and one gets the feeling that one must either sign (or pray) on the bottom line, or be told, "Fine, you had your chance; now *go* to hell."

Or words to that effect.

And I think that people who dislike evangelical Christians do so for the same reason that most people dislike bullies. We all have a natural aversion to being pigeonholed and discomfited, particularly when the perpetrators appear close-minded and two-dimensional.

Religion, politics and lifestyle decisions all arrive with baggage when we ascribe them to our characters. And it seems to me that there are three ways to make them tolerable, or even palatable, to our readers.

Exfoliation

The first is a process I like to think of as "exfoliation." In this, you introduce your character with his or her baggage all intact. Then, in a process similar to peeling away the layers of an onion, you reveal at least some of how and why that baggage got there in the first place.

This is the approach that Stieg Larrson employs with Lisbeth Salander in *The Girl with the Dragon Tattoo*.

We first see her through the eyes of her employer, the head of a private security agency. He remembers being on the verge of firing her, and only then discovering her extraordinary investigative powers.

We soon understand that she is a crusader of sorts, uncovering and exposing men who abuse women and children.

Later we see her visiting her mother, a dementia sufferer, in a nursing home.

We learn that Lisbeth was bullied as a child and met violence with violence, after which (because she refused to answer psychologists' questions) she narrowly averted institutionalization, and was placed instead under the care of a guardian.

Bit by bit, we have learned to see past Lisbeth's hard-shell exterior, and appreciate the sensitive young woman who lives within.

It takes some time. Lisbeth is the title character of *The Girl with the Dragon Tattoo*, but she does not meet its protagonist, Mikael Blomkvist, until the second half of the book.

Larrson had good reason to wait so long; he needs to develop both characters. Lisbeth has been victimized physically and socially, and Blomkvist—a journalist convicted of libel after refusing to reveal an off-the-record source—has been victimized professionally. In that manner, they are soul mates of a sort. By the time they meet, readers know them well enough to understand—and expect—that Blomkvist will treat the young woman fairly.

Environment

A second way to make the baggage-encumbered character accessible is to place that character in surroundings in which his or her beliefs or actions are seen as everyday or even expected.

Let's say, for instance that you have a character who so literally accepts the word of the gospels that he gives away all his worldly goods, prays five times a day, adopts uncomfortable clothing on the premise that comfort is too worldly, and avoids sex whether it is outside of or within marriage.

In most environments, such a character is an oddball, a weirdo. But place him within the world of a fourteenth-century Catholic monastery, and that character and his habits become absolutely normal.

That's what the Italian novelist Umberto Eco did in his murder mystery *Il nome della rosa* (English title, *The Name of the Rose*).

In it, a traveling Franciscan monk in the year 1327 investigates several mysterious deaths at a Benedictine monastery. The Franciscan, a learned man of science, applies scientific principles to study the deaths, and is in every regard a monastic Sherlock Holmes (Eco even names him "Brother William of Baskerville").

But the book requires characters who live ascetic lives, so Eco places them in a setting in which such lifestyles are not only commonplace, but mandatory.

Development

And a third approach is to begin with a character who is not remarkable or distinctive in terms of politics, lifestyle or religion, and then develop that character—grow him or her into the person that is necessary for the story.

This is a technique I use often. In my 2004 novel, *Turn Four* (a book I mentioned in the last chapter: the one set in the world of NASCAR) my character Chance Reynolds is a preacher who travels with an organization that ministers to NASCAR drivers and teams.

But he doesn't start out that way.

As the book opens, Chance is a NASCAR driver with excellent prospects for winning a championship, and a thinly veiled feud with his main competition, an old-school driver who isn't afraid to wreck everybody else to win. Then, in an off-track accident (a helicopter crash), Chance loses most of the vision in one eye, a condition that renders him incapable of driving competitively. He has trained all his life to be a driver, and has no other employable skill, except one—he is an armchair theologian and a committed Christian, and he uses that as a springboard to become educated and ordained as a minister.

I use this approach a lot because, once readers like a character, they will tolerate or even embrace the choices that character makes, even when they differ dramatically from choices the readers might make on their own.

Putting It All to Work

So, back to the novel that got triggered by the quarter that I found in my change....

As I considered who to place at Seneca Rocks in that novel set in the summer of 1976, I knew that my main character was going to be a rock climber.

Rock climbing is a subject with which most readers are likely to be profoundly unfamiliar, so I decided to make him a younger rock climber—a teenager who was still somewhere on the learning curve. That way my readers would be able to discover some of the details organically, as my character discovered them in the story.

I decided on a young man, rather than a young woman, for a couple of reasons.

One is that I have had—albeit decades ago—experience at being a young man, and so could draw from that well.

And the other was that, while there were young women who climbed in 1976, they were the exception and because of that, they stood out. I didn't want my lead character to be conspicuous in that regard.

So I made my main character a young man with the somewhat-Irish-American name of Patrick Nolan. And for that summer of 1976, I placed him in the latter part of his sixteenth year.

Because I was going to take my time writing this novel, I figured Patrick was going to be with me for several months (it turned out to be several years), and purely out of selfishness, I decided to make him a kid I could like. He'd be smart, athletic, relatively outgoing, and not yet rebellious.

And although I didn't belabor the point, I made him successful enough at sports that it would guarantee him a certain level of popularity at school.

Done. Now who else?

Think back to your own sixteenth year, and chances are the world seemed a little dizzying back then. Life tends to revolve around friends and family. And because high school tends to operate on a group dynamic, the friends seem to come in packs.

Packs provide a lot of superficial interaction and camaraderie, but little in the way of emotional depth. To engage the interest of a reader, one needs a more profound relationship. So I wanted to free Patrick from the usual high-school dynamic of friends in groups, without making him moody or a loner.

That was what I wanted. I just wasn't certain how to get there.

Then there was the family. Family relationships complicate exponentially with each additional member, and I didn't want this to be an ensemble piece with a large and varied family, such as John Irving had in *The Cider House Rules*. In fact, I wanted the opposite, so I went for that and made Patrick an only child.

That left his parents, and even a very small nuclear family of a husband, a wife and a child can quickly lead to a complicated mixture of relationships. There is the relationship each parent has with the other, the relationship each has with the child, and the relationship the child has with each parent as seen from the child's perspective. That's a book in itself.

Also, because I had a sixteen-year-old boy as my protagonist, I figured I would eventually have a girl of about the same age. It would be natural, and it is also a fact that, of all the potential relationship stories out there, stories about love tend to resonate best with readers.

We all enjoy the like-new, discovery-filled feeling of falling in love, and the most ethical (and least dangerous) way to experience that feeling over and over again is to do it vicariously, through story.

So, knowing that Patrick would have a love interest later in the story, I wanted to simplify to the greatest extent possible the relationships I would be working with in his family. I also wanted to take Patrick away from the clique-and-class dynamic of being a popular boy in high school.

And it occurred to me that the simplest way to accomplish both would be to eliminate one of his parents early in the story. In my mind's eye, Patrick's father—Kevin—was the individual who introduced him to rock climbing. As I wanted Patrick to stay in that world, it was important to me to keep Kevin alive.

So my mind was made up; I killed off the mom.

The "Dead-Mom Story"

I say this sheepishly, not only because I rather heartlessly decided to do away with what turns out in retrospect to be a warm, loving, dedicated and hard-working woman, but because killing off a wife or a husband is a fairly common method of getting swiftly into a parent-child story—so much so that, at age five, my daughter had already identified the device and begun to describe family movies as "dead-mom stories" or "dead-dad stories."

Be that as it may, the device is used often because it works well.

And as I thought about this, I decided that, if I made the mother's death a tragedy, it could draw father and son together.

Moreover, if I made the death such a tragedy that Kevin (the father) decided to run away, and if I made Patrick the responsible and protective sort of son who would not let his father leave alone, but would accompany him, then that would remove Patrick from all of the friends he would have made to that point. For a time at least, he and his father would be stuck with one another.

Casting Call

I knew, of course, that there would be other characters in this novel. At least one would be based, generally, on a real person.

Seneca Rocks in the 'Seventies had a general store, an old-fashion mercantile with gas pumps out front, that was run by a middle-aged West Virginian who distrusted anyone and anything that came from up North, or the big city. He also had an opinion on everything and was more than ready to share it. He was the sort of guy who looked like he'd walked straight out of Central Casting—bib overalls and grain-elevator hat, and a constant chaw of tobacco in his cheek. I knew he'd be in the book somewhere, and probably sooner, rather than later.

But outside of Patrick and his father and that one local-color character, I did not at that point have a clear view of anyone else in the story.

That didn't matter; I knew that they would come to me as I wrote.

So—father and son in a fresh location. An interesting location: Seneca Rocks, West Virginia in 1976.

My mind was made up.

I was definitely writing a dead-mom story.

And the next questions I had to deal with were these: Who tells the story? And how will it be told?

| THREE: The Storyteller

We have to dare to be our selves, however frightening or strange that self may prove to be. — MAY SARTON

ASK A CHILD to tell you about his or her day, and you'll hear, "We went ..." or "I saw ..."

First person: first person is the language of truth, the point of view of verisimilitude; it is the way of speaking we all naturally resort to when conveying personal history.

But ask the same child to tell you a story, and you're likely to get, "Once upon a time, there was ... "

Third person: "he," "she," "they," "it." When we resort to third person, we immediately imply that what we are talking about did not happen to us personally. It is the language we use when reporting the behavior of someone else and, because it takes the spotlight off of us as narrator, it is also the language most people default to when creating fiction: the natural language of storytelling.

As long as it is clear that a story is being told, third person is the point of view in which it is socially permissible to lie, and that's probably why it is the point of view in which most fiction is written. We are naturally disposed to view prevarication unkindly, and third-person eases the sting of what we've been raised to believe is a sin.

You'll get arguments from fiction-writers on this point. They'll point out that third person allows them to share the thoughts and viewpoints of multiple characters, and that it eliminates the need to marry the narrative to a single character—and these things are certainly true.

But I still suspect a large part of the reason for writing in third person is social conditioning. It is simply the most comfortable voice to use for wholesale fabrication.

Second Person

There is, of course, another point of view—second person: "you."

Normally the language of direct address, such as personal commands, condemnation and praise, second person was also in vogue for a time with French historians: "You are standing with Napoleon on the smoke-filled battlefield at Waterloo…"

This point of view is rare in contemporary fiction, but it does exist, and it is usually literary poison.

There are exceptions. It was used by Jay McInerney in his 1984 bestseller, *Bright Lights, Big City*. Recalling that book on his website (jaymcinerney.com), McInerney writes:

"When I told my best friend and future editor Gary Fisketjion what I was doing he said that he hoped I wasn't trying to write an entire novel in the second person. I was too embarrassed to tell him that that was precisely what I was doing."

For *Bright Lights, Big City*, it worked. The first six sentences of that novel look like this:

You are not the kind of guy who would be at a place like this at this time of the morning. But here you are, and you cannot say the terrain is entirely unfamiliar, although the details are fuzzy. You are at a nightclub talking to a girl with a shaved head. The club is either Heartbreak or the Lizard Lounge. All might come clear if you could just slip into the bathroom and do a little more Bolivian Marching Powder. Then again, it might not.

Second-person point of view is a language that suggests a dream state (or, in future tense, fortune-telling or prophecy). In present tense, it is also an ideal way to present intoxication and confusion, which happens to make it ideal for McInerney's debut novel. But used incorrectly—and nine-hundred-ninety-nine times out of a thousand, its use will be incorrect—it is simply a handy way to irritate and alienate one's readers.

So, except for the odd prologue, most novelists avoid the second-person point of view, and stick instead to the third and, to a lesser degree, the first.

Time and Scope

As classically defined, there are a couple other elements that factor into a narrative point of view.

One is tense.

Most novels are narrated in past tense: you are being told a story that has already occurred.

More of a rarity in contemporary fiction is present tense. It is generally used when the writer wants to create a very fast-paced, edgy story, one that unfolds literally as it is being told. It is more of a challenge in terms of suspension of disbelief—the reader is tempted to ask, "If this is happening as I read, then how did it come to be written down in the first place?"

But, just as audiences at Broadway musicals accept and expect the fact that the characters will occasionally break into song, present tense can be used successfully if the tense is appropriate to the genre and the focus of the novel.

The Story Yet to Happen

Then there is future tense.

I cannot think of a single instance in which a novel has been written in it successfully—that is, a novel that does not leave its readers wanting to rub ground glass into their eyes so they won't have to go on.

A novel written in future tense has no choice but to sound like a virtually endless visit to a palm reader.

But I have seen it used successfully in dream-state prologues. It is, however, like sipping an extremely sweet aperitif—interesting only if taken in very small and occasional servings.

Knowledge

I said earlier that there were a couple of other elements that factor into the traditional classification of points of view. Actually, there are three, but the last two are so closely linked that they may be thought of as almost a single component, and that is the level of knowledge and emotional content being conveyed by the narrator.

If the narrator knows everything, then the novel is being told from an "omniscient" point of view, while a story that tells us what just one character knows (or does not let us into any characters' heads at all) is said to be "limited." And if we know the emotional condition of one or more of the characters (how the character feels about what is going on), the story is being told in a "subjective" fashion, while a story in which we don't know how the character feels is a story that is being told in an "objective" fashion.

Most novels are written in past tense, from a third-person omniscient point of view.

And this, in part, is where many first-time novelists go off the rails.

Intonation Versus Information

Because most of us have been reading for practically longer than we can remember, we tend to think of reading as a way of conveying information.

And it's not—not directly at least.

When we write, the marks we put on paper or onscreen do not represent thoughts.

They represent phonemes—*sounds*. The sounds join together to form words, and it is the words that represent thoughts and concepts.

This is a fine distinction, but an important one.

I make it because, as a result of our over-familiarity with the acts of writing and reading, we often skip right past the phonemes and the sounds and go straight to the thoughts they represent. And the sound of the narration can add to the dream-state of the novel, or it can (just as easily) confuse, muddy or detract from it.

Point of view can compound this. Because an omniscient narrator knows everything, newer novelists are often tempted to just tell us what the narrator knows. And while it is possible to download a whole bunch of information that way, information downloading is not what fiction is all about. To put the readers there with you, in the dream of your story, you have to do more than give them the background. You have to present them with the same environments, the same actions, and the same dilemmas being faced by your characters.

Just delivering information is a mistake in most kinds of writing, and it is doubly so in fiction. The point of fiction is not simply to convey information; it is to illuminate relationships, to place the reader in the characters' emotional context, and to allow the reader to share in the perils, victories, joys, loss and growth of the characters. Clunky data-dumping will not accomplish this.

After all, if the point of the novel was simply to convey information, *The Great Gatsby* could be reduced to a single sentence: "Money cannot buy happiness." And *The Old Man and the Sea* would become, "Santiago caught the fish, but the sharks ate it."

The points of those books are in relationships and emotional context, and you get that by going above a simple conveyance of information. It's not mere story-telling. It's not even, "Show; don't tell." It's more along the lines of "Sing and share and show; don't tell."

The same guidelines hold true for subjective viewpoints; just because your point of view allows you to get into the character's head doesn't mean that you can get away with telling us, "Mary Jane was worried."

On the contrary, your duty as an author is to let us *see* Mary Jane worried and, if you want to use those subjective privileges, to let us feel the tension in the back of her neck and the rapid beat of her pulse.

The reason you need to do this is because, while we are wired to be emotional beings and to invest emotionally in those around us, we don't reach out to make that emotional investment unless we first enter the dream-state of the story.

And to do that, we need that full, five-senses experience.

Heartstrings

That's why those commercials seeking support for overseas children always show the kids: once you see them, you care. Presented without that sensory connection, they are simply statistics. And statistics don't tug at our heartstrings.

So while a less restrictive point of view can certainly be a useful tool for sharing the thoughts, views and emotions of your characters, it's a mistake to rely solely on that tool to do the work for you; you'll write a boring book.

This doesn't mean that successful novelists never story-tell. On the contrary, practically all of them do—in moderation. But the way to develop a feel for that moderation is to err on the conservative side.

Finding the Conservative Side

A few years ago, after dispensing that same advice to legions of writers-workshop participants, I decided to take my own medicine and write a novel from a purely third-person objective point of view. My protagonist would be my anchor, but he would not be my point-of-view character. Rather, my narrator would be able to see (and hear, touch, taste and smell) practically everything that my protagonist saw. The narrator would be able to observe everything that my protagonist did, but the narrator would not be allowed to share that character's thoughts ... or any of the other characters' thoughts.

If a character was upset, that character would have to express it through, say, the way he cooked dinner. Or he could simply say so. But otherwise the reader would not know about it.

That novel was *Wind River*, published by Bethany House in 2008. It opens on a mountain trail, an environment in which it would be entirely natural to hop into a character's head and describe his reaction to nature's grandeur. But it doesn't. In *Wind River*, this is the opening sentence:

The morning sun had just cleared the summits to the east, and the grass in the small valley was still thick with dew, wetting the boots and the shins of the man and the boy.

It is observation, pure and simple, with an emphasis on "simple;" the entire sentence is composed of one- and two-syllable words.

Then that scene proceeds to description of the two characters:

The man, tall and unstooped, wore bib overalls over a flannel shirt, his feet shod with cream-soled tan work boots, white hair crowned with a faded green John Deere ball cap. Carrying a heavy Kelty backpack topped with a rolled tent, he walked confidently. His oaken walking staff, gripped just beneath the fist-size burl at its top, seemed to be more for cadence than support. The whiteness of his hair, his wire-rimmed bifocals, the crow's feet next to his eyes, and a longish nose, just beginning to thicken, were the only hints that he was well past his middle years.

The boy wore a hooded sweatshirt and blue jeans bought too long and cuffed short so they wouldn't drag. His pack was little more than a rucksack, and in his right hand he carried an Orvis split-bamboo fly rod, fully assembled and bobbing before him like a slender, overlong divining rod. Like the man, his blond-streaked light-brown hair was also topped with a John Deere cap, only his cap was still brand-new.

This is more character description than I usually indulge in, particularly on the first few pages. But part of the older man's character is that is he a little eccentric, and I wanted to convey that through details such as his choice of bib overalls for backpacking attire.

As I described him, I also described the boy, who is going to become my protagonist. And I didn't mind indulging in so much detailed description of my protagonist as, the next time the reader meets him, in the next chapter, he will be thirteen years older and a grown man.

Part of the distinctive point-of-view in this book is that the third-person narrator makes the sort of judgments that an everyday person observing events might make.

He observes, for instance, that the man walks "confidently." He says that not only are the boy's blue jeans too long for him, but they are "blue jeans bought too long and cuffed short so they wouldn't drag."

The narrator also chooses details that are, to some degree revelatory, especially to readers who are attuned to the world of this book.

For instance, the boy carries an "Orvis split-bamboo fly rod" and readers who are experienced anglers will know that this is a very expensive piece of equipment—thousands of dollars apiece today, and certainly worth hundreds of dollars whenever it was purchased back in the day, before the start of the book. That the boy would be trusted to carry such a thing implies that either the man is reckless, or that the boy is trustworthy and the man loves him very much— and my hope was that my angling-educated readers would assume the latter. But the narrator does not lead the readers into this assumption. It is a nuance left there for the reader to discover.

Then the scene proceeds to action:

A small movement in the woods high on the hill to their right brought both hikers to a halt. They stood there, silent, for a moment, the bright mountain sun reflecting off a thousand beads of water on the foliage around them.

Then the man made a sound halfway between a cough and the caw of a crow.

Up on the slope, a deer stepped out from the trees, velvet nubbins of horn sprouting on his tawny head. The deer stared at the man and boy, took a tentative step in their direction, then turned and bolted back uphill, his white tail upright in alarm, the snapping branches marking his flight for several seconds after he had vanished back into the forest.

The man tamped his staff on the ground and chuckled. The boy looked his way.

It is a moment with magic, the kind of thing that, if it happened to you, you would remember it for along time.

And only at this point, after the introductions have been made, and the tone of this scene has been set, does the narrator share any dialogue:

"Why'd he come out like that?"

"I called him," the man said. "That sound I made? That's the sound his mama made when he was just a fawn, how she told him to stop doin' whatever he was doin', and get over to her. They hear it when they're growin' up, and they never forget it. Even if you can't bring a deer to you with that, you can freeze 'em in their tracks for just a second when they hear it. It's how they was raised."

The boy made the sound, a tenor echo of the man's warm baritone.

"That's it," the man told him. "You've got it."

The setting in this opening scene could be rugged, challenging, or out-there tough. But the scene is none of these things. Instead, it is warm and endearing (and not simply in my opinion: I have hundreds of emails from readers who have told me as much). And the thing that makes it this way is the implied narrator, and what he chooses to convey through this third-person limited point of view. It is a powerful tool that every novelist has available, should he or she choose to employ it.

But, when the story is the kind in which character observation and reflection need to be shared, first person can be an equally potent implement.

The Personal Voice

As fiction writers, we always talk about wanting to achieve the "reasonable suspension of disbelief" with our readers. A major point of good fiction is to create the illusion of truth, to present fiction in such a manner that the reader accepts it as a sort of personal history, a recounting of fact.

In *Ernest Hemingway on Writing*, edited by Larry W. Phillips, Phillips presents a portion of an unpublished manuscript by Hemingway, in which the novelist says:

When you first start writing stories in the first person if the stories are made so real that people believe them the people reading them nearly always think the stories really happened to you.

And Papa's right.

The first time I noticed this was many years ago, when my best friend, Al Lee (an old MFA classmate of mine from Bowling Green), got a job editing a new magazine for stamp collectors, *Stamp World*.

Part of Al's vision for the magazine—a part that was central to him landing the job—was that each issue would contain what Al referred to as "philatelic fiction." Each issue would contain a short story in which stamps and stamp collecting would be central to the story.

The problem was that, once Al started looking, he found there was very little of such short fiction available—very little, at least, that modern-day readers would find relevant and palatable. So he turned to me and asked me to write him some stories for the magazine.

Of course I agreed, and I decided that one of the first of those stories would be about a boy who lived in secluded circumstances, a boy to whom stamps and the places they suggested would be a portal to the great world beyond.

To do that, I would need to set the story in a place and time when all the most obvious means of modern communication—things such as radio and television and regularly delivered newspapers and magazines—either did not exist or were not available.

As it happened, I had just concluded a long and rambling climbing and fishing trip out West. And as part of that trip, I had stopped in at Old Faithful Lodge in Yellowstone Park.

The stop was not long. I had friends with me who were eager to get some trout-fishing done. But we were there long enough for me to wander about the lobby for twenty minutes or so, and to stop into the gift shop and buy a book-length history of the lodge.

The brief quarter-hour or so was enough for me to get a semblance of feeling for the place, and the history gave me interesting period details: the fact that, back in the early years of the Lodge, the iron telephone wires were often pulled down by winter ice storms; that the hotel staff would sometimes pour soap down a geyser to coax it into erupting for the edification of the guests; and that there once was a carbide-gas spotlight atop the Lodge that could be used to pick out wandering bears and other wildlife as a form of evening amusement.

I decided to place that boy in Old Faithful Lodge as the son of the assistant manager, back in a time leading up to and including the first years of World War I, when the assistant manager (as low man on the management totem-pole) would stay in the hotel with his family during the winter off-season, to keep enough heat in the place to keep things from freezing, and effect any repairs needed by winter weather-damage. Think the setting and premise of Stephen King's

The Shining, only told from the first-person point-of-view of a grown man who had once been the assistant manager's son, and set in an earlier time, without any of King's horror elements.

I wrote that story. It was called "Old Faithful," and it was published in *Stamp World* in 1984.

And about a month later I received a letter, sent to me care of the magazine. It was written in fountain pen, in a thready and quaking hand, and it was from a lady who was obviously well up in her years.

She told me who she was, and that, as a young girl, she had lived in the Yellowstone Park region. And because my details in the story matched so vividly to her memories of that time, she assumed that I had also grown up in the park just prior to World War I, and she was wondering how it was that she did not know me.

I kept that letter and treasured it until it was lost in a subsequent move, because it told me that I had succeeded in one aspect as a fiction writer; I had written a story that rang so true that at least one reader well acquainted with my setting had accepted it as fact.

And that is part of the power of the first-person point of view.

In Hemingway's manuscript, he used the phrase, "When you first start writing stories in the first person…"

He used that, I believe, because if you write in first person regularly, and a reader is familiar with your larger body of work, that reader soon realizes that the various stories represent a multitude of characters and those characters (particularly if they are of different genders or of different ethnicity or backgrounds) could not possibly all be the same author, disguising his or her personal history as fiction.

But if a reader has not read you regularly, and especially if that first-person piece is the first of yours that particular reader has read, the story (if well-crafted) will almost always convince the reader that you are actually writing about yourself.

And since that first thready letter, I have received a great many letters and emails, and read a number of reviews and Amazon comments, in which the reader was led to believe that one of my first-person stories or novels was actually a slice of my own life.

Even now, when I have seen many such reader comments and letters, I am always a bit in awe of the fact that fiction can ring so true when the main character is a narrator telling the story in the first person.

Other Options

There are seemingly endless variants on point of view.

One is the "epistolary novel." In its classic form, this is a novel written as a series of letters, usually between two people, although more than two is certainly possible. And in its modern form it can also be a series of letters … or emails, Tweets, texts, Facebook postings, or any of a myriad of personal communications.

The advantage of the epistolary novel is that it allows multiple characters to provide the narrative from a first-person point of view. And the downside of it is that the narrative is delivered in the sorts of small missives in which everyday people are usually not particularly eloquent.

But with the right characters, it not only will work, but will allow the novelist to present the sorts of didn't-see-it-coming twists that are possible in third-person objective stories, while preserving the purity and immediacy of a first-person narrative.

Another variation—and one that I employed in my 2009 novel, *Pirate Hunter*—is to use more than one type of narrator.

Pirate Hunter is a novel that is composed of paired stories: two separate but parallel stories told in an alternating fashion throughout the length of the book.

One story, set in the eigthteenth century, is that of a young African man who is freed from a slave ship by pirates.

The other story, set in contemporary times, is that of a young marine archaeologist who takes a job working with a Key West treasure-salvage company.

As the two stories echo and parallel one another in the novel, I distinguished one from the other by writing the historical story in third person, while using a first-person point of view for the contemporary story.

The tactic worked well, and one thing that surprised me was that, when I spoke to readers who were not writers themselves, many were surprised when I told them that the narrative point of view was different in the two stories; they only remembered that they could easily tell one from the other, without being distracted by the switch.

While it is unusual to write a novel in this fashion: half in first person and half in third, many writers will use narrative-point-of-view shifts to convey dream sequences, flashbacks, backstory and the like.

And there is no reason it has to be restricted to first- and third-person narration. It can also be done in the first and second person, or second and third.

Choosing

I had worked in, or at least experimented with, all of these narrative points of view before I began *In High Places*, so I was aware of the advantages and disadvantages of each as I prepared to write the book.

Initially I thought of this project, as I usually think of each project early on, as a third-person subjective novel. That is the viewpoint that allows the most latitude; it allows you to fly using all of the controls.

But the more I thought about the story (for I usually think things over for quite a long time before I sit down to begin to write), the more I realized that this story would require several things to happen offstage, without the main character's knowledge. And to most effectively do that, I needed to write in first person from the point of view of my main character—who is a teenage boy throughout most of the book.

This posed an interesting question: exactly *when* is the story being told?

Interesting because, if I told the story contemporary to the time of its actions—i.e., in 1976, when my main character was turning

THE NOVEL & THE NOVELIST

seventeen, I would be limited to the memories, experience, attitude and maturity of a seventeen-year old. And even though this particular seventeen-year-old was going to be more mature than most, I thought the story would require a level of depth that might not come across as believable if the story was told in real time.

Another hurdle, and this was a big one for me, was that if I told the story as it happened in 1976, I would be limited to the vernacular of the 'Seventies, and if I did that, I would run the risk of making the language sound corny. Fans of Holden Caulfield may tar and feather me for saying it, but this is one of the things that I loved about *A Catcher in the Rye* when I was fifteen years old, and learned to detest as I grew older; Salinger's main character was cool when I was his contemporary, but became more than a bit of a jerk when I looked at him from the perspective of adulthood.

What I needed then, for *In High Places* (the title, by the way, was in my head before I'd so much as written a word), was a filter—the diffusing perspective of age. And I decided to write the book as a first-person narrative, written from the perspective of a forty-five-year-old man, looking back on the summer he turned seventeen.

The Narrator as Character

To do this effectively, I had to think about this grown man. What would he be like, and how would he have matured from his younger self? And what would have influenced that maturity? What would have happened to him in the intervening twenty-eight years that would have affected those changes?

It was an interesting puzzle because, while I only needed to consider the experiences of seventeen years to arrive at the composition of my main character at the time of the story (or at least the time of the bulk of the story), I would need to consider roughly two-and-a-half times as much to arrive at the composition of my *narrator*.

In other words, it took me much longer to figure out and get a feeling for my narrator than it did to do the same thing for my main character.

I needed to understand his path both geographically and philosophically: where he would go to school, who he would meet and what effects they would have on him, what career he would pursue, and what he valued as a grown man (as opposed to what he valued as a young man). I needed to endow him with both the strengths and the imperfections that I would build into him, were I crafting him as a character.

So while the story of *In High Places* focuses on one summer in the life of the seventeen-year old son, it is told from the perspective of a narrator who really has more in common with the young character's father.

Here's a sample. Following the death of Patrick's mother, Patrick and his father have moved from urban Ohio to rural West Virginia, where Patrick's father buys and is renovating an old, hunting-lodge-style log home. The renovation is not yet done (among other things, they are waiting for a valve to come in for the LP gas tank), so they are living in an old Airstream trailer while they do the work on the house.

In this scene, it is early summer and Patrick and his father have just finished splitting a load of wood and stacking it in the woodshed so the wood will have time to dry and cure for the coming winter:

"There," my father said when we had put the last of it away and squirted WD-40 onto the tools. "Even if that valve comes in tomorrow, we've got a good, solid week's worth of backup heat in there for this winter. And if we want a roaring fire Christmas Eve, well, we've got it."

We started toward the trailer and then he stopped walking, looking at the house.

"What?"

"Oh, I was just thinking about Christmas." He shook his head. "This will be a great place at Christmas, Sport."

And the look in his eyes was so hollow that I shivered, despite the warmth of the evening.

That scene tells us a lot about who the narrator is. He remembers and recounts this particular small scene because it points directly at a main theme of the book, the theme of loss. And because the narrator is mature, he doesn't feel the need to state the obvious: that Patrick's father is haunted by the fact that his wife is dead. The narrator is sufficiently wise to understand that the reader will understand this implicitly.

At this point, I need to insert a warning. What follows next is a spoiler. Not a spoiler in the classic, you find out whodunit, sense, but certainly enough that it reveals out of context several things that a reader would otherwise discover organically as the book proceeds.

So once again: if you have not yet read *In High Places* and you intend to (and you don't have to—this book will "work" for you whether you read it or not), then you should probably stop reading this now and go do that.

First-Person, Personified

To tell my story from the perspective I desired, I decided my narrator would be the pastor of an evangelical Christian church in semi-rural Michigan, looking back on three great losses in his life. And he would recount these losses in the manner of a man who is grieving, yet tempered by hope—simply because, if one lives long enough and grows sufficiently, grief tempered by hope is a significant part of what corporeal life eventually amounts to.

Initially, I had only intended for *In High Places* to recount one year—and especially one summer—out of my main character's life.

But as my narrator took shape before me, his life-shaping moments had such impact on the story that key events from the following twenty-eight years found their way into the book.

And as to when those events and others would be presented, and how, I would need to consider that element which builds to the crux of any novel or truly complete story. And that is *conflict*.

| FOUR: The Ladder of Jeopardy

"To live is to war with trolls." — HENRIK IBSEN

WERE I TO ASK YOU, "Tell me your story—the story of you," very likely you would tell me where you grew up, possibly what your parents did for a living, where you went to school, your first job, how you met the love of your life, and how you got to be where you are now. You might even throw in details: a description of your first car, how long (or short, or bleached or spiked or dyed) your hair was in college, or the house that you live in now. You might talk about your children. You might talk about your pets.

But none of that is a story. A description of that sort is known as a "chronicle." And while a chronicle can be a story, what we just ran through lacks one critical element that all narratives must have to be recognized as a story by the vast majority of people.

It lacks conflict.

The prototype of all stories is the story of the overcomer. A character—generally the lead character or main character—wants, desires or needs something, and something or someone is preventing that character from reaching his or her goal.

What makes it a story is that conflict, and how the character deals with it. And that's been the case since Ulysses tried to get home from the Odyssey (and before).

Seeking Strife

Human beings arrive on Earth seemingly pre-wired to seek out such stories. We even gravitate to them in our daily news. If a candidate runs unopposed for office, hardly anyone notices. It may make the news, but if it does, it probably won't be front-page news. Ask any newspaper editor, and they'll tell you, "There's no story there."

But put another candidate into play for the same office, have each do his or her best to defeat the other, and it's not only news; most people will follow it as a form of entertainment.

It's the same with most of the media we digest. Two rock idols or movie stars who get married and live happily ever after may draw our admiration, but they won't attract our attention. But let the marriage go on the rocks, and people will buy magazines to read about it.

The principle is even wired into the ways our children play. Leave a bunch of little boys alone and they will probably find a way to play a heroes-versus-bad-guys game, the opening gambit of which is the quarrel over who has to be the bad guy. And little girls long to be princesses—a role that, in fairy tales, is almost always the result of a conflict successfully overcome.

In speaking engagements, Kurt Vonnegut, Jr., used to give the same lecture over and over. To assure a good turnout, he often called it, "How to Get a Job Like Mine." But the lecture (I had the privilege of seeing it twice, years apart) was really on what it is that constitutes a story.

Vonnegut's example in that lecture was the story of "Cinderella." He said it was perfect because it contained two goals, each with its own conflicts (getting to go to the ball, and getting to try on the glass slipper), with the bonus of a countdown (the strike of midnight) in between.

Not Just the Protagonist

I think Vonnegut gravitated to "Cinderella" because of the dual conflicts.

Just about everyone in that story is looking for something they cannot immediately attain: Cinderella is longing to be restored to her former station in life, the prince is looking for a wife, the king wants a wedded son, the stepsisters want husbands, and the stepmother wants money.

And while Cinderella is a fairy tale, it mirrors life in that fashion, because the truth is that just about everyone wants something that is not within his or her immediate grasp. Acknowledgement of this fact is one step that helps lead to very readable fiction.

One of the fundamental differences between a character and a caricature is that virtually all good characters share the very human trait of having aspirations and goals.

The coincidence and contradictions of these multiple wants can produce stories readers will remember forever.

In the O. Henry short story, "The Gift of the Magi," there are only two characters. They are a young married couple, quite poor, and each wants more than anything to buy the other the perfect Christmas gift. But, being poor, neither has the money. So, unbeknownst to one another, they arrive at the same means of overcoming that conflict. They both sell their most precious possessions—she, her knee-length hair, and he, his heirloom pocket watch—in order to buy the other a gift.

Those gifts, unfortunately, turn out to be a set of ornamental hair combs and a watch-chain.

I read this story to my daughter the Christmas Eve that she was six, and she—partly because she was a little girl with hair that fell past her waist—gasped, put her tiny hand theatrically to her chest, and said, "Again, Dad. Read it again."

Which is a reaction that we, as fiction writers, should all aspire to elicit from our readers.

So, while the language of the writing workshop customarily speaks of "the conflict," it is actually "conflicts"—*plural*—that produce the most readable fiction.

When everyone wants something that is just (or more than just) out of reach, we reproduce in our stories an environment that sounds like life, because hope is the spark plug that stimulates our heartbeats: the reason we go on living.

Even in very short stories, then, there are multiple desires and multiple conflicts that stifle or prevent the realization of those desires. In longer fiction, the main character or characters may face several conflicts during the course of the story.

And it is the structure of these multiple conflicts that turn a story into a novel, because in a novel, two things happen.

The Winding, Uphill Road

First, the paths followed by the lead characters are going to parallel, intersect, contrast or collide with the paths of other characters, each pursuing their own aspirations.

This can happen in a story as well, but it always happens in a novel, and because the construction of that path can seem similar to that of charting the course of a ship through treacherous waters, this part of fiction is referred to with a word borrowed from maritime vocabulary; it's referred to as "the plot."

The second thing that happens in a novel is that the plot takes a distinctive form, in that the conflicts faced by the lead character escalate and render his or her situation increasingly perilous (oftentimes, and even usually, the work of an antagonist).

Think of the plot as a ladder and think of the conflicts as rungs. With each rung, the character becomes increasingly committed, and with each rung the character is placed in increasingly dire circumstances—in further and further jeopardy.

This is part of the narrative arc we mentioned a while back, and there is a name for it: "rising action."

Reading a novel without this rising action is like tuning into the last twenty minutes of a movie. The hero may be in jeopardy, but our concern for him is superficial at best, because we do not know him. We have not attained the sympathy that comes with familiarity.

The conflict will probably also lack meaning because one of the points of the novel is for us to watch the main character (or characters) grow, and one of the central ways we are going to see that growth is by watching how the ultimate conflict is handled by the character. Presented alone, it lacks context.

And finally, presented without preamble, the immensity of the final conflict may ring as false or far-fetched to the reader.

Our mission, then, as novelists, is to lead the reader up the ladder of jeopardy, and past those ascending rungs of conflict.

And the first step of doing that is the first step …

… The first conflict.

Common Ground

Conflict has a purpose beyond the mathematical utility of a plot point. It reaches back to why we choose reading as a form of entertainment in the first place.

Ever watch three-year olds at play? They may start out with what their parents refer to as "playing nice." But left to their own devices, children at play (and adults at play, and even dogs and cats at play) will gradually escalate to the point that the participants are flushed and hyperactive.

And the reason they appear this way is because they are anxious. A product of play—and, indeed, what many psychologists believe is the basic reason for play—is *anxiety*.

Why anxiety? Because anxiety requires the players to exercise social skills to resolve that anxiety. It teaches the players how to live in relationship with one another: from who gets to lead, to how to be a peacemaker.

When they are at play, even the children who are not actively involved in finding a resolution benefit, because they are observing usable social skills that help them deal with the world around them. And whether active or passive, those at play are energized by the experience. It makes them more hopeful. And it helps stave off depression: boredom and the blues.

This is important because it may be the deep, latent reason that human beings crave story. This mounting conflict, this narrative tension, triggers within us essentially the same reaction that is brought about by play-induced anxiety: a thirst for a return to equilibrium—resolution of the conflict or solution of the problem.

The "Relaxing Read"

I know that this seems counter-intuitive. After all, when we think of reading, we think of relaxation: an Adirondack chair on the beach, or a comfortable wingback chair on a winter's evening, next to a crackling fire. We talk about "curling up with a good book" … and not curling into the fetal position.

So how in the world does reading equate to anxiety?

The answer is that it equates in the same way that play feels pleasurable. Children seek the anxiety of play because it is fun. And when deprived of it, they complain that they are bored. We innately desire a disruption to normal—particularly those sorts of disruptions that can then be alleviated through personal intervention or social skills.

Still not convinced that reading and play are primally related? Consider then, what you tell your friends when you've read a truly extraordinary novel:

"I couldn't put it down…" or

"It was a real page-turner…" or

"I couldn't sleep until I'd finished it…" or even

"I had to remind myself to breathe."

Do these sound like the reactions to a relaxing and peaceful activity?

There is such a thing as writing that is read for its soothing and calming effects. But that is pastoral poetry.

Fiction—the sort of fiction that people like to read—requires conflict. And fictional narrative requires tension.

Used correctly, then, conflict strikes a chord with the reader; a chord that is both primal and emotional. In order to strike that chord, we first have to help the reader identify with the character who is facing—or about to face—the conflict.

There are a number of ways of doing this. In fact, in most cases, the writer will use one of four approaches.

Doorway One: Beginning with Normal

One method—often employed in suspense and horror novels—is to set the stage for a conflict by starting out with a scene that is pleasant, normal and ordinary.

This is a technique that Stephen King has used often. People are depicted doing unremarkable, everyday things, the sorts of things with which most readers will readily identify (in one case, sitting on the toilet, reading a popular mail-order catalog). Then, shortly thereafter, the unspeakable begins to happen.

This momentary tranquility can last for a sentence, or it can be even briefer than that. The first half of the first sentence of Tolstoy's *Anna Karenina* is this charming statement:

Happy families are all alike ...

But then the second half of that sentence crops up:

... every unhappy family is unhappy in its own way.

From there, we proceed to learn snippets of an affair that caused one family to dissolve.

The conflict doesn't need to come that quickly. In my novel, *Wind River*, the entire first chapter is a picture of pastoral bliss: a young boy and a grandfather-figure on a fishing and camping trip in the mountains.

Then the second chapter opens and that young boy has become a young man, trying to keep his fellow Marines alive in a combat zone in the Middle East.

A short chapter is about as much of the pastoral approach as most readers are going to find acceptable. And even then, you'll want to leave them with a reason to go on to Chapter Two.

In that opening chapter of *Wind River*, my two characters have stopped to fish and rest along the hiking trail. The boy—his name is Tyler—has stepped into the creek to land his trout, and he's had to change to a dry pair of socks. Then the chapter closes this way:

The boy beamed and the man seemed to dim a little, his smile straightening, eyes moving back to the jagged edge of the distant ridgeline.

"What are you thinking?"

The man smiled at him. "About how much I love coming here. About how I like being here with you."

"Then why did you look sad there for a little bit?"

The man cocked his head and studied the boy a

moment, then turned his attention toward the ridge again, tucking the Bible back into his bib pocket and buttoning the pocket shut.

"I've been coming into the Wind River Range for more than fifty years, Tyler. Started when I was barely shaving. And now ... well, now I'm old."

"You're not old."

The man took his cap off and his white hair shown in the sun.

"There's snow on the mountain," he said, laughing.

"But you're still strong."

"Am now." The man nodded. "But I won't be forever. And I was just thinkin' that there'll come a day when I won't be able to do this anymore. When I won't be able to just pack up and go."

The boy looked at the ridge as well.

"Then I'll bring you," he finally said.

"How's that?"

"When you can't come on your own. I'll come and I'll get you and I'll bring you. I'll come to your and Miss Edda's house, and I'll put you in my truck and I'll bring you."

"You have a truck now, do you?"

Tyler shook his head. "Not yet. But I will when I'm a man. And I'll come and I'll get you and I'll take you into the Winds, just like you take me now."

The man smiled, tan skin wrinkling more deeply behind his glasses at the corners of his blue eyes.

"Well, I'd like that," he said. "You wouldn't have to do it all the time. Who knows? When you grow up, you might live somewhere way across the country. But maybe when I'm too old to come up here all by my lonesome ... maybe you can come get me sometime and bring me back up for one last trip. Could you do that?"

"I'll do that."

"You promise?"

The boy spat on his palm and held his hand out.

The man spat on his own and they shook. No laughter. No jokes.

"It's a promise," Tyler told him.

"All right then." The man looked around the valley and took the boy's wet socks, putting them under the straps that held the tent on his back so they'd dry as they walked in the sun. "One last time. One last trip into the Winds."

"When you're too old."

"That's right. When I'm too old."

One reason conflict works so well in a story is because conflict raises a question in the mind of the reader. The reader wants to know if or how the conflict will be overcome.

This chapter, while largely devoid of conflict (other than the challenge of catching a fish) keeps the reader going by likewise ending with a question: whether the boy is going to make good on his promise and, if so, under what circumstances.

So even though there's no conflict yet, there is still that answer-seeking reason to continue.

And in *Wind River*, when Tyler—now a man—returns to take his mentor back into the mountains, Tyler is haunted by his past. The conflicts quickly escalate. And Tyler discovers that his mentor has ghosts as well.

Uneasy Peace

The peace of a novel's opening scene can also be relative. In *Danger Close*, a 2010 military espionage thriller I co-wrote with Lt. Gen. William G. Boykin, the book opens with a Special Forces team on a hilltop in Afghanistan. The characters are warriors in wartime.

But the scene begins on an evening that is calm, peaceful, and very nearly beautiful. The only hint of what's to come is what the protagonist is doing; he's placing Claymore mines to form a protective perimeter around the team's bivouac site. And by the time that chapter ends, a firefight has erupted.

Doorway Two: In the Thick of It

A second approach is to open with a character already in the throes of a conflict, dealing and fighting with it from the very first line.

Carl Hiassen's 2004 novel, *Skinny Dip*, does this. As the novel opens, Hiassen's character, Joey Perrone, has just been thrown overboard from a cruise ship, and we are getting her thoughts as she plummets several stories into the vast and empty ocean.

Starting in mid-conflict is a classic way of opening an adventure or an epic. In *The Iliad*, by Homer, the story starts with a quarrel that takes place between Achilles and Agamemnon. And the technique is old enough that it even has a Latin name: *in medias res*.

Doorway Three: Right After

A close cousin to beginning in the middle of things—so close that it still qualifies for the same *in medias res* label—is to begin in the immediate aftermath of a conflict. Something significant, something big, has just happened, and we start with what comes next.

Here, for instance, is the opening of Stephen King's novel, *11/23/63*:

> **I have never been what you'd call a crying man.**
>
> **My ex-wife said that my "nonexistent emotional gradient" was the main reason she was leaving me (as if the guy she met in her AA meetings was beside the point).**

And so Jake Epping, King's hero, begins his story with a broken heart, supposedly for being unable to demonstrate that he was broken-hearted.

But this soul-crushing experience—having the love of his life stolen away by another man—is going to be eclipsed in a few chapters by another issue. Jake's going to slip through a time warp and start making his way back to 1963, where he will try to keep Lee Harvey Oswald from assassinating John Fitzgerald Kennedy.

Doorway Four: The Teaser

There's one more approach that works very well: to open the novel with a teaser—the ultimate or penultimate conflict, or at least a conflict that significantly imperils the protagonist—glimpsed but not resolved.

One example of that is the opening sentence from Dennis Lehane's 2012 novel, *Live by Night*:

> **Some years later, on a tugboat in the Gulf of Mexico, Joe Coughlin's feet were placed in a tub of cement.**

Does that grab your attention?

Lehane's first sentence sparks several questions:

Several years later than what?

And …

What did Joe Coughlin do that made somebody mad enough to want to do away with him?

And …

How is he going to get out of this situation?

Or …

Is Joe even going to make it out of this situation at all?

So you keep going, and the rest of the paragraph reads like this:

> **Twelve gunmen stood waiting until they got far enough out to sea to throw him overboard, while Joe listened to the engine chug and watched the water churn white at the stern. And it occurred to him that almost everything of note that had ever happened in his life—good or bad— had been set in motion the morning he first crossed paths with Emma Gould.**

So here's another question:

Who is Emma Gould, and what does she have to do with this?

And then, within three paragraphs, we have jumped back in time and Joe and his partners are robbing what they have been told is a run-of-the-mill poker game ... only to discover that the players are all heavily armed mobsters.

This conflict introduces even more questions in the reader's mind: *Is the planned execution in retribution for robbing the game?*

We don't know.

But Lehane's novel is off and running.

Applied Theory

In *In High Places*, then, I had my choice of four proven ways to introduce conflict within my novel. But I had already decided that the novel would revolve around rock climbing, so that helped me to zero in on a technique.

You see, whenever psychologists rank common fears, acrophobia—the fear of heights—is always in the top five, and usually in the top three. And having been a rock climber myself, I knew that while a rock climber would not be a chronic acrophobe, an occasional lapse into fear is not only possible, but highly probable. It is common enough that circa-1970s rock-climbing parlance even had a term for it: being "gripped."

So I decided to open the book by having my lead character and narrator, Patrick, face the conflict of having to come to terms with that fear:

It was not the rock—it was never the rock; it was the air. Air: gusts and threads of it, rustling my hair at the edge of my faded red rugby shirt collar. Air: swaying the thin red climbing rope that dropped beneath me in a single, brief, pendulous loop. Air all around me and above me and behind me, open and empty and unsubstantial, drying the sweat on my dread-paled, beardless face, an

entire sea of air, an ocean of it, lying vacantly beneath my jutting, quaking heels.

By fingertips and the thin soles of my shoes, I hung over a deep pool of nothing, a drop one could pass through for an eternity before being swallowed by the bright green, spring-leafed treetops of the Monongahela National Forest.

The Gendarme was an exceptionally airy place, a thirty-foot, twenty-ton, top-heavy block of Tuscarora quartzite, perched tenuously upon the soaring, thin, cloud-feathered ridge that joined the twin summits of Seneca Rocks.

From the valley floor below, hundreds of feet below, it seemed very insubstantial, a blip in the naked stone skyline, the slightest thin twig of stone. But from its base, it was a gray, orange-lichened obelisk, a tower, soaring high into the stark, blue West Virginia sky.

You didn't step onto the Gendarme, you boarded it, a stretching traverse to the initial foothold, a tentative and overbalanced tiptoe, like stepping into an empty canoe.

Only the Gendarme was built to repel boarders—just fifteen degrees of westward tilt separated it from dead vertical. And that very first step left you open and exposed, as hung-out on the rock as one would be after a rope-pitch or two of straight-up conventional climbing.

Still, I felt absolutely ridiculous.

There I was, the sixteen-year-old who'd won four column-inches of praise for his junior-varsity football heroics, the cocky kid who'd waltzed up the considerably more challenging Thais face just the afternoon before. I'd climbed much harder routes than this; I'd *styled* much harder routes than this. Yet on this fine, early spring morning, I was clinging to the rock with all the urgency of a terrified primate. My rubber-soled shoes and my two clammy hands we smeared against the climb's rain-worn

holds, trying vainly to become one with the rock. I was gripped: frozen into immobility. And I was both of these things less than six feet away from my father.

Clinging to a rock face hundreds of feet in the air—even though he is on a rope being belayed by his father, and even though his father is near enough to talk with him—what's at stake here for Patrick is nothing less than his very life. And that's important because those conflicts that are a matter of life and death are the conflicts that interest readers the most.

It doesn't even matter that the reader knows that this particular conflict will be resolved with Patrick emerging safe and sound at the end of it. After all, unless Patrick is speaking to us from beyond the grave, he has to come out okay, because he's the one narrating the book. But the situation still works as a conflict, because the potential for loss exists here on several levels.

At one extreme, Patrick could lose his life; that's not going to happen, but the potential is there. At the other, he could chicken out, be unable to complete the climb, and lose credibility as a climber. Patrick's self-confidence is at stake as well.

But the chief risk that is at play here is the trust that exists between Patrick and Kevin—his father.

This first conflict is there, not simply to open the story with conflict, but to establish, in the very first scene, the relationship between these two. It is going to be the longest-running relationship in the book, and we are testing it from the very first sentence.

Again, No Rules

We don't have to stress and test the pivotal relationship in the very first scene. There is no rule that says we have to do that, just as there is no rule that says we have to open in conflict. But the option to do both is open, and for *In High Places*, it got the story going nicely, with an absolute minimum of throat-clearing.

We get a little more information as the early portion of the book progresses. Both Kevin and Patrick are feeling guilty that they're off playing while Laura (Kevin's wife and Patrick's mother) is home, studying and trying to finish her bachelor's degree. They also regret that they've not yet put in a brick patio that she had been asking them to add to the house. So they resolve to keep that promise to her, and to bring her along the next time that they go climbing in West Virginia.

Rising Action

So that's how the novel opens. Now the action needs to rise, and continue rising. It needs to take us to the focus of the book—the central conflict of the novel—and keep rising until we get to the climax, where everything is going to work out or fall apart.

And now that we have that introductory, easily resolved conflict out of the way, the best way to continue that rising action is to present a series of ascending conflicts, each one serious enough that it could, potentially, comprise the focal conflict of the novel.

The hint of discord in the household suggests that this is where we are going to find the central problem of *In High Places*. But that changes in the opening scene of the next chapter, as Patrick and his father arrive at their house, in Toledo, Ohio, and this next scene transpires:

> **At least we weren't the ones who found her. I've often wondered which one of us it would have damaged first if we had—my poet-engineer father, or me: his coddled and protected only son.**
>
> **But that's moot, because it was a neighbor, Dr. Marion, my mother's classical-literature professor, who came home after brunch at Churchill's on Sunday morning, and saw the blue-gray exhaust vapor creeping out from under our closed garage door.**
>
> **And it was Dr. Marion who had been watching by his window when we pulled into our driveway past nine that Sunday evening.**
>
> **Our house was a white, two-story Italianate,**

unremarkable in Toledo's historic Old West End. We hadn't finished wondering about the fact that there wasn't a single light showing anywhere in it when the old professor was there at the curb. First he came to my side and then, when he saw that I was driving, he scuttled around to my father's side and opened the door, tugging him out to the slim, dark lawn of the parkway, whispering urgently. Except that, from half-deaf Dr. Marion, even a whisper was like normal conversation and I heard every word.

He blurted it out awkwardly, an odd departure for a normally fastidious man, except, of course, there wasn't really a way to tell a person such a thing gracefully. And I was glad that he did it the way he did, raised voice and awkwardness and all, because it spared my father the agony of having to repeat the whole thing to me.

As I write this, I'm referring to *In High Places* on an e-book reader—the kind that has a progress bar on the bottom of the screen, showing how far along I am in the book. And this fresh conflict—which appears exactly five percent of the way into the story—is of a different nature from that with which we opened the book. There has been loss; there has been death.

Irreversible

Death is a special sort of conflict. It cannot be reversed; there is no resolution that will set things back the way they were before, so it requires a change in the character affected by the death; that character will either grow or crumble.

Patrick's mother has not appeared as a living character anywhere in the book; the only place we will see her in real-time is at the funeral home, as she is lying in the coffin for the viewing. But even though we have not met her, we feel her loss with him. And we will continue to feel her loss as he remembers her and mourns her absence.

This conflict raises a significant question for this book: how are Patrick and his father going to get along after the loss of the most important person in the world to them?

Dealing With It

Kevin attempts to deal with this by changing virtually everything. He quits his job as an automotive engineer and decides to leave Ohio and go start a climbing shop in West Virginia (the place he and Patrick had been visiting when they'd decided they'd been neglecting Laurie).

He even offers to leave Patrick behind with friends, so Patrick can play varsity football at the high school he'd already attended for two years. But Patrick insists on moving to West Virginia with his father.

At first, this tactic of changing everything appears to work. The two are engrossed in starting the new business.

Although they have moved their belongings into their new home—what was once a hunting lodge—they are living in a trailer on the property while renovations are completed on the old house.

The house—they call it "The Lodge"—is complete enough that Kevin goes into it to escape the cramped and cluttered confines of the trailer as he does his paperwork. And Kevin is doing that and has been in the house for quite a while when Patrick decides to go in and check on him.

But Kevin is not in the office. And from the footsteps he hears above him, on the second floor, Patrick deduces that his father has gone up to the master bedroom—the bedroom where they have stored all of Laurie's belongings.

Escalation

This is eighteen percent of the way into the novel:

Indian-quiet on my bare feet, I padded up the broad wooden staircase to the second floor, made my way down the short hall and paused the master bedroom door.

Guilt ran hot in me. There was no possibility of mistaken perception now; if my father discovered me, he would know I was spying.

But then there was the matter of the door. It was partway open, and inside I could hear my father. At first I thought the sound I heard was laughter—the gasping-for-breath, deep-in-the-throat laugh a person might reserve for a truly tremendous joke. But after a second or two, I realized that the sound was not laughter after all. My father was sobbing.

He was weeping.

In my life, I have had many regrets. There are friendships I wish I had not allowed to fade and words I wish I had not said. But chief among my regrets is that I did not rush into that big, unused room right then, did not wrap my arms around my father and tell him that I loved him, did not assure him that he still had me. Had I been even a year older, I might have. But as it was, I was frozen into inaction, embarrassed at my uncertainty over what to do next.

This fresh conflict, then, is really an escalation of the earlier conflict. Patrick has turned the page, or is at least making the attempt to do so, but his father cannot. Because Patrick is by nature a peacemaker, a mediator and a care-giver, he is frustrated by his failure to comfort his father.

It's a lot to put on a pair of sixteen-year-old shoulders.

But the load is going to get even heavier ...

It Goes Public

The two drive in to the climbing shop, where Patrick decides to stay in the shop, do some make-up homework, and tidy up while his father goes up to the rocks to do some bouldering—practice climbing in which one never gets more than just a few feet off the ground.

Patrick sweeps the shop and then goes out and sweeps and tidies the common area in front of the shop and Judd's store—he notes that Judd watches him from inside but does not come outside to offer a word of thanks: probably because, in doing so, he would feel obliged to offer Patrick payment for his troubles and Judd is, by nature, a skinflint.

Finally, Patrick is finished with his chores and comes out to sit on a bench on the front porch of the climbing shop.

This scene occurs twenty percent of the way into the story:

Judd came out on his porch, as well, having decided, apparently, that sufficient time has passed to allow him to emerge without talk of remuneration for my sweeping services. He gazed up at the Rocks—it was hard not to do so from his porch; they filled up nearly half the sky. Then he bent forward, looked again, and turned my way.

"You ain't up climbin' today?"

Which, admittedly was a pretty stupid question, what with me sitting there in front of him and all. But to point that out would not go well with Judd. I'd already heard him mention to my father that, in Judd Horton's worldly and wise opinion, kids from up north had a tendency to be "uppity."

I shrugged. "Had to finish some homework."

Judd looked back up at the rock and squinted, which was unusual for Judd. He had a little pair of drugstore half-spectacles that he used for reading, but at a distance, Judd's vision was legendary. Mountain people practically lined up to go hunting with him. He could spot a deer standing in thick brush from half a mile away.

Scowling, he looked back at me a second time.

"Then who is yer daddy up climbin' with?"

"Who?" I leaned forward. There was a huckleberry bush we hadn't cut back yet, growing wild off the east side of our porch, so I couldn't see much of the Rocks.

"Nobody," I told him. "He's by himself."

Judd looked dumbfounded. It was the one and only time in all the years I would know him that I would ever see him speechless.

Looking back at the rock, he scowled again and then asked, "All the way up there?"

It's accurate, what people say about having your heart fall. Mine did, and it didn't even bother to stop in the abdomen; it dropped all the way to my knees and quivered a bit. Still, I got to my feet and stepped out onto the turnaround. Sure enough, halfway up the wall beneath the South Summit there was just the suggestion of limbs emanating from a red dot. Red shirt, I remembered. My father was wearing a red shirt.

Still scowling, Judd shuffled quickly back into his store, his potbelly bobbing with urgency. The bell of his cash register sounded, and a moment later he was back, a quarter in his hand.

Judd had a tourist binoculars mounted on the front railing of his porch—one of those coin-operated, weatherproof, twin-lensed monstrosities that look like a cross between a gas mask and a bedpan. He thumbed the quarter into it, initiating a faint whir. Then he stooped and put his eyes to it, twisting the focusing knob.

"My, my, my," he whispered as he peered into the eyepieces. "My, my, my, my, my"

"What?" I asked.

"Yer daddy," Judd muttered. "Boy, he ain't on no rope."

This is a complication and, coming as it does at the end of a chapter, it is literally a cliffhanger.

But it is not a conflict in the usual sense, as it is not within the powers of Patrick, our protagonist, to circumvent or overcome it.

After all, if I'd simply made Patrick's father a risk-taker and a daredevil, the issue would have simply been one of Patrick having a father with poor judgment.

That is an issue for Patrick, but the sort of issue that he could eventually overcome by growing out of it.

But there is an actual conflict that lives within Kevin's action, and it shows up several pages later.

We are twenty-six percent of the way through the novel when Patrick confronts his father about what he and Judd saw, and his father responds this way:

> **"It was like I can't begin to describe it to you, Patrick,"**
> **he murmured. "Like seeing the sun come up after a long,**
> **dark, winter's night. I mean, the higher I got, the more**
> **things started to drop away. Losing your mom, the way**
> **she went, the questions that I keep asking myself every**
> **single day. The endless stream of 'if-onlys." It didn't**
> **banish them, but it kept pushing them back, further and**
> **further and further, until finally there was nothing in my**
> **life but that rock. Just that hold I was on, and the one I**
> **was going for. Nothing more."**
>
> **Not even me.**
>
> **"And finally … " He smiled. "When I got to the top?**
> **When I stood there? It was like, oh man—there was a**
> **phrase they used in my philosophy class, back in college.**
> **What was it?**
>
> **"*Tabula rasa*. That's it. It's Latin, from what's-his-**
> **name … Locke. *Tabula rasa*. It means 'a blank slate.'**
> **And that's what this climb did for me, Patrick. It wiped**
> **the slate clean, if only for the moment."**
>
> **I looked at him for a long, weighty second.**
>
> **"And you needed that," I finally said.**
>
> **"Yes." He looked me in the eye as he said it. "I really**
> **did."**

Grow or Crumble

Again—when faced with the death of someone close, a character has two choices: grow, or crumble. In the aftermath of Laurie's death, Patrick has grown, but Kevin is crumbling.

So, a little more than a quarter of the way into the novel, Patrick has encountered yet another conflict that seems and feels large enough to be *the* conflict for the book. Kevin has resorted to reckless behavior to ease his pain and Patrick is faced with a dilemma; he is grown enough to sense the potentially mortal danger of the situation, but he is young enough that he is hesitant to take action. He is, after all, a stranger in a strange land—outside of the passing acquaintance with the nosey Judd Horton, he knows no one in West Virginia. So he is trying to address the situation by himself, but doesn't know how.

Patrick appears to be in a situation with no way out. And this is exactly the sort of conflict that I wanted at about this point in the book: the kind of conflict that gets the readers worried about the main character. I want them putting themselves in his shoes and running through his options. And I want them to come up short.

Allies

At this point—when my protagonist is boxed in with no place left to go—I began a chain of events that resulted in the introduction of the third main character in *In High Places*: Rachel Ransom, Patrick's love interest in the story.

Rachel is pretty, going on beautiful. She is smart. She is compassionate. And she is the daughter of a local pastor, and shares her father's zeal for his calling. Theirs is an evangelical Christian church that has extremely conservative views, and while Rachel's father holds more progressive views personally, he conforms to his church's views so as not to offend his congregation.

Patrick meets Rachel a little more than a third of the way through the book (thirty-six percent of the way in, according to my e-book reader). This may seem late in the game to be introducing a major character, but actually it is not.

Fashionably Late

When you are writing a novel, a good rule of thumb is to write sparingly. When you enter a scene, for instance, it works best to enter the scene as late as you possibly can. You also want to end the scene as soon as it accomplishes its purpose. Brad Whittington, a novelist who does this extremely well, tells me that he has heard this technique described as "cutting off the heads and the tails."

And the way you apply this to characters is to introduce major characters as late as you can do so, while still allowing them time to develop and accomplish their purpose. So, in *In High Places*, I did not bring Rachel into Patrick's life until he needed her to help address the fresh conflict in his life.

As the novel progresses, their relationship develops as a chaste infatuation. Then the situation with Patrick's father escalates.

The background to this escalation is very much in keeping with the atmosphere and politics inherent in the rock-climbing world of the mid-1970s. Patrick, the narrator, reveals that, for years, local climbers have been trying to complete a route on Seneca Rocks known as "Zardoz." The climb is so difficult that every attempt on it has required "aid"—a climbing term for using equipment to make progress on the climb, rather than just using equipment as a backstop in case of a fall.

But even as an aid climb, Zardoz has yet to be completed: one critical section of the climb is devoid of the cracks climbers usually use to place their equipment, so a Washington, DC, climber by the name of Phil Tapia (named after Rick Tapia, an old climbing buddy of mine) has suggested placing a bolt—just what it sounds like: a concrete expansion bolt driven into the rock, so a climber can hang a stirrup from it and get past the featureless section of the route.

But others in the rock-climbing community are against defacing the rock in this fashion.

There is a heated argument in the climbing shop about this. Ultimately, Tapia declares his intention to return in a week's time; he is going to place the bolt, regardless of what the others say, and complete the climb.

But when Tapia comes back to do just that, he sees gymnast's chalk—the substance climbers use to dry their hands while climbing—all the way up the route.

Tapia goes to the shop, where Patrick's father shows him the route book—a book in which climbers record the details of new routes—and Tapia learns that not only has the route been completed without placing the bolt: it has been completed without using aid. The route listing is signed, "Anonymous," and this scene ensures:

"'Anonymous?'" Tapia turned around and looked past me, eyes wide, at my father. "Oh, come on, Kevin—some guy waltzes in and says he topped out on, says he *freed* Zardoz, and you just accept the claim even though he won't sign his name? Do you even know who wrote this entry?"

"I do," my father said.

Tapia stepped around me.

"Then who is it?"

"Anonymous. He doesn't want his name known, and that's cool with me. No rule that says you have to sign the route, as long as you climbed it."

"Well who was the second?"

"No second."

"He self-belayed?"

"He free-soloed."

Tapia had his back to me, but I'm guessing he rolled his eyes.

"And you're buying this? I can't believe what I'm hearing, Kevin. Someone's put you on. They rapped down the route, spotted it with chalk marks, and then came in here and claimed to have bagged it."

My father shook his head.

"Not how it worked, Phil. He got it fair and square."

More bird sounds.

"And how are you so sure?"

> My father shrugged.
>
> "I was up there yesterday. I saw the whole thing. Free solo, bottom to top."
>
> He began collecting the carabiners and returning them to their shipping box. I could hear the *clink, clink, clink* as he stacked them atop one another.
>
> "You saw it." Tapia said it straight, a statement, but there was still a question in there somewhere.
>
> My father nodded. "With my own eyes. And trust me, Phil. I know this guy."
>
> So did I. Maybe a little too well. I'd known it before I'd even seen the route book, but I was certain once I'd seen the first word.
>
> The description was in my father's handwriting.

This scene happened a little over halfway through the book—my e-book reader tells me it transpires fifty-two percent of the way in—and it places Patrick on the cusp of panic. In his ongoing quest to return to *tabula rasa*, Patrick's father has been seeking more and more difficult climbs, and doing them without a rope to protect himself in the event of a fall.

The situation has progressed to the point that Patrick's father has now completed what is generally acknowledged to be the most difficult climb at Seneca Rocks—without a rope.

To Patrick, it is obvious now that, left unchecked, his father, while not suicidal, is nonetheless engaged in a suicidal activity. An easy climb cannot provide Kevin with the release he craves, so he has been seeking harder and harder ones.

And Patrick, wise now in the ways of the sport, knows that eventually his father will encounter a route on which he will slip and fall—and die.

But Patrick has an ally now. He shares his fears with Rachel. And she tells him what he already knows and rephrases what is—to this point at least—the central issue or conflict in the novel:

"Patrick," she whispered. "This is serious. This is your daddy we're talking about here. You've got to do something. You have to tell somebody."

"Who? The police? He's not breaking any laws. And if I get ... I don't know, social workers and whatnot involved, they'll think he's not fit as a father."

"Well? Is he?"

I thought about that for a long moment, and we were so still that a jay landed not two feet from where we sat and looked at us with one eye, head cocked. I cleared my throat and the bird flew away.

"He's hurting, Rachel. He goes upstairs in the house, he goes through her things, and he gets buried by the memories. Then he does these climbs just to ... to clear out the garbage. He's not suicidal, not trying to harm himself. He's just carrying too much, and he thinks the climbing helps ... takes it away for a while.

"But, trying or not, he could still die, couldn't he?"

I nodded.

"Then what are you going to do?"

The two teenagers decide to go to the unfinished house and get rid of the material that is feeding Kevin's ennui.

And they do that, sorting through and packing up and removing virtually all of Patrick's mother's belongings.

In the process of doing this, they encounter what is, to Rachel, a crucial piece of evidence: a small copy of the New Testament and Psalms, in which Patrick's mother has recorded, in her own handwriting, her decision to become a Christian.

To Patrick, this is a bit of a mystery. He thinks of Christianity the way most people do, as a cultural tradition. In this way of thinking, if your grandparents and great-grandparents went to a Christian church, then that was the category you fell into as well.

But Rachel, an evangelical Christian, has an entirely different view on the matter. She believes Christianity hinges on an individual choice: a choice that, once made, assures eternal life with God. And having found evidence that Patrick's mother made that choice, she is ecstatic. It is, from her point of view, the best news possible.

Patrick gets swept up in her enthusiasm. They go find Rachel's father, and then the three of them go to the climbing shop to tell Patrick's father the news.

The tactic backfires spectacularly. Kevin is not pleased with any of the news: not pleased that the teenagers have packed his wife's things behind his back, not pleased that his wife signed the testimony (which he says she probably did to appease some religious kook), and not pleased with the idea of a God that would welcome a new child into his fold by allowing her to go into the garage and kill herself.

He declares his wife dead—dead and gone—asks the pastor and his daughter to leave, and begins what will turn out to be several days of the silent treatment with Patrick.

Shut out from the only family member he has, Patrick goes to church where—mostly because he thinks it's what Rachel wants him to do—he comes forward during the altar call. He agrees to be baptized, thinking that it's going to involve moistening his forehead with water, but Rachel's church baptizes with total immersion, and they do that in a nearby creek.

As the pastor baptizes Patrick, he tells him that his decision is going to assure that he will see his mother again and, in that instant, Patrick truly accepts his new faith. He becomes a Christian—according to the evangelical definition, and not the cultural one—even though he knows that it will open even wider the gulf between him and his father.

That night, Patrick decides to hide that decision from his father. He gets home to the trailer before his father arrives, goes to bed and feigns sleep when the Volkswagen pulls in and parks. Then he hears the sounds of his father coming in, going to the bedroom in the rear of the trailer, and getting into bed.

Here's the rest of that scene, sixty percent into the novel:

I thought of all that had happened since I'd last seen him, of all the news I had to share but couldn't share: not with him, and not right now, and maybe never. I thought of the invitation, of me raising my hand, going forward, of the cold water in the creek, of Preacher's words.

"My son, who was dead, is alive."

Was dead.

Is alive.

"Just as all are dead who have not claimed Christ Jesus as their savior."

I thought of my father lying still, silent, hands folded upon his chest, on the small, square bed at the back of the Airstream.

"Your mama. She lives." I pictured my mother vibrant, still young, never growing old. I thought of her as Preacher thought of her, as Rachel did, as she was to every member of their church—of my church.

So my mother was dead in my father's eyes, and if what Preacher had told me was true, my father was dead in my mother's eyes. I examined that thought, turning it like the Mobius strip that it was. And then squeezing my eyes shut again, I took a deep breath and drifted by fits and starts into troubled sleep—the shallow, restless slumber of an orphan.

This scene takes place nearly two-thirds of the way through the book, and it is important because it is here, in this wholly internal scene, as Patrick lies on his bed, that the true and ultimate conflict of the book is revealed.

Patrick now believes his mother is alive for all eternity and that he will live forever as well.

And the thing he wants most is to see his father accept the same eternal life—a hope on which his father seems to have firmly shut the door.

Late to the Ball

If you've been tracking the locations of these scenes as I have introduced them, and where they are in relation to the rest of the book, and if you are new to writing novels (or even if you are not), then you may be surprised by how late things are happening.

True, *In High Places* opens in conflict (albeit one easily resolved). And true, the catalytic event of the story, the death of Patrick's mother, happens just a few pages later, only five percent of the way into the book.

But Rachel, a very important character in this novel, doesn't even appear until the story is better than a third of the way told. And the final conflict of the book—the conflict that the book is actually "about"—doesn't appear until well into the second half of the novel.

That is not a fluke.

Lisbeth Salander, the title character in *The Girl with the Dragon Tattoo*, is not there at all in the first several pages of the book, and does not meet Mikael Blomkvist, the protagonist, until the book is half finished. Sadie Clayton, the main character's love interest in Stephen King's *11/22/63*, is first mentioned a little over a third of the way into that novel, and King's ultimate conflict shows up very, very close to the end.

Important characters and important events often occur a third of the way along—or better—in novels.

If this seems unusual to modern writers, it is probably because, in the novel's closest visual cousin—the feature film—major characters are typically introduced very early on, as is the central conflict of the film.

But films are not novels and, in fact, films have very little in common with novels. The closest cousin films have in the literary world is the short story.

Novels—most classically constructed or literary novels—depend on fairly deep character development. It takes a long time to explore the circumstances surrounding a character and get the readers to the point where they, grasp, understand, appreciate and—most importantly—sympathize with the issues with which that character is wrestling. Films, which depend upon visible action, don't deal well with such highly internal issues.

That's one reason why it is so very hard to make a successful movie out of a successful novel—especially a successful movie that can be appreciated and understood by viewers unfamiliar with the novel on which it is based. Novels cover more territory than one can cover in the running length of a typical feature film, and much of that territory is usually difficult, if not impossible, to represent in dialogue and pictures.

In fact, a 2004 film by Tod Williams called *The Door in the Floor* is notable because it is not only a comprehensive and successful feature film, but it is also a faithful depiction of the characters, situation and plot elements of a well-known novel: John Irving's 1998 work, *A Widow for One Year*.

But to pull that off, Williams limited the scope of his film to the first third of that novel: the most visually vivid portion of the story, one that could be portrayed with a minimum of internal reflection, and a section that was brief enough to be covered in a movie.

The only recent successful film adaptation of a full, standalone novel that comes to mind is Ang Lee's 2012 adaptation of Yann Martel's Man Booker prize-winning novel, *Life of Pi*. But Martel's novel, like *The Old Man and the Sea*, is a much more linear story than most novels (so linear that, to make a film of it, Lee added a love interest that does not exist in the book).

I distinguish *Life of Pi* as a standalone novel, because, as with most things concerning the writing of a novel, late introduction of significant characters and late conflict discovery, while characteristic of most modern novels, are not characteristics shared by all modern novels.

There are numerous exceptions.

In genre romance, for instance, the readers (and the editors) expect the love interests to encounter one another much earlier on in the story. In short-form romances, that meeting pretty much has to occur in the very first chapter or the readers (and the editors) will stop reading.

The full cast of characters can also appear much earlier in novels that feature a well-known series character, or novels that have an extremely well-known historical figure as the protagonist.

Proving the Rule

Examples of the former would be Agatha Christie's Hercule Poirot mysteries, or Ian Fleming's James Bond thrillers.

In 1953, when Fleming first introduced Bond in *Casino Royale*, Bond was an unknown quantity, and the book had to be structured fairly conventionally, even though it was the briefest of the James Bond novels. But as Bond gained a following, it was no longer necessary to develop the character in each subsequent book, and by the time Fleming published *Goldfinger*, in 1959, his secret agent was known all around the world.

Particularly when Bond began to appear as a character in films, it was difficult to find anyone in the English-speaking world who didn't know that James Bond's codename was "007," that he wore a Rolex Oyster wristwatch, and that he drank his vodka martinis "shaken, not stirred."

By 1963, when Fleming wrote *On Her Majesty's Secret Service*, the novel could be structured almost exactly like a feature film, so much so that the motion-picture version of that book (released in 1969, and the only Bond film to star George Lazenby as 007) could follow the plotline and structure of the novel very, very closely.

So ... let's say that you are planning a series of books that share the same main character and complement one another chronologically. Does this mean that, once you have the first book or two out of the way, you can move all your essential characters and your focal conflicts to the front of the remainder of the novels?

Absolutely, it does ... provided you are certain that the first couple of novels in your series will sell hundreds of thousands of copies apiece (actually, in today's cluttered market, we'd better make that "millions of copies apiece").

If you are not certain of that, then abandoning conventional construction in your latter books will almost certainly make you fall victim to "the sophomore curse." The later books will fail to sell well because readers will be justifiably convinced that, without having read the earlier novels, they won't know what's going on.

As for the other major exception to the late-in rule—the well-known historical figure—the pertinent adjective here is "well-known."

For instance … certainly, we have all heard of Dwight D. Eisenhower. But do you know where he was educated, what his pet peeves were, or what his focus was after leaving the Presidency?

Neither do I. In fact, other than knowing that he lived on a farm in Pennsylvania during his retirement, I don't know the answers to any of those questions, so it would not be reasonable to expect my readers to be familiar with them.

Only a handful of historical figures enjoy such widespread familiarity that they needn't be extensively developed in a novel: Jesus, certainly … Mark Twain, possibly. Other than that, I would tread carefully—and structure conventionally.

An Author, Not a Director

The thing to remember then is that, for most of us—and I most certainly include myself in this group—we've grown up on the fiction equivalent of junk food. Yes, I read a lot when I was a kid, but I'd bet that, if you'd kept a clock on me, I spent much more time staring at a television screen than I did reading novels. And I spent more Saturday afternoons in the movie theater than I did at the library.

That's not all bad. There are some screenwriting techniques that translate well into the world of book-length fiction. But structure is not one of them.

Nor is the way that the novel ends.

| FIVE: Solution and Resonance

There is no real ending. It's just the place where you stop the story. — FRANK HERBERT

OF ALL THE pages in your novel, which are most important?

If you answered, "The opening pages" ... you're right. At least, from a sales perspective, you're right.

Opening pages are the front door and the entry hall of your book. If readers don't like what they see there, they will go no further, and all your hard work will be for naught.

This is true for acquisition editors who are weighing whether to dedicate rolls of paper and a barrel of ink to your book.

And it is true for the potential buyer looking for a summer read in the bookstore.

This has always been the case. It was when the only way one could get one's hands on a book was to go to the bookstore or the library and pick one up.

And it is today, when many online retailers and all of the major e-book platforms allow readers to look at or even download a free sample of the novel—a sample that consists, always, of the opening pages.

So, particularly for the newer novelist, it is critical to open with work that is eloquent but not overwritten, work that will prove engaging even to complete strangers, and work that leaves the reader aching to turn the page and learn what happens next.

That is why, when it comes to getting readers, editors, marketing people and other key stakeholders interested in your work, your opening pages are your most important pages.

But in terms of your reputation and your stature as a writer, the most important pages are those with which you *end* your novel. Why? Because those comprise the most lasting impression you will leave with your reader. People remember—viscerally, emotionally, and sometimes even literally—the part they read last.

Cognitive Bias

This is true with any written work—be it a novel, a work of nonfiction, or even a short story or a term paper or (and this is where it was first researched and discussed) a list—because of something psychologists refer to as "cognitive bias."

Cognitive bias, as the phrase implies, holds that when we are recalling something too large to hold in one's head all at the same time—and a novel certainly qualifies—we place more importance on, and remember better, certain elements of the work. And those same psychologists maintain that cognitive bias is driven by two effects.

Four Score ...

Quick—without Googling it or otherwise looking it up—what are the opening words to Lincoln's Gettysburg Address?

Chances are, you replied, "Four score and seven years ago ..." and possibly " ... our fathers brought forth upon this continent a new nation, conceived in liberty, and dedicated to the proposition that all men are created equal."

A+. That is the first full sentence of The Gettysburg Address.

Now, just as quickly, and without Googling it: what is the *fourth* sentence of that same speech?

Unless you were a genuine whiz-kid in American history, the kind who committed the entire speech to memory—or even if you were such a whiz kid, but are now several decades removed—chances are that you are drawing a blank.

Primacy

This is because of the first effect involved in cognitive bias—something known as "primacy."

We tend to remember beginnings. In a brief work such as The Gettysburg Address, we will oftentimes remember beginnings verbatim. And in a longer work, such as a novel, we will usually recall vividly at least the gist of how the book begins.

Recency

The second element of cognitive bias is something called the "recency effect."

If you look up The Gettysburg Address right now, and read it through a couple of times and then set it aside, fifteen minutes later you will probably still be hard-pressed to remember the exact wording of that fourth sentence. But if I ask you for the last eighteen words—and especially if I prompt you with the first six: " ... and that government of the people"—you will probably be able to recall the rest: " ... by the people, for the people, shall not perish from the earth."

Because of the recency effect, we tend to remember—and remember nearly as well as we remember beginnings, or *even better,* in the case of a longer work—the last thing that we read.

In a novel, recency is a moving target. If all you have read of a work is the first three or four chapters, and you have set the book down for a couple of days, you can easily re-find where you left off by simply skimming until you get to the last thing you remember reading. It "sticks," and you can distinguish the familiar words with very little effort. Keep reading, set the book aside, and come back to it, and you can find the new stopping point with similar ease.

But the parts in-between will eventually tend to blur and run together.

This moving-target effect continues until we hit the end of a book. At that point, the final pages, being the last ones that we read, are also the ones that have the potential to stay with us for a long, long time—oftentimes better than the beginning.

So that's one reason the conclusion of your novel is so important; *your readers are going to remember it.*

Why This Matters

Another, and more important reason that endings are so significant is this: the way your novel ends—the quality of it—is going to have a significant impact on how your readers think of your novel, your work in general, and you as a writer.

You know this as a reader yourself. A good ending sticks with you. You find yourself thinking about it, talking about it with your friends.

This is called "word-of-mouth," and it is word-of-mouth—not advertising, not marketing, and not book reviews—that is most responsible for generating book sales. If people are talking about a book, it sells. And if they are not, all the other effort is like shouting into a vacuum.

A good ending also gets you thinking about the book and the author who wrote it. You find yourself Googling the name to see what else is out there by the same person. And when a new book comes out, and you see that name on the cover or the listing, your impulse is to buy it.

Endings, then, are important: crucially important.

So why are there so many novels out there with predictable, trite, contrived, weak, or otherwise mediocre endings?

Lights! Camera! Keystroke?

Part of the problem is the temptation to write a novel along the lines of something that is not a novel.

We are now several generations into a society that sees several feature films for every novel it reads. Yes, we are developing a theme here (see my other rants about books imitating films in Chapters Two and Four). As I said earlier, while feature films, like novels, are the long form of their medium, by and large they are not novels and do not act like novels.

And part of the reason for this dissimilarity is that they do not end like them.

Films are written by screenwriters, created by directors, and shaped by producers and marketing departments. The practice for many years now has been to test-market films, oftentimes with alternate endings, and to conduct focus groups with audiences who see the film prior to its general opening. The information gathered is used to fine-tune the film, its editing, and especially its ending, in order to generate the maximum buzz possible among theater-goers.

Case in point: *Fatal Attraction*, the 1987 film starring Michael Douglas and Glenn Close.

As originally shot, Glenn Close's character, having been rejected by Michael Douglas's character after he has an affair with her, commits suicide by cutting her own throat (to the tune of an aria from "Madame Butterfly"). She does this in a way that frames Douglas's character for her death.

But in watching test audiences, the producers decided the ending was not giving the audience what it wanted (the story is that they had this conference standing by the popcorn machine in the lobby of a theater where the film was test-screened). The audience was obviously sympathetic to the character played by Anne Archer (the wife cheated on in the affair), and wanted her to do away with the other woman. So the ending was re-written to make that possible.

Now, true, both films and novels live and die on the power of word-of-mouth. But—and this is important to grasp—the things people rave about after watching a sub-two-hour movie are not the same things they are looking for when they dedicate several evenings, or even several weeks, to a book.

Junk Food

Because most readers are also moviegoers (or at least movie-viewers) the expectation of movie-like endings has bled over into the world of popular fiction. Many writers are now producing work that meets that expectation—and sells all right, at least in the short term. But it sells well for the same reason that Big Macs sell well; it is satisfying a shallower appetite.

My opinion is that writers better serve their readership if they try to create novels that are truly outstanding, rather than merely good. If you're going to put the time, sweat and angst into crafting a story, you may as well make it a story that will still be amazing to readers several decades down the road.

And those novels aren't like your typical Friday-night feature.

In great novels, the guy doesn't always get the girl. There isn't always a miraculous turn at the last moment that snatches victory from the jaws of defeat. Justice is not always served. The characters may not always live happily ever after; they may not even live. And before you open the laptop to send me that email, let me add that, in great movies—truly great movies that win critical acclaim as well as a decent box office, and do not follow plot points dictated by the marketing department—this is also the case. Or usually it is.

Folding Under Pressure

Mediocre endings also occur when novelists find themselves rushing to finish a book.

All sorts of conditions can cause this. Maybe the writer took a year off to produce a novel, and now those twelve fleeting months are coming to an end. Maybe an opportunity arose to show it to a valued critic, or an editor, and the writer felt the need to put a bow on it before that reading. Maybe a milestone birthday is looming.

What all these situations have in common is *pressure*. And even among those of us who are natural-born crisis workers, stress and pressure are rarely conducive to producing a novel with an extraordinary conclusion.

Then there is a situation that seems almost custom-made for creating a high-stress, pressure-filled writing environment.

That is the second book in a new novelist's contract.

The Sophomore Curse

I can't count the number of times I've had the conversation…

"I sold my novel," a newer writer will tell me breathlessly. And then comes part two: "And they like it so much that they asked for a second book in the same contract."

Not exactly.

When you sell a book, quite often you'll wind up with an offer for more than that one book. Two- and three-book contracts are relatively common in the publishing industry.

With established writers, the multi-book contract affords the publisher a level of price protection. The contract guarantees that, even if the first book in the deal takes off as a runaway best-seller, creating a huge appetite for more of the author's work, the publisher is not going to be priced out of the market on the second book.

That's because the advance for all of the books in the contract is arrived at and agreed upon by all parties long before the initial copies of the first book roll out.

And with newer writers, a multi-book contract is a tool with which the publisher hopes to grow the author's brand.

The first book establishes that writer in the marketplace, gets his or her name known, and may or may not prove to be profitable for the publisher.

Then the second book goes to market on the shoulders of the first, and hopefully does better.

In a perfect world, the second novel can even breathe secondary life into demand for the writer's debut work.

But that's assuming both books are equally good.

The Big "If"

Now, think about it… If you are working on your debut novel right now, chances are you've been at it for a while. You probably have worked on it, off and on, for several months or, quite possibly, several years.

You may have taken it to workshops, gotten critiques, and revised it several times on the basis of that advice. If you have an agent, it's likely he or she coached you on how to make it stronger, and you took that advice. Or an acquisitions editor may have said, "We like it a lot, but we'd like it even better if…" and so maybe you revised it again.

The bottom line is, you'll put in a lot of time creating a first novel that is really and truly ready to sell. And once it is sold, you'll be revising it, checking galleys, approving (and perhaps writing) catalog material and back-cover blurbs, and then promoting it as the launch approaches.

So, understanding that: what do you think the chances are of you writing an equally good, or even better, second novel, and having it in to the publisher *a year or less after the acceptance of the first*?

Second novels often suffer from that multi-book-contract deadline pressure.

And as most people write the ending last, it is the ending—the part that people remember, and the part that helps set your reputation—that suffers the most.

The pressure for a second book, written quickly, affects even authors who manage to land standalone, one-book contracts—contracts that do not require delivery of a second manuscript—or authors who are self-published and beholden to no house. That's because, even when clock is not ticking at the publisher, it often is ticking, or seems to be ticking, in the marketplace. You establish a name with a first book, and now the heat is on to bring out another before your readers forget who you are.

Grace Under Fire

One solution to all this is to refuse to bend to the pressure, don't sign a two-book deal, and take the time to write a great second book, having faith that, if your work is good enough, your readers will wait for it. But having that faith is more easily said than done. And it may be very difficult to find a publisher who is willing to take the increased gamble of a one-book deal.

Another, vastly preferable, solution is, after you have written a great first novel, to write a great second novel as well—a novel that both begins and ends well—*before* offering the first to a publisher, or bringing it out as a self-pub.

Say What?

To most unpublished novelists, this sounds like heresy, because the thing they want most in life, or at least want only slightly less than oxygen, is to have a book in print. Their book. With their name on it.

But the eventual aim of most novelists is *books*—plural—and, unless you are simply working on your novel to cross it off your bucket list, you will end up far, far happier in your work (and your life in general) if you can get yourself ahead of the curve... if, when you send your great first novel out, you have an equally great (or even better) second novel warmed up, on deck and ready to follow.

This especially makes sense if you are writing a series. And it is precisely what Stieg Larsson did with his "Millennium Trilogy."

All three books in that trilogy—*The Girl with the Dragon Tattoo, The Girl Who Played with Fire*, and *The Girl Who Kicked Over the Hornets' Nest*—were written, revised, polished and ready for their close-ups before Larsson ever submitted them, as a trilogy, to potential publishers.

I'm guessing Larsson did this because he was a magazine editor, and he understood the challenge inherent in creating greatness under the pressure of a deadline. Plus, as a magazine editor, he probably already had all the deadline pressure he wanted, and then some.

That's not to say the writing schedule for the trilogy was open-ended. Larsson wrote the novels for a purpose; his hope was that he would sell enough books to pay off his apartment. But he allowed himself time to do the job right.

Partly because each of the books was well-crafted to and through its ending, the trilogy sold better than forty-six million copies in its first five years of publication. And Larrson became the first author to sell more than a million e-books on Amazon's Kindle Store.

So great endings matter, and you'll do yourself a favor if you allow yourself the room and the time to work out a great ending for every novel you ever write.

Which leaves one huge, burning question …

… What, precisely, is it that constitutes a great ending?

Two Things

Personally, when I write a novel, I am aiming for an ending that does two things.

The first is an ending that over-delivers on the promise of the book.

The second is an ending that is resonant.

Let's take a look at what these two mean … .

Over-Delivering on the Promise

When I say "the promise of the book," I mean the expectation that is established by the novel, its premise, its action and its genre. Readers develop an image of how they believe the work is going to conclude: how the ultimate conflict is going to be handled, what is going to happen to the characters, and how they—the readers—are going to feel about this when they finish the last page. In essence, they play an ongoing and evolving game of "guess the ending."

My job, as the novelist, is to understand and anticipate what the reader expects, and craft instead an ending that *goes beyond* that expectation—that ends the novel at a place that is entirely logical, yet completely unexpected. If I am successful, the ending I come up with is one they never would have guessed, and far, far better than what the readers expected.

Do novels always have to end this way?

No. They do not. In fact, in some genres, ending outside the readers' expectations will be a disappointment.

I do not, for instance, write genre romance. This is not a criticism of that sort of novel: merely my admission that I am clumsily unfamiliar with the form and don't know how to do it.

But I have friends who make their livings as romance writers, and they tell me that one of the biggest mistakes newcomers make is that they write manuscripts in which they try to "shake things up" … and then are amazed when publishers say the work is not for them.

Now, contrary to popular criticism, romances—good romances—are not written by formula. If they were, someone at MIT would have developed a computer program by now that could churn them out by the thousands, no human intervention required.

But my romance-writing friends tell me that the form does come with certain expectations that have to be met for the book to be considered a success.

The ending is expected to deliver a certain situation (the guy is going to get the girl, and vice versa). And so there is a loose sort of road map that the narrative follows.

The book in this case is similar to a dancer performing a

variation of a known dance, or a jazz musician interpreting a popular tune.

Readers come to the genre not to see how the story goes, but to see how this particular writer, at this particular time, tells the story. It's all about performance.

But in non-genre books, it's almost always preferable to avoid that predictable circumstance at the end.

Resonance

The second thing I strive for in an ending is *resonance*.

The best definition I can give for "resonance" is that I want my readers to be haunted by the way my novel ends. I want them to be thinking about it hours, days, or weeks after they have finished the book. And months later, when a friend mentions the novel, I want them to be bursting to talk about its conclusion—but to be unwilling to do so, for fear of spoiling the ending for that friend.

I know of two good ways to create this type of resonant ending.

One is to leave some questions unanswered.

The What-Ifs

Leaving unanswered questions allows the story to continue in the reader's mind long after the narrative has ended. They can imagine their own, further, outcomes to the story. In fact, many writers have a following of readers who imagine and share stories based around these open-ended situations in exercises known as "fanfiction." Recently, an entire high-school class wrote alternative endings to one of my novels, and sent the best ones to me.

Or the readers can compare the experiences in the book to those in their own lives and, on the basis of how you ended your book, speculate on how their own lives could have been different, if events had simply turned a certain way.

Much fiction is, after all, based on speculation—the "what ifs." And leaving room for "what ifs" in your reader's heads allows your story to take root.

The Oh-No-You-Didn'ts

So one key to a resonant ending is to answer questions and resolve the open-ended situations in the end, but to do so in a manner that the reader did not expect.

Better still, if it can be done without cheating the reader, you can achieve an extremely resonant conclusion by wrapping things up in a fashion that is *the opposite* of what the reader expected.

Or ... Use Them Both

For *In High Places*, I chose to employ a combination of these two techniques.

That novel is thirty-seven chapters long. The initial thirty-two chapters take place entirely during the spring and summer of 1976—in fact, altogether, they encompass less than half a year.

And in that space, if I have done my job correctly, the reader has developed five hopes for the characters in my novel:

1. That Patrick will learn and prove that his mother's death was not a suicide.

2. That Kevin (Patrick's father) will cease his potentially self-destructive practice of making difficult, solo, ropeless climbs.

3. That Patrick and Rachel will fall completely in love and live happily ever after.

4. That—because it has become Patrick's most fervent prayer and a crucial element in his life—Kevin will adopt his son's faith as his own.

5. That, as a result of all these outcomes, Patrick (whom I hope the readers like) will find peace and have a fulfilling life.

Those are the reader's hopes. Or, at very least, these are the things that I want the reader to expect to happen.

At the same time, I am bearing in mind that *In High Places* is a *Bildungsroman* (a particular type of coming-of-age story) in which a forty-something narrator is remembering things that happened the summer he turned seventeen. So there are two mental filters active here: those of the seventeen-year-old adolescent, and those of the forty-something adult.

To the teenage Patrick, getting to the roots of his mother's death is crucial; if he can prove that his mother's death was not a suicide, he can remove the cause of his father's feelings of guilt. And with that guilt removed, his father will no longer seek the relief of his dangerous ropeless climbs.

At the same time, Patrick is falling in love with Rachel. She is becoming his world. And because of that, she nearly eclipses all other concerns.

But the narrator of the story—the adult Patrick—is a faithful and believing pastor, and a man of the cloth. Because he is telling the story, he is very conscious of its ultimate conflict. And that conflict is not the issue of getting Patrick's father back to inner peace or even finding lifelong happiness for Patrick and Rachel. It is the fate of Kevin's—Patrick's father's—soul.

Legerdemain

Now, here's the trick. Throughout the initial thirty-two chapters, even though we are in the adult Patrick's voice and narrative, we are in the teenage Patrick's head.

And because of this, even though we are aware of the story's priorities and what is most important the way the adult Patrick sees it—in light of eternity—we gravitate toward that element of the story that consumes the teenage character, and that element is Rachel.

The novel is specifically written to work this way, and after hundreds of reader letters and more conversations than I can count, I think I can safely say it works as designed. Through much of the rising-action portion of the narrative arc, we're thinking mostly of the love story.

So how do you satisfactorily conclude a novel that has two different agendas proceeding simultaneously?

In this case, I gave each agenda its own ending. And I also included a resolution that precedes either of those endings.

The Initial Resolution

The reader's first two expectations—that Patrick's mother's death will prove to be other than a suicide and that Kevin will stop his potentially self-destructive behavior—are both resolved by the close of Chapter Thirty-Two. In other words, they are resolved during that long-ago summer of 1976. And this takes place during the climactic scene of the novel, when the rising action is at is zenith.

Like most novelists, I detest summarizing my work. Nonetheless, for the sake of brevity, I'll grit my teeth here and share how that climax occurs…

- Patrick realizes that a rare medical condition affecting a friend may, in fact, be something that was affecting his mother. But he has to talk to his mother's doctor to be sure.

- He knows the doctor is unlikely to talk to him about it over the phone. So he decides to drive back to Toledo to plead his case, and he decides to do this on an overnight trip at the end of the fourth-of-July weekend, when his father is unlikely to miss him.

- He shares this plan with Rachel, and she insists on coming with him.

- They find the doctor and he says he suspected Patrick's mother had a condition that could cause her to faint. She would wake after fainting when she fell over, but a seat belt would have prevented her from doing this. So it is likely, albeit not provable, that she simply started the car and passed out before she could touch the garage-door opener (the way Patrick learns this is *way* more involved that what we have here, but this is the end result). And then the exhaust did her in.

- Patrick and Rachel return to their distraught fathers and share what they have learned. Even though the information is not conclusive, Preacher Ransom observes, "Sometimes hope is enough."

- So Laurie's death appears to have been an accident and (we actually learn this in the beginning of Chapter Thirty-Three) Kevin stops making his dangerous solo climbs.

I'm leaving out a ton of stuff in this summary—amongst other things, I am leaving out Patrick's and Rachel's first kiss. But that's how we handle the reader's first two expectations, and as you can see, while they may not have been resolved in a manner the reader expected, the climactic outcome is pretty much what the reader has been hoping for.

But Patrick's mother's death, and Patrick's father's behavior, while central issues in the book, are not its most crucial issues.

Those are handled in the following five chapters.

The Roller Coaster

I visualize the construction of *In High Places* as being similar to a roller coaster. For thirty-two chapters, the cars have been climbing the hill, and—in the world of the novel—all of that rising action has taken place within the space of about 150 days. The progress bar on my e-book reader tells me that this climb has occupied exactly ninety percent of the novel's total content.

From Chapter Thirty-Three onward, the car drops. We are now into the falling action of the narrative arc. The tempo of the book changes—dramatically. While previously the novel had progressed by weeks, days, hours and even minute-by-minute, the action in the final chapters is delivered in elements of months, years, and even decades.

We are in the final ten percent of the novel, and the change in tone and tempo lets the reader know that the novel is moving to a new place. The narrator's adult point-of view becomes more and more prevalent; we are seeing fewer things filtered through a teenage mindset. And as a result, the tone becomes bittersweet, because growing up is bittersweet.

Unwelcome News

With the "why" of Patrick's mother's death removed, and Patrick's father taken out of immediate danger, the two most pressing, burning-platform issues of *In High Places* have been resolved.

The next issue that the reader is most likely to be concerned with is the future of Patrick's and Rachel's relationship.

After all, in the first thirty-two chapters, Rachel is a character who has been present in either the foreground or the background of the novel better than half the time. She has exerted a progressively greater influence on Patrick as the novel has progressed.

Because the novel is written from Patrick's point of view, the reader understands and has empathy for Patrick's feelings about Rachel. And in Chapter Thirty-Two, both Patrick and Rachel profess their love for one another.

So the novel is structured to get the reader rooting for the romance.

We have also set up a certain expectation because of the way the first two major issues of the novel—the matter of Patrick's mother's death, and the problem of his father's potentially self-destructive behavior—have been resolved at the novel's climax. While the readers may not have foreseen the precise manner in which these issues were resolved, they have, nonetheless, taken place in a manner that is in keeping with what the readers' desire. The readers are now expecting something similar to transpire with the romance. The novel has been written the way it has to *make* them expect it.

Stacking the Deck

By writing this novel from a first-person point of view, and by voicing Patrick's desires, I have made his wishes the reader's wishes. Patrick is a likeable character. Even for readers who have never rock-climbed and will never rock-climb, he is very easy to identify with. And the reader is naturally going to root for the home team.

So, now that the reader desires and expects that Patrick and Rachel will fall even more deeply in love, I have an obligation as a novelist to act on that expectation.

And the way I act upon it is simple. I deny it.

Going to Pieces

Here, in short, is what happens:

- Because Rachel ran off to Ohio with Patrick, their future relationship becomes constrained. Their families understand that nothing untoward has happened, but to the wagging tongues of the community, Rachel's reputation is, at the very least, sullied.

- Patrick realizes that this threatens more than Rachel's reputation. It threatens her family's reputation and, because of that, it threatens her father's ministry.

- Patrick wants the relationship to continue, but because of what's at stake, he realizes that it has to continue in a fashion that will be beyond reproach.

- So the two don't date—no dinners, no movies, nothing of that sort. Rachel's family doesn't dance, so they don't go to Patrick's or Rachel's proms. They don't even sit together in church. The only time they get together is when Patrick goes to the Ransom's home after church: something he only does if they have no other company. The two young people are never, ever alone together.

- When Patrick goes away to West Virginia University, he does not date other girls. Rachel never comes to visit him, and their only contact is by phone. They still see each other when he is home, but again the contact is limited, to home visits—her home, after church.

- This puts a huge strain on their relationship, particularly from Patrick's perspective. In effect, he has a girlfriend to whom he cannot display affection.

- When, after his sophomore year at university, an opportunity arises to take a summer job as a rock-climbing guide in Yosemite, Patrick takes it … over the objections of his father, who would rather not see the couple apart for so long. But when Patrick explains the difficulty of seeing Rachel every week, but never feeling as if he can even hold her hand, his father understands.

- Patrick goes to Yosemite and remains loyal to Rachel, even across the distance. In his words, "Monks on mountaintops had more of a social life than I did."

- When Patrick returns to the university, Rachel is beginning her own away-from-home school experience at Oral Roberts University (having completed her first two years of college as a commuter, at a junior college in West Virginia). The two remain in touch by phone, never dating other people. But they are beginning to show the emotional distance that results from physical distance

Everything comes to a head at Christmas. Patrick and Rachel are both on college break, and he visits her family's home for dinner on Christmas Eve. They have been perfectly loyal to one another for four years now. Patrick's father has developed a healthy mail-order business, in addition to the shop, and Patrick is still considered an equal partner in that, even though he is away most of the time for school.

So Patrick has a secure future in a place that Rachel has always called home. When he takes her to a corner of the family room for a talk, everyone—the readers included—has every reason to expect that he is going to propose.

He does not. What Patrick tells her, instead, is that an expedition is being formed to go to Pakistan, to climb K2 (the second-highest mountain on earth) and that he has been invited to go as the junior member of the team. The climbers are scheduled to train in the Swiss Alps through the winter, and then travel to K2 in the spring.

Rachel is surprised that Patrick is going to disrupt his university studies for a climb. She is also deeply concerned.

Because climbing is important to Patrick, it is important—as a subject—to Rachel. She is well-read on it, and she knows that K2 is an extremely dangerous mountain: one on which a number of climbers have perished.

So she protests. And the protest turns into a discussion, which transpires like this (Rachel is the first speaker):

"It's just ... I don't know, Patrick. Is this what we are going to do from now on? Am I going to wait while you go off to places you might not come back from? I mean— I know that this is who you are, has always been who you are. But ... "

Her eyes were welling as she looked at me, took both of my hands in hers, held them.

"I've tried to wait, Patrick," she'd told me. "I have. I want to. But I'm not as good at it as I'd like to be. I'm running out of 'wait.'"

She looked me square in the eyes. There it was. My turn.

"Then don't," I'd told her. "Then don't."

Say It Ain't So

At this point, I'm fairly certain that 100 percent of my readers would like to strangle me.

Because the novel is being told from Patrick's point of view, and because he is a likeable character, readers are naturally going to sympathize with him. And actually, they will do more than sympathize; the book is deliberately slanted to help the reader to identify with him. So when Patrick falls in love with Rachel, so, in a manner of speaking, does the reader.

Now, here comes the writer, threatening to ruin this wonderful relationship. It's unsettling.

Unsettling, and unforeseen, but not unthinkable.

Here's why.

First, we've established that, while Patrick understands he must keep Rachel at a distance—indeed, keeping her at a distance is his idea—he has grown increasingly uncomfortable with the arrangement. He is a young man, and it is hard for him to be in love with a young woman whom he cannot, in good conscience, so much as touch. While he remains loyal to Rachel during his summer in Yosemite, his willingness to go there is proof of his discomfort with the relationship.

Second, although he does not say so, Patrick appears to think that being invited on the expedition is an extraordinary coup for a climber of his age and experience. It is something to be excited about, and when Rachel is not excited, that may be an unexpected reaction.

Third—and this is the part that I feel makes the reaction in-character for Patrick—he is a young man, with the emphasis on the noun: man. And while it may be politically correct to say that gender has nothing to do with personality and how one handles oneself socially, my experience is that women and men think, interact, and react differently.

In this conversation, Rachel is thinking and acting as the sensitive young woman that she is. In her mind's eye, she is already looking ahead to a time when she and Patrick might marry, and she is reading the present situation in light of that anticipated future. Her inclination is to protect Patrick and keep him safe and, by doing so, to protect and safeguard the family she hopes they will become.

Patrick, on the other hand, thinks as a young man thinks and lives more in the moment. He sees the expedition as a once-in-a-lifetime opportunity. And the manner in which Rachel objects makes it clear that she is not simply troubled by him going to K2; she is troubled by the idea of him going on potentially dangerous expeditions, period. She is threatening his plans and trying to change him, and Patrick reacts the way men often react when someone is trying to make them change; he rebels.

It is a lapse for him, but it is a plausible lapse. And the book has been designed from Page One to make the reader hope it will be a temporary lapse—something that can be fixed. That is what will keep the reader reading.

But the lapse not going to be fixed: not immediately, at the very least. Patrick goes on the expedition.

The Other Side of the Earth

After winter training in Switzerland, Patrick continues on to the other side of the earth from West Virginia—Pakistan and the Karakoram mountain range.

In a single chapter, we are with him high on K2 when, in an attempt to beat a storm that is due to arrive in days, the expedition orders Patrick, an older Italian climber, and a single Balti porter to make an attempt for the summit.

Things go well until, on a steep section, the team is hit by falling rock and ice. The Italian falls to his death, but Patrick manages to save himself and the porter, although the porter's leg is broken.

The porter begs Patrick to leave him, but Patrick refuses, and manages to get the injured man down to their high camp, where they wait for a rescue party to arrive and help carry the injured man the rest of the way down.

But the porter's injuries go beyond his broken leg. At midday the next day, he dies. Patrick also learns that there have been avalanches in the night, and the four-man rescue party has disappeared. Had he left the porter as the man had requested, two people would be dead. But because Patrick insisted on trying to save him, the death toll now stands at six.

Alone, Patrick descends in the rising snowstorm, and staggers into base camp, where he is warmed and cared for by the rest of the team.

The storm continues unabated for weeks, making further climbing impossible. Then, when it subsides, melt-swollen rivers make it impossible for the team to leave. They are forced to wait for two months until a pack train can get into them. And during all this time, Patrick has had ample opportunity to think about the life he has chosen.

In the most literal sense of the term, he repents. He thinks again about his life choices, and decides that he is going to get educated to become a pastor and that, if Rachel will have him, he is going to spend the rest of his life with her.

By the time the expedition team gets to Islamabad and dependable long-distance phone lines, they have been out of touch with the world for better than eight months (remember, this is long before satellite phones or cell phones were common). Patrick's first phone call is to Rachel's father.

Patrick tells Preacher that he has re-thought his life and asks him if he can help get Patrick into a Christian university for the coming term, so he can study to become a pastor.

And after Patrick spills all of this out, Preacher is silent—silent so long that Patrick asks if he is still there. The scene continues:

> **"I'm still here," he told me. "And yes, sure. I can do all of that, Patrick. Happy to do it. I know people at several schools where you could start in the fall; you'd have your choice. But, Patrick, there's something you need to know … something about Rachel."**
>
> **Visions of car accidents, of house fires, of plane crashes, of disasters of every sort and magnitude raced through my mind.**
>
> **"Is she all right?" I asked him.**
>
> **"She's fine," he assured me. "But, Patrick … well, she met someone. They were married last month."**

This time, rather than wanting to kill the author, I imagine my readers are simply stunned. Patrick has finally done the right thing, but he's done it too late. Rachel is married, and marriage is something that she would take very, very seriously. Philosophically, the love story is dead; it has reached a place from which it cannot turn back. Patrick has lost Rachel forever.

It's a moment of high anxiety—anxiety: the product of play and so the product of fiction.

So while the reader was reading first to follow the love story, and then to see how Patrick will fix the damaged relationship, the reader now continues in order to learn what will become of Patrick.

Denial

In the chapter that follows, Patrick follows through on his promise to go to a Christian university (Liberty) and study to be a pastor. But he understands that any hope he might harbor of a life with Rachel is simply denial on his part. He becomes a profoundly unhappy young man, and channels his anger into his studies, where his professors mistake it for a passion for learning.

At Christmastime, he decides not to come home—the chance of seeing Rachel with her new husband is more than he can bear. So his father shows up at his dorm room and tells him that he's brought him a packed suitcase and they have a flight to catch. Patrick protests that he does not want to go climbing, and his father tells him climbing is not on the agenda. So they leave.

The destination turns out to be Kauai, in the Hawaiian Islands. It's a place that looks and feels like paradise, and—slowly—it drags Patrick out of his funk. He begins to rise early and run every morning on the beach, the run followed by a swim, and the endorphins lift him further from his depression.

One morning, after his swim, he crosses paths with a beautiful young woman on the beach. She seems familiar, so he takes a second look, just as she does the same. They realize that they are both students at Liberty and have seen each other on campus. They introduce themselves—her name is Sarah—have breakfast together, and then lunch.

The two families spend Christmas together. Patrick's father starts reading novels on the beach, to give the young people time together. And when the holiday is over and they go back to school, Patrick and Sarah realize that theirs is not an island infatuation. They fall in love and marry the following June.

In terms of seasons, passage of time, and other details, I—the author—have made sure that the beginning of this new love story mirrors elements of the end of the old. Patrick and Rachel break up at Christmastime; he meets Sarah the following Christmas. Sarah, like Rachel, has a biblical name (in Hebrew, Sarah means "princess"). And just as Rachel met and married someone very quickly after Patrick pushed her away, Patrick and Sarah marry just half a year after they begin seeing one another. The echoes are there to show Patrick healing.

The First Ending

Now the story accelerates. The couple starts a family. They work—she in counseling and he as a church pastor. Because

Patrick's father insists on giving him part of the income from the mail-order business, they have enough money to meet their needs, so while their marriage is not all sweetness and light, it mostly is. They are happy. But while the wound has healed, the scar remains.

The adult Patrick sums it up this way:

> **But sometimes, when I am alone in my study, or early in the morning, when I get up to shave and Sarah is still warm and asleep in our bed, my mind wanders back to Rachel, and to what might have been, if I had been as selfless as she … if I had chosen two other words in that Christmas Eve conversation. Words like, "I'm sorry."**
>
> **Or, "Forgive me."**
>
> **Or even, "Marry me."**
>
> **And when I think of Rachel, or rather of Rachel-long-ago, I remember that faint taste of peppermint when she kissed me, of the scent of her hair as it closed around our faces, of the touch of her hands at the small of my back. And I wonder if it is a sin to think of things like that: a sin, or human nature, or—as so very many things are—both. And I ask for forgiveness, because I believe it probably is, and I place that memory under the blood of my Savior, and I go to find my Sarah and I kiss her.**
>
> **And life?**
>
> **Life goes on.**

This passage feels like an ending. It works like an ending. And it *is* an ending—the ending of the love story.

I consider it the "first conclusion" of Patrick's narrative.

But it is not the conclusion of the novel, because the novel still has unfinished business.

Remember, while the conflict inherent in the relationship between Patrick and Rachel occupies much of the reader's attention, it is not the ultimate conflict, not the focus of the book.

The focus of the book was revealed in Chapter Twenty—it is Patrick's concern with the state of his father's soul. And that has not yet been addressed.

It gets addressed in the final chapter.

The Last Chapter

Chapter Thirty-Seven, the last chapter of *In High Places*, still takes place in what is, to the narrator, the relatively distant past, but it is a past approximately a decade removed from where we were when the book first opened.

In the final chapter, Patrick is recalling the autumn of 1985, when a hundred-year flood struck the region around Seneca.

We established earlier in the novel that Patrick's father provided rescue service, when called upon to do so by the Forest Service, and he does that during the flood, helping to evacuate people from the more distant mountain hollows, and get them to the school gymnasiums and other buildings being used as emergency shelters.

As the flood ravages the valley, Patrick calls and offers to drive down and assist his father with the evacuation efforts, but Kevin refuses. He tells Patrick that the roads coming into the valley would probably be impassable by the time he arrived, and besides, he doesn't want to see Patrick burn the gas to make the trip from Michigan, where he now lives.

"I'll need you after Thanksgiving, to help me clean out and shore up the shop," Patrick's father tells him. "But there's no use in making two trips down, one right after the other. Just stay where you are, and I'll call you when it's over."

So everything Patrick relates in the rest of the chapter is told to him by other people in the Seneca Rocks region.

The Second Ending

Members of Preacher Ransom's church tell Patrick that his father arrived with his rescue team at the gymnasium at the local college, late on the final evening of the flood. The gym was being used as a shelter, Preacher's church people were staffing it and, after the rest of his team had left, Patrick's father stayed on to have a bowl of chili before heading home.

Preacher joined him. The two followed the chili with coffee. And they spoke for a long time—better than an hour. As one of the church ladies later tells Patrick, "I cain't say for surely, but it looked to me powerfully like Preacher was witnessing to your daddy."

A call came in on the Forest Service radio—a woman at another shelter believed her elderly mother to be stranded by the flood in her up-hollow home. Kevin's team members had all gone home, so he agreed to respond to the call, and Preacher went along with him to help. Witnesses recall that the two men were still talking as they walked out into the storm and the dark.

The old woman, it turned out, was not stranded—she turned up the next morning at a different emergency shelter. But Patrick's father and Preacher did not know this. They made their way by four-wheel-drive to her home. The evidence points to that: the vehicle was found on the half-washed-out road the next morning, one of Patrick's father's climbing ropes lying on the ground behind it, still tightly coiled. But both men were gone, swept away by the flood.

Conclusion

Patrick recalls that Preacher's body was found a week later, several miles downstream. But, despite weeks of searching, his father's body was never discovered.

Patrick has been denied that closure, and he does not have closure on his one, great, lasting concern about his father—whether his father made that final, spiritual decision.

Here are the final 326 words of *In High Places*:

That's the hardest part: the uncertainty. Sometimes, late at night, lying awake in my bed with Sarah sleeping silently beside me, I think of him being borne down the river on those floodwaters, the roar and the dirty foam of the North Fork giving way to the swollen Potomac. I think of him drifting in the night down, downstream, past

the early morning lights of Washington, and then out into Chesapeake Bay, being pulled by the outgoing tide into the great Atlantic proper. I think of him being swept up into the great, glacial circle of the broad Gulf Stream, being pulled in that slow, eternal journey, under stars so bright they appear to be jagged points of ice, under skies where the horizon is always a flat and featureless blue.

Adrift.

Apart.

Alone.

And I wonder what he was talking about with Preacher Ransom on that last night: what views were exchanged, what points were conceded, what decisions, possibly, were made.

Because I believe what Preacher told me long ago in the cold, swift waters of Seneca Creek. I believe that when I close my eyes on this life and open them in the next, the first face I see will be that of my Savior, and the second will be that of my mother. But I wonder—and this is the thing that keeps me awake in the small, dark hours—I wonder if, after that second face, I will turn and see, perhaps, a third.

On that, I haven't a shred of certainty.

But I have hope. And on those long nights, when finally I rest and yield to slumber, it is always because I have remembered another time—the evening of the very last day that I was alone with the first girl I loved. And I remember and I cling to the other thing that her father told me...

That sometimes, hope is all we have.

And sometimes, hope is enough.

It Takes Two

So—in *In High Places* I have, for all intents and purposes, two endings. One resolves the state of the principle character, and the other brings the central conflict of the novel to solution (or dissolution, depending on how you look at it).

A couple of thoughts here…

One is that you might be wondering how common it is for a novel to seemingly come to a conclusion twice. And the answer is that it is very common. I'd venture to say it happens more often than not.

But the way it is usually done is that the initial conclusion brings the main conflict to an end, usually at the climax. And then the last chapter happens in a sort of afterglow and ties up the affairs of the characters in a final resolution.

I'm not sure why that happens. I've done it myself in some novels, and I cannot say for certain why *I* did it. Although I suspect one reason is that the "afterglow ending" is the one that is often used in (you guessed it) movies.

In my opinion, a far more powerful and resonant ending is achieved if you save the solution of the ultimate conflict for the end, preferably for the final sentence of the book. Books that end like that end like the striking of a great, huge bell—you can still hear it ringing long after the book's been closed.

Another thought is that, if you flip back and read those two endings that I used in *In High Places* again, you'll see many similarities.

Both endings contain references to Sarah—who represents Patrick the narrator's present life—asleep in their bed. Both contain references to exactly the same evening in that long-ago summer of 1976, when Patrick and Rachel returned from their clandestine trip to Ohio. In the first ending (which deals with the characters), Patrick remembers the kiss. And in the second ending, he remembers what Rachel's father had to say about hope.

And finally, at the conclusion of the first ending, Patrick goes to Sarah and kisses her—he wakes her up and they get on with their lives. But in the final paragraphs of the novel overall, Patrick refers to going back to bed and falling asleep.

And there is a reason he is going back to bed. It's because he can. Now he is past the anxiety.

Now he has peace.

More than a few readers have noticed the similarity of these two "conclusions," and they have written to me or spoken to me and asked how it was that I got the conclusion of the novel—the second ending—to echo the elements of the first. And they're surprised when I tell them my answer.

You see, I wrote the second ending—the novel's conclusion—first. I wrote it before I wrote the end of Chapter Thirty-Six.

And, truth be told, I wrote it before I wrote Chapter 1.

Chapter Thirty-Seven—the last chapter of *In High Places*—was the first part of the novel that I put on paper. Yes, it was a first draft, and yes, of course, it was later revised. But essentially all of that final chapter's elements were there in the beginning. I wrote the ending first, and everything else came later.

Hatfields and McCoys

Now, if you ever want to get a lively discussion going among a bunch of novelists, asked them whether they outline their books or not.

By "outline," I don't mean the classic, indented document with Roman numerals and capital letters that you learned in fifth grade. I don't know a single novelist who does that before they write.

A novel outline can be as simple as a list of sentences, with each sentence representing a scene, a series of note-cards containing scene or chapter prompts, a document created with a dedicated novel-writing program (such as Literature and Latte's Scrivener), a customized series of mindmaps scribbled in a notebook, or a whiteboard with a timeline and notes.

What these all have in common is that: a) the novelist knows where the book is going before the novelist begins to write, and b) he or she knows it in sufficient detail to be able to write it down.

At the other end of the spectrum is the pure, seat-of-the-pants novelist. This is the writer that does not know where the book is heading, and discovers the novel's direction during the course of writing it.

Typically, neither of these extremes can understand how a person could possibly produce a novel using the opposite technique.

Outliners say that a book written without an outline is going to lack form and direction, will likely require extensive rewriting, and runs a very real risk of losing its way or otherwise failing to "work" a hundred pages or more into the process. To an outliner, writing any other way is simply too fraught with risk.

And to a seat-of-the-pants novelist, the idea of following an outline seems devoid of discovery or spontaneity. They also often say it's less enjoyable—that it robs the novelist of those moments when the characters take off and start thinking and acting on their own. They lose, in other words, the joy of seeing the characters and the stories come fully to life.

And then there is the middle-of-the-road option, what some colleagues of mine refer to as the "headlights" approach. In this, at the end of a day of writing, you outline what comes next as far as you can clearly see (thus the "headlights" analogy). Technically, this is what is referred to as a "running outline," and I have heard a number of novelists say that it is something they often use.

Potpourri

Over the years, I have used all of these techniques. And quite frankly, I continue to employ a mongrel blend of plotting tools as I plan my narrative.

At the moment, for instance, when not working on this book, I have been working sporadically on a novel. I know what sort of novel it is going to be, where it will be set (at least at the beginning), and I know my principal character very, very well, as he is one I have used before. I don't know how the book ends, and I have only the most general idea of its principal conflict.

But I do have a very clear idea of the opening conflict and the details of the first several scenes. So I have gone ahead and written them, and now I have set them aside until the rest of the book comes to me. When it does, if those first scenes are still germane, I will use them, and if they are not, then out they go.

In contrast, when I was working on my novel *Wind River*, that book had a fairly short deadline, and I knew I did not have a lot of time for rewrites. So I outlined the entire book in bulleted sentences or phrases, each bullet representing a scene, and I did my plot revision in that skeleton of the book, rearranging, adding and deleting scenes until I was comfortable that I had what I needed. Then I wrote the novel in the same Word document, burning my bridges as I went, and deleting each bullet after I had written the scene it represented.

For *In High Places*, as I had no contract for that book, and thus no deadline, I had the luxury of thinking about it a long time before beginning to write.

Some chapters, I outlined scene-by-scene; for others, I had a summary paragraph that I wrote out to remind me of what needed to happen.

And others, I simply carried in my head.

But I did not begin to write that novel until I knew how it worked, beginning to end, and to remind myself where I was going, I wrote the last chapter first, and the first scene I wrote of that chapter was the final one.

Now, is this as fun as making it up as one goes? I think it can be, if your idea of fun is avoiding extensive rewrites. And besides, although I do find the writing process entertaining, I bear in mind that the ultimate purpose of the book is not to entertain me, but to entertain my readers. And I believe I can do that better if I know from the onset where the book is headed.

Expertise

I am happy to say I am certainly not the only novelist who feels this way. I've spoken with dozens of others who agree. And not long ago, at the end of the e-book version of *A Widow for One Year*, I came across an interview with John Irving, in which he said:

I have to know the end of a story before I can imagine the best beginning.

Later, in that same interview, Irving elaborated:

When I start telling a story, I already know the story. There must be authority and authenticity in a storyteller's voice; readers must trust that the storyteller is an expert, at least on this particular story. How can you be an expert if you don't know what happens?

"Expert"—I like that. We talk about the storyteller as a workman; even the subtitle of this book refers to the novelist's work as a craft. But the absolute truth of it is that making a novel is an art, and great artists design before they begin the works that others are going to see.

In that respect, novelists have more in common with artists and architects than they do with craftspeople. Great books—great novels—are designed before they are written. And an integral element of the design is the conclusion. Argue with me if you want (and many will), but I sincerely think you have to know how it ends before you can make a worthy start.

Book Two

The Novelist

| SIX: Reading to Write

If you don't have time to read, you don't have the time (or the tools) to write. Simple as that. — STEPHEN KING

IN WOODY ALLEN'S MOVIE, *Midnight in Paris,* aspiring novelist Gil Pender travels back in time to the Paris of the 1920s, where he meets Ernest Hemingway. They have this conversation:

Gil
Would you read it?

Hemingway
Your novel.

Gil
Yeah. It's ... it's like 400 pages long, and I'm ... I'm just looking, just for ... you know: an opinion.

Hemingway
My opinion is I hate it.

Gil
I mean ... you haven't even read it!

Hemingway
**If it's bad, I'll hate it, because I hate bad writing.
If it's good, I'll be envious and hate it all the more.**

This is feature-film dialogue, and thus invented, but it sounds shockingly realistic to me.

This is probably because—confession being good for the soul— it rings perilously close to the way that I read other people's novels.

I realize this is not a very Christian thing to admit, but it is what it is. We all have our frailties. I suspect I have more than most. Besides, I think this is pretty much the natural state of all artists.

Was Michelangelo able to look at a painting or sculpture by Leonardo da Vinci without mentally setting his own work on the opposite side of the scales? I strongly doubt it; Giorgio Vasari, the biographer of both artists, suggests that the two men were openly contemptuous of one another, to the point of insulting one another's work.

Sounds like professional jealousy to me.

And when I read another novelist's work, be it an advance reader's copy sent to me for review, the season's most recent runaway bestseller, or a student manuscript from a workshop, I constantly compare it to my own work.

Yes, if the novelist is a close friend who has done well, I rejoice at that success. But for the most part I find myself thinking, "If I live to be 100, I will never, ever, write this well..." or, "Please, Lord, please ... if I ever write anything this bad, dash the keyboard from my hands..." or (most often), "Look at this—I could write this... so why on earth didn't I?"

Yet, despite the accompanying emotional turmoil, I read other writer's novels all the time, finishing one and starting another pretty much every week. And I have been doing this, quite literally, for decades.

I make it sound like work. It is not. Reading fiction in general, and novels in particular, has always been a favorite entertainment for me, and it remains that, even if I read today with a much more critical eye.

Before I was ever a writer of fiction, I was a reader of fiction, and I think of that as a prerequisite for the vocation. To me this just seems obvious. Apparently to some people it is not.

If You Don't Love It, Set It Free

I say this because, several times now, I have been contacted by individuals who wanted to be novelists, but were woefully unfamiliar with the genre. Sometimes they were businessmen who wanted to create a book-length allegory to illustrate some philosophy in their field. At others times, they simply wanted the title of "novelist," believing it had the same cache as, say, "rock star" (they were sadly misinformed).

But what they all had in common was that, other than *The Great Gatsby* and a few other books they had read under protest in their high school and college days, their last encounters with book-length fiction had been as children. And the manuscripts they showed me looked as if they had been written by people whose only familiarity with the form had been Tom Swift and The Hardy Boys, thirty or forty years removed.

It gets worse.

Not once, but twice, when I looked at these clumsy and juvenile manuscripts, and asked their authors if they read novels, they told me (knowing, mind you, that I was a fiction writer), "No. I don't have time to waste on fiction. There's no point in it."

Which made me want to ask them if they had ever bothered to fall in love, because there is certainly no point in that, either.

Writing a novel is a task that consumes hours, days, weeks, months or even (in my case, at least) years. And putting that much effort into something you don't respect—something that you don't flat-out love—is worse than crazy. It's stupid-crazy.

Over the decades, my life has been enriched, my horizons have been broadened, and my heart has been stirred by the work of other novelists. Some of those books were so powerful that they are still moving me, years or even decades after I first read them. Part of the reason I write is to add to that tradition, to offer readers the same depth of experience that other novelists have offered me. So I read, I write and I read to write.

Books written without that depth of background are doomed from the get-go. That being the case, if you are not an avid reader of fiction, yet you wish to be a writer of it, my best advice to you is to close this book right now and go spend a decade or so reading great novels. We'll be here when you get back.

You are What You Read

Still with us? Good—I thought you'd be an avid reader.

But now let's talk about what it is that you've been reading.

That's important. Reading, to a novelist, is what nutrition is to an athlete. Some forms are better than others. In fact, some forms are *much* better than others.

I say this as a survivor of the junk-food wars.

I arrived at elementary school already knowing how to read—the work of my paternal grandmother, whose favorite way of keeping me from pestering her was to sit me down with the family Bible and have me sound out the words. So once I got to first grade, I supplemented *Fun with Dick and Jane* with the *Encyclopedia Americana* and (once my teacher made certain I wasn't spending all my time ogling pictures of bare-breasted tribal women), several decades' worth of *National Geographic*.

Outside of school, I read what most boys read … boys who read, that is. Adventure novels, Robert Louis Stevenson, Rudyard Kipling and *Boys Life* magazine during the years when I could cage someone in the family into buying me a subscription for Christmas.

And then there was the library. I grew up in a little farm town in Illinois, and the local library was a portal into the world beyond the cornfields.

The problem with our library was that it wasn't all that large, and there wasn't a bookstore within twenty miles. I think my voice was getting ready to change before I realized that there were stores where one could buy virtually nothing but things to read. So I made my way through all of the boys' fiction in the library, supplementing it with military histories and how-tos on camping and fishing.

It was not that I was exclusively bookish. I rode my Schwinn cruiser, participated in Scouting, played baseball, fished for crawdads in the local creek and built creaking tree houses with my friends.

But even when I did these things, I usually had some reading material stuffed away in my jeans pocket.

During the summers I would live for a month or more at a time with an aunt and uncle who ran a public golf course. This was my introduction to work, and I would caddy, rake sand traps, sell shag balls through a window in the pro shop, and finish each day practicing putting and chipping with my uncle, who had never made it onto the pro tour and suffered from the delusion that I could someday do so in his place.

Then, when it got so dark that we could no longer see the flags on the greens, we would retire to my aunt's and uncle's spacious apartment above the pro shop, where I would delve into Aunt El's back issues of the *Reader's Digest* and those accompanying hardbound volumes of literature with all the goodness boiled away: the *Reader's Digest Condensed Books*.

I entered high school, then, thinking that I was well read, but I was not. I was widely read.

There is a difference.

Particularly when it came to fiction, our little public library's collection was made up mostly of books bequeathed to it from the estates of some of the area's wealthier families. My English teachers in junior high and, indeed, in my first years of high school, either stuck to the classics, or books that had been contemporary when they, or the professors who'd taught them, had been in college. So I wasn't really reading anything more modern than Hemingway, Fitzgerald, Dos Passos and their peers.

It was not that I didn't read anything modern at all. I did—my uncle, the golf pro, was fond of Ian Fleming's James Bond paperbacks and handed them down to me. And for some reason, the little town library always had a good supply of recent books of real-life adventures written by mountain climbers and ocean explorers and the like.

But it wasn't until I was in my last two years of high school and we got a new English teacher—Miss Coulter was her name—that my eyes were opened to the fact that real literature, actual extraordinary writing, was being produced by people who were still alive and breathing.

To me, this was an epiphany, but it was not yet an awakening. Most of my high-school classes, and later almost all of my freshman and sophomore literature classes, glorified the past and paid scant attention to the present. No one bothered to state what now seems obvious: that their intention was to provide me with that as a foundation: something upon which to build. To me, and I suspect to legions of would-be writers, the message I got was, "If you want to write the really good stuff, you'll write *just like this*."

So, stylistically, I was being taught to appreciate stovepipe hats and bowlers, long after the state of the art had moved on to—and beyond—fedoras.

The Disconnect

Even as an undergraduate in college, I had some success selling my nonfiction writing. Advertising copy for local businesses, pieces for the *Toledo Blade Sunday Magazine*: it was far from a fulltime job, but I got paid for it, and I could say that I was a professional writer.

So I figured getting some fiction published would not be that great a leap.

I was re-reading Arthur Conan Doyle at the time, thought I could do a good job of writing something like that, and wrote a story about a master detective, as seen through the eyes of his companion. I set it in London—a city I'd never so much as laid eyes on at the time—and in the Victorian era, a period with which I was all but unacquainted. But I figured the story was a lot like Doyle's work—I'd done everything but name my characters "Watson" and "Holmes"—and Doyle was supposed to be a master of the form. Then I sent it in to *Ellery Queen Mystery Magazine* and waited for my paycheck.

I got a rejection slip.

I tried again, and this time the slip came with a note suggesting I read a couple issues of the magazine.

Which was great advice, because while I had glanced through it before, that was all I had done: glance.

And it turned out that mystery writing seemed to have moved on considerably since the days of Arthur Conan Doyle. Now, the writers were working in forms with which I was unfamiliar.

I never did sell a story to Ellery Queen (although, now that I'm thinking about, I may try again). But I learned a valuable lesson, which is: *write—and read—for your readers, not for generations past.*

This has been an uphill sell for me with some of the writers in my workshops.

"I don't understand," they'll tell me. "My story is just like _____ (fill in the blank with "Hemingway," "Tolkien," or whomever); why doesn't it sell?"

I usually don't tell them the first part of the answer, which is that their writing is probably nothing whatsoever like that of the famous writer they've just named. But I do tell them the second part, which is that, if modern readers want to read, say Hemingway, they already have twenty-five volumes of that writer's *own* work to choose from.

Imitations of other writers' works fall into one of three general areas. They can be a *pastiche* (in which the style and tone are imitated, sometimes with the original author's characters); if the original work is still under copyright, these can be and often are the targets of lawsuits. Or they can be a *parody* (comedic criticism of the original work, usually allowable under copyright law). Or they can be *fanfiction*, which uses the characters of another author, sometimes in an alternative setting.

What all of these have in common is that they are derivative; the writer has depended on someone else to provide the foundation.

And they generally don't sell. Pastiche usually works only if the style of an earlier writer is used to explore a theme that resonates profoundly with a modern audience—mere imitation is usually not enough to do the job. Parody has a tendency to just be silly. And the audience for fanfiction is so specialized that it circulates almost exclusively online, or through outlets that are only accessible online.

So imitating dead writers not only smothers your own style and creativity—it's generally unprofitable as well.

This doesn't mean you should avoid writers of another age. I still read Twain, Hemingway, Dickens, Dinesen and the rest for the sheer enjoyment of it. And they do provide a good foundation on which to build your craft.

But if you want to write fiction that sells to a modern audience, you also need to read quality modern work.

Where the Puck is Going to Be

Every time I give this advice, I think of the great Wayne Gretzky, the hockey player who said that the secret to playing the game was not to skate to the puck, but to skate to *where the puck is going to be*.

The application for this in writing—or in any field in which one markets a good or a service—is that you study what is currently successful, not in order to imitate it, but to predict what the next big thing will be.

And then you create that next big thing.

This is not the technique used by most writers. Nor, quite frankly, is it the technique used by most publishers. Every publisher takes on measured risk with each book that they publish, and many seek to ameliorate that risk by making up the majority of their catalogue with books that are similar to those that are already doing well in the marketplace.

So writing books similar to what is already out there does give the newer writer a somewhat better chance of selling a book. But it is a two-edged sword; books that simply imitate other books rarely become breakout bestsellers. And eventually trends run their course, which means you may be left with a book written for a genre that has simply dried up.

As selling a novel is an extraordinarily risky venture anyhow, I think it is better to look at what sells extremely well right now, and then—based on that market knowledge, plus trends in world affairs, culture, and just generally what people seem to be getting interested in—write the novel that is going to satisfy the taste that has not quite emerged yet.

Steve Berry, a bestselling novelist who was raised in Georgia and now lives in northeastern Florida, did exactly that.

Before he was ever a novelist, Berry was a successful attorney. When he decided he wanted to write, he spent several years making the pilgrimage to a writer's group several hours away from where he lived, learning and practicing his craft.

As a seasoned attorney, the logical thing for him to do—the expected thing for him to do—would have been to write legal thrillers. And when Berry began writing novels in earnest, several writers, including such notables as John Grisham and Scott Turow, had achieved extraordinary fame and fortune writing such books.

But Berry probably realized that the legal-thriller boom had been going on for quite a while by the time he began writing. And besides, one of the reasons Steve Berry started writing fiction in the first place was to incorporate a lifelong passion of his: the study of history.

So he began to write contemporary suspense novels that had a strong and significant historical backstory—books in which the protagonist was seeking knowledge or an artifact from another time. These books had action, adventure, history, mystery, suspense, detective-work and some elements of the thriller, all rolled into one, and at first, the publishing world did not know what to do with such books.

So it ignored them.

Then publishing insiders began to get excited about a forthcoming book by another writer: Dan Brown. His novel, *The Da Vinci Code*, was being brought out by Doubleday and, late in 2002, it was the talk of the upcoming publishing season. It was a fresh approach, combining—you guessed it—action, adventure, history, mystery, suspense, detective-work and some elements of the thriller, all rolled into one.

Everyone agreed it had "bestseller" written all over it. Publishers began looking for novels with those qualities.

And Steve Berry had just such a novel, ready to go.

That debut novel, *The Amber Room*, was published by Ballantine and immediately made the national bestseller lists. So did his second novel. And when Berry introduced his popular series featuring a former Justice Department operative by the name of Cotton Malone, the very first book in that series, *The Templar Legacy*, debuted on the New York Times bestseller list at Number Four.

True, many critics have referred to Berry's works as "*Da Vinci Code* knock-offs." And Steve Barry himself jokes that, every time he passes the Dan Brown shelves in a bookstore, he pauses to pay homage. But Berry's first novel was in print and on shelves a mere four months after *The Da Vinci Code* was launched. Clearly, his novel was written and ready to go long before Dan Brown's appeared in print, which means that Berry was either smart enough or lucky enough to predict where the fiction market was headed long before *The Da Vinci Code* hit the bestseller lists.

Reading Fiction "In-Season"

The trick to this, of course, is having enough time (and money) to read what's coming out in the areas in which you like to write, and learn enough to make an educated guess as to where the market is headed.

One way to take money out of the equation is to take advantage of the local library. The key here, though, is being the early bird that gets the worm; while most public librarians are wise enough to get in multiple copies of a potentially popular title, it's simply not cost-effective to buy more than a few. So while your local library might have five or six copies of the latest bestseller, there could be hundreds of patrons waiting to get their hands on it. And with each book out on loan for a week or two at a time, it could be months before you actually have a copy in hand.

As a college student, I learned that this issue was compounded at university libraries, which exist to support an educational mission, and so generally do not invest heavily in those titles that they would classify as recreational reading. One of the universities I attended

(Bowling Green) had an entire library devoted to popular culture, but even that tended to specialize in research materials, so the inhabitants of the *New York Times* bestseller list remained difficult to find.

Back then, the only alternatives left were bookstores. As I went to school in northwestern Ohio and often made the relatively short drive north to Ann Arbor and the University of Michigan libraries, I always made a trip to the original Borders bookstore, as well as the mega-bookstores that were just then beginning to appear.

The problem on a student's budget, of course, was how to buy books and have enough left over to pay rent and eat.

Which made the bargain bins—sitting near the front doors of the bookshops, and oftentimes outside the bookshop, on the sidewalk—a seductive alternative.

It wasn't just that they were merely cheap books. Some of them were from well-known authors: writers whose work I recognized and knew to be exceptional. And when I was riding a bicycle most places, not for my health, but to save money on gasoline, $2.99 for a novel by Kurt Vonnegut or Saul Bellow seemed like one heck of a deal.

So I bought a lot of books from the remainder tables and the bargain bins. To this day, I don't regret the purchases; they provided me with hours of good, quality entertainment, and they filled my head with excellent prose, which I hoped would soon crowd out the less-than-excellent verbiage that I was putting on paper in those days.

Those books were bargains, they were good investments, and they were quality company. But what they were not was *missional*.

I'd recognized that I needed to read more—much more—contemporary fiction. I needed to steep myself in the kinds of literature that book-buyers were seeking out then, in that season. But the books on the remainder table were just that: remainders—which is a marketing-savvy term for "leftovers." They were copies that had not sold the season before—or the season before that ... or several seasons before even that.

So I was not staying up to date on the current trends in fiction. I was staying up to date on those trends that had preceded them. I was getting closer—but not close enough. And on a student's budget, I simply could not fill my shelves with the sorts of fiction I needed to be reading if I wanted to get smart on what was in demand in the moment, to get a sea-sense on where the currents of popular taste were shifting.

The solution to this conundrum came about when, through friends of friends, I was introduced to the local National Public Radio affiliate, which was in need of someone to do a weekly book-review spot.

I auditioned and got the role, which is much less of an accomplishment than it sounds like, as it was unpaid.

But the book-review gig got me access to just-published and yet-to-be-published novels, as well as the occasional sit-down with a real live author. For a voracious reader such as me, access to all-you-can-eat books was a sort of heaven, and even though the most I ever got paid for that was a cup of coffee from the producers' lounge at the radio station, I enjoyed doing the spot and continued to record it until I was finished with grad school, at which point the harsher realities of making a living took up all of my time, and I relinquished my weekly five minutes before the microphone.

I seriously doubt that I was the first fiction lover to happen upon book reviews as a means of getting my hands on top-quality, current fiction, and I certainly know I was not the last. Plenty of people still blend their avocation and vocation in this manner, and if they do it in the right media, everybody wins.

By "right media," I mean outlets in which a publisher can be assured that enough people are hearing the opinions about a book to justify dealing with that person as a book reviewer.

The radio station where I did my reviews, for instance, was supported by tens of thousands of members; that was an easily verifiable fact. And for each member who belonged to Public Radio, there were dozens of listeners who tuned in but did not buy memberships to support the station (a fact that Public Radio stations remind the world of at every pledge drive).

So publishers knew that my reviews, which aired in good, daytime spots, would be heard by hundreds of thousands of people. The radio station spent most of its day broadcasting classical music and news, and people who listened to that sort of radio tended to be people who bought books.

And finally, as I sent air-dated copies of my scripts to the publishers who provided books for review, they knew I was fair, objective, and not afraid to give a bad review to a well-known author who'd turned out a clinker of a book, so it was obvious that my listeners trusted my judgment.

There are still a variety of outlets for such reviews; large-circulation magazines and newspapers with audited circulation, commercial and public radio and television all serve up audiences of a size that can make it worth a publisher's while to send review copies. But the number of such gigs is limited, which means conventional media, if they want a book reviewer, can pretty much take their pick.

But conventional media is no longer the only media, and "book reviewers" now seem to be cropping up like dandelions. Sometimes their only outlets are the product pages on Amazon (where the "Customer Reviews" are not really reviews, but customer comments—the actual reviews are in the "Editorial Reviews" section, higher up). And sometimes the outlets for their reviews are blogs.

The Cargo Cults

I know about the rising tide of Internet book reviewers because every publisher I know of gets solicited by them. Many would-be reviewers also do something no self-respecting conventional book reviewer would ever do, which is approach the *authors* of the books and ask for review copies.

And while a few kind souls in writer-world occasionally answer such requests by sending books out for review (usually to readers whom they know have been following their work for quite some time), most publishers and most authors politely decline.

This usually results in hurt feelings. The people wanting to do the reviews can't understand why they are being refused. After all, they usually send links to their pages, so you can see that they are real reviews.

But the thing is, from the industry's perspective, they are not.

Before they will work with media and provide them books for review, publishers want to know three things.

They want to know how many people are going to see the review—not how many clicks or how many views, but how many unique individuals ... and they usually want this information to come from an objective third party. They want to know the demographics of that group of individuals—their income, their levels of education, and other data that can indicate how likely they are to be buyers and readers of books. And they want to know that the reviewer has been vetted by a professional and reliable source, such as an editor or, in broadcast, a producer.

Traditional media can provide all of this information, and so can some professionally run websites, but the typical blog or amateur e-zine cannot, either because they don't know how, or they would rather not share the dim truths thus revealed. So even though standalone reviewers may be able to provide samples of book reviews laid out on nicely designed web pages, they are not considered viable by the industry.

In a way this reminds me of the Cargo Cults.

These were tribal groups who lived in Papua, New Guinea in almost Stone-Age conditions; they had rarely been contacted by the outside world, and most of their members had never seen an airplane. Then, during World War II, American Seabees and British Royal Engineers arrived and carved out airstrips in the jungle, and when they did, a marvelous thing happened: airplanes began arriving, and the airplanes were full of food, medicine, Coca-Cola, Spam, Hershey bars, T-shirts and other wonderful products of the Western world, which the Allies shared with the local people.

Then the war ended, the military went away, the airstrips were reclaimed by the jungle, and the tribes missed the huge, noisy, metal devices that had come down from the sky and brought them so many amazing gifts.

So, since airstrips had apparently attracted them in the first place, the people cleared land and carved out new airstrips; they even used bamboo to construct likenesses of control towers and hangers, and fashioned near-life-size facsimiles of aircraft out of natural materials, parking them along the runways. But the airplanes never returned, and this mystified the tribes because, as far as they could tell, what the military had constructed and what they had fabricated were almost exactly the same thing.

First Impressions

To a Western mind—to a mind that understands how things really worked—the efforts of the Cargo Cults seem misguided and naïve.

And to the publishing industry, self-proclaimed book reviewers seem the same.

If reading is all would-be reviewers want to do, they may not care what the publishing industry thinks of them. But for those who hope one day to join that industry—those who wish to become professional novelists themselves—"misguided and naïve" is not the best first impression to make.

So I don't suggest the roll-your-own review page route.

Fortunately, we live in an age that offers a viable, and even preferable, alternative.

The Virtual Library

I have always loved books. Not just the contents of books, but the physical objects: the look and the feel of them in the hand. When I see a shelf full of books that I have read and enjoyed, it gives me a sense of comfort. At one time, I had bookcases and bookshelves in literally every room of my house, the kitchen and the bathrooms included. And my study was lined with bookshelves; there literally was no wall space visible, anywhere.

Then our family moved from Michigan to Florida. The movers were being paid by the pound.

And books ... are heavy.

So, three days in a row, I loaded up my pickup truck with books and donated them to the county library. I only kept those volumes that had been inscribed to me by their authors, and a few others to which I felt great sentimental attachment.

It was still hundreds of pounds of books.

This diminished, somewhat, my love affair with books as physical objects.

Then the second shoe dropped when my wife and I took a transatlantic cruise.

I confess that I truly enjoy cruise-ship vacations. You only have to unpack once, there isn't the familiar vacationer's pain in the wallet every time you sit down for a meal, and I like to sit on a balcony and watch the ocean rolling by. As far as I'm concerned, it doesn't even matter where the cruise is going; they could just take the ship out in the ocean and steam around in circles, and I would be fine with that.

Plus, cruise ships don't seem to care how much luggage you bring; if it fits in your stateroom, they're apparently fine with it. So, as we live in Florida and can drive in less than a morning to five different cruise-ship terminals, we're accustomed to taking pretty much as much luggage as the trunk of the car will hold.

But the transatlantic cruise posed a hurdle, because, unlike most cruises my wife and I go on, this one would not start and end at the same port. It would finish up in Europe, so we would be flying back and, unlike the cruise ships, airlines do care about how much luggage you bring—and charge dearly for the excess.

Which posed a problem because, while I customarily read a novel or two during the course of a workweek, I'll read twice as much when I'm on vacation—four or six novels during the course of a fifteen-night transatlantic cruise. Plus, as I will do some writing even while on vacation, I like to have reference volumes at hand: a dictionary, a Bible, perhaps a history book or a guidebook or two—maybe more when I'm aboard a ship, where internet access is erratic. Even in my pared-down-and-ready-to-travel mode, I might want to take along eight to twelve volumes for that two-week transatlantic trip.

And books, as we've already established, are heavy.

Fortunately, I had an alternative. My wife had gotten me an e-reader—a Kindle—for my birthday, and all the books I wanted, plus hundreds and hundreds more, fit into a slim device that weighed less than a paperback. During that cruise, I began to use it in earnest. It was a model that could do data transfers by cellular signals, as well as by Wi-Fi, and one evening, as we were leaving the Azores, we realized we still needed guidebooks for both Lisbon and Paris so, as Ponta Delgada diminished on the aft horizon, I held the Kindle as far out over the balcony railing as I could, purchased the books we needed, and received them, wirelessly, in less than a minute. In all, I suppose I accessed and used more than twenty books over the course of a fortnight.

But when we checked in at the airport in London, my bag was under the maximum allowed weight by nearly half a kilogram. And it wasn't just that. I'd also saved quite a bit by buying e-books rather than books printed on paper—saved enough that I didn't feel guilty at all buying a title on a whim.

And there was one other highly significant advantage to reading this way.

Endless Free Samples

Remember what we said earlier about the importance of an opening of a book? Well, on my Kindle—and on Barnes & Nobles' Nook, Apple's iBook reader, and most other popular e-readers—that opening is available as a free sample, downloaded instantly and delivered wirelessly.

For novelists new and old, this is a godsend. It is now possible to read, on the day of release and without making a trip to a library or a bookstore, the latest releases from virtually every publisher's line ... and to read the initial portion (generally the first chapter and then some) without spending a cent.

I'm not saying I no longer read traditional, printed-on-paper books. I do, and my family knows there is no gift I enjoy more than a new novel by a favorite author, especially if it is signed.

But for the salt-mines reading, the reading that I do to strengthen craft, e-books excel, and the free samples are a veritable candy store.

As a writer, I take liberal advantage of them. If a novel comes out that I am even remotely interested in, I download the sample and read it. Then, if the sample hooks me, I'll buy the book. I also use the same method for nonfiction I'm reading as background—I read the sample first to see if it's really what I'm after.

The difference is that, with fiction, oftentimes just the sample is enough to give me a taste of a fresh technique, or raise my antennae to an emerging trend. The book may not be my cup of tea, and I might not decide to buy it, but the glimpse afforded by the sample may very well have increased my market awareness and sharpened my art.

Method to the Madness

For the newer novelist, e-book sample browsing is most productive if it is done with a purpose. Let's say you've heard in a workshop that your dialogue needs work; you can read the openings of a dozen (or more) recent, high-quality novels, look for dialogue that you find engaging, take note of the things that make it that way, incorporate that into your work, and see if anyone notices an improvement. And you can repeat the process as many times as it takes for you to start writing professional-caliber dialogue.

By "take note," I mean that literally. Many e-readers have provisions for note-taking right on the reader, and you can use that if that works for you. But I find it more productive to have all my notes on a subject in the same place, so the easiest way for me to do this is old-school. I keep a good, old-fashion notebook next to whatever I'm reading, and collect all of my notes in it.

The object here is not to imitate one particular writer, but to look for consistencies in technique. If you read the openings to twenty really good and really current novels, and jot down the speaker attributions as you find them, and notice that "he exclaimed" or "she whined" are uncommon, while "said" seems to predominate, that might tell you something about what readers (and editors) prefer right now. And if you search the samples for words ending in "ly" and find very few of them, then that might tell you how contemporary readers and editors feel about adverbs.

Jot down those elements that surprise and delight you, as well. Stephen King has a way of describing commonplace things—even the sounds of lawn sprinklers—that adds dimension and texture and makes you look at them in an entirely new way. And I know that because I made a note to myself when I encountered it.

Can you learn this stuff by osmosis—just by reading a lot of good, current writing, and letting the elements soak in? Certainly, you can. But I believe that note-taking, especially when you are early in your career as a novelist, shortens the learning curve considerably and makes you more aware of style and technique, and how they work.

The Spice of Life

Earlier, I said that reading, to a novelist, is what nutrition is to an athlete.

To continue along that train of thought: you need to have a varied diet when you read.

It's surprising how many newer writers ignore this. There are people trying to write speculative fiction who have never read anything but speculative fiction. There are people trying to write historical romances without regularly reading outside of that genre. I assume the same thing is true for virtually every popular genre of fiction, and the results of this siloed approach to reading are predictable. Only reading in the genre in which you write produces storylines and structures that tend to be familiar and echoic. It results in what I refer to as "inbred fiction"—fiction that is weak and pale because it has not had the benefit of influence from outside its genre.

But when you read a variety of genres and a wide range of material, it opens new windows into your world.

Here's one example: history.

For decades, historians tend to read a lot of history, and little else. And as history is usually thought of as the objective record of past events, most histories tended to be on the dry side.

Shortly after World War II, Bruce Catton started producing a different sort of history. He was not a traditional academic historian; his background was in newspaper journalism, a field in which he had also worked as a book reviewer. As such, he had great familiarity with popular novels, and when Catton—who had moved on to become founding editor of American Heritage magazine— published his first well-known history, *Mr. Lincoln's Army*, he wrote it using the techniques of a popular novelist, adopting the point of view of a narrator actually witnessing the events, and even inserting dialogue for which there was no verifiable record.

Catton's books about the American Civil War became some of the most popular histories ever published, and some of the strongest examples of "popular history," a genre that blended historical documentation with fictive narrative technique. And I imagine that one reason he was able to write such successful books was because he was not only widely read—he was well read outside his genre.

Black and White and Read All Over

I think it also helps, no matter what genre you are writing in, to be well read in current events.

Years ago, when I was an undergraduate at The University of Toledo, I had the opportunity to attend a lecture by Leonard Nimoy—the actor who played the alien first officer, "Mr. Spock," on the original *Star Trek* television show. He talked about the series, and how an episode was created, and he said that, almost invariably, the process began with the show's writers reading the newspaper.

They would come across a story that piqued their interest, and then imagine what it would be like if a similar story, or some element of it, were to take place in the future, in intergalactic space.

This process worked, Nimoy said, because the tastes of the writers tended to be about the same as the tastes of the viewers who watched the program. This meant that a topic of interest to the writers would usually be of interest to the fans and, as the shows were written relatively close to their airdates, they could exploit popular themes and well-known current events, and incorporate them into the fabric of the series. It was a technique that served the series' writers very well: so well that reflecting popular themes and current events became a hallmark of the television shows and feature films that were later spun off from the original series.

The Second Most Important Thing

So reading—reading current fiction, reading widely, and reading about current events—is one of the essential habits of successful novelists. Bodybuilders pump iron, and musicians have to endlessly practice scales for their art, but novelists get to read other people's books. It almost seems unfair that one of the central practices of the vocation can bring such great pleasure. Yet it is a central practice.

In fact, in the world of the professional novelist, there is only one thing more important than the practice of intelligent, well-guided reading.

And that is the practice of putting words on paper.

| SEVEN: Writing to Write

One day I will find the right words, and they will be simple.
— JACK KEROUAC

SEVERAL YEARS AGO, during a trip to London, my wife and I paid a visit to the Tate Gallery, in Millbank, adjacent to the Thames. The Tate (now known as "Tate Britain") is immensely popular with locals and tourists alike. I have heard that it surpasses even the Metropolitan Museum of Modern Art in annual visitation.

We'd come on a mission. My wife had seen pictures of *La Petite Danseuse de Quatorze Ans*—"Little Dancer of Fourteen Years"—by Edward Degas, and wanted to see the sculpture for herself.

Actually, what the Tate has is a casting of the original. Degas chose wax, a potentially perishable medium, for his original work, placing a natural-hair wig on its head, and dressing it in a linen bodice, gauze tutu and pink satin hair ribbon, coating both the wig and the bodice in wax, and exhibiting the finished and fragile work in a glass case, which observers of the day said made it look like a medical specimen.

In 1922, five years after Degas' death, his entrepreneurial heirs used the wax original to make a mold and created a limited number of bronze castings of the sculpture. In these, both the hair and bodice are bronze as well. The tutu is crafted from artificially aged muslin, and the hair ribbon is, as in the wax original, made of satin.

Degas, who was also a painter, made his wax sculpture in 1881, coloring his material naturally to convey as exact a representation of life as possible. I imagine he was reacting to the by-then-established technology of photography, which he sometimes used himself to create extremely detailed images: one of the more famous of these is a self-portrait that he shot in 1895.

But with his wax sculptures Degas was able to do something that photography could not: he created highly lifelike, three-dimensional renditions of the human form—like full-color photographs one could view from every angle.

At least, I imagine that was his intention. And while he might have achieved that with his wax original, the bronze copies that the relatives created, while still considered exceptional works of art—they have sold for upwards of ten million dollars apiece—are a step removed.

In the Tate's version of *La Petite Danseuse de Quatorze Ans*, the bronze bodice is of a lighter patina than the rest of the statue. While in some of the bronze copies the muslin tutu is very nearly a canvas white, the tutu on the Tate version is a dark and greenish brown, as if dyed in very dark, dirty tea. By contrast, the satin hair ribbon is pristine, a bright yellow-gold in color.

My wife found the work touching and entrancing: an immortal moment lifted from the ballet studios of nineteenth-century Paris.

I found it just plain creepy.

I've since learned that these polar opposites are quite common reactions to this particular work. When Degas exhibited the original, some critics found the mixture of materials breathtaking, while others referred to it as nothing less than evil.

So, while my wife gazed, awestruck, and whispered, "Isn't she amazing?" … I was experiencing the sort of repulsion one might feel if brought face-to-face with one of the flying monkeys from *The Wizard of Oz*.

Not wanting to spoil the moment for her, I excused myself to go have a look around.

And a minute later, in a nearby gallery, I found myself surrounded by something I'd never even heard of before: cloud studies.

Practicing the Ephemeral

Most were paintings by the English landscape artist, John Constable. And I understood immediately why he painted them.

After all, think about it; most of the elements of a landscape composition, even those in motion, can be studied in repose. Trees and wheat fields are not always waving in the wind. Horses and carriages come to a standstill occasionally. Except for the passage of sun and shadow or the dusting of snow, mountains and hills are eternal. But clouds move and change, often by the second.

Constable died in 1837, only ten years or so after the creation of the oldest surviving photograph, so it's possible he never even heard of the medium. And even if he had, early nineteenth-century photography required exposures that went on for several hours— useless for recording a subject as changeable and fleeting as a cloud.

So Constable made a concentrated effort to hone his skills in the most difficult aspect of his art. Landscape painting is a process of composition, observation and rendition, and in making his cloud studies, Constable forced himself to remember what he had observed—possibly for only a moment—long enough to render it faithfully in the time-consuming processing of painting with oils.

Possibly because of the concentration required to create them, the paintings are rather small; I don't recall any that were more than a couple of feet wide.

And I have since heard that, of the scores of cloud studies Constable produced over the years, only one was exhibited during his lifetime. These were works he created, not for sale or to increase his reputation, but simply to make him a better painter. Constable centered in on that part of his art that was, for him, the most challenging, and he made himself a master of it.

I am indebted, then, to Edward Degas, or at least to his avaricious relatives, who carted his wax sculpture off to the foundry and creating that little bronze flying monkey of a ballerina. It was the catalyst that sent me wandering deeper into the museum, where I encountered John Constable's cloud studies. And for me and for my craft, those cloud studies were nothing less than an epiphany.

Strength Training

It is human nature, I think, to gravitate toward what we do effortlessly and well. Some writers just "get it" immediately when it comes to plot and structure. Others understand intuitively how to create characters that seem human and three-dimensional and very, very real. And for some writers, these strengths are so great that publishers and readers both are willing to overlook flaws elsewhere in their writing.

Admittedly, writers seem to read with a more critical eye than the average reader. Elmore Leonard once told me that, when he read someone else's published work, "Invariably, I'll find myself pausing and thinking, 'Why did he decide to use "if" instead of "when" right there? And why did he use a comma?'"

I'm much the same way. And there is no published work I am more critical of than my own. When I come back to something I wrote a year or so earlier, I am often surprised by how much better the work looks, overall, than what I remember writing. Yet the rough spots—and there will always be rough spots—seem to leap at me from the page.

Back when I was writing mostly short fiction and had just landed the contract for my first novel, two of those leap-from-the page elements were dialogue and voice.

My work conveyed the sense of what my characters were talking about, but I was having a difficult time arriving at that happy medium: getting the dialogue to the point where it sounded like real people talking, without descending into the fragmented gibberish that usually results if you transcribe an actual conversation between two people.

And as for narrative voice, my writing either sounded like me (which is good, in a way) or it sounded forced. I was having a difficult time adopting a narrative voice outside the realm of how I naturally would speak and write.

I'd realized after a while that these two issues were related, but I was at a loss as to how to address them.

Then, standing in the Tate Gallery, looking at Constable's cloud studies, the solution came to me.

To make himself a better landscape painter, Constable had chosen to work regularly on canvases that concentrated exclusively on his area of greatest challenge. So to make myself a better fiction writer, I needed to channel a larger portion of my everyday writing into forms that would force me to write in other people's voices.

Tough Choices

By the time I had this epiphany, I was making my living exclusively as a writer.

I realize, of course, what a rarity and a privilege that is. Anton Chekhov, the most famous short-story writer in all of Russian literature, worked as a doctor to support his family—including his bankrupt father. He once wrote of his life, "Medicine is my lawful wife, and literature is my mistress."

And Wallace Stevens, certainly one of the greatest poets of the twentieth century, made his living not from his poetry, but from his career as a vice president of The Hartford Accident and Indemnity Company (admittedly a fairly cushy job: it allowed him to spend his winters in Key West). Stevens stayed in this role even after he'd won the Pulitzer Prize for Poetry, and later turned down an offer to join the faculty at Harvard, on the grounds that doing so would require him to leave the insurance business.

So being able to spend all of one's days putting words on paper is a privilege: one for which I am deeply and constantly grateful.

On top of this, at the time I had that epiphany at the Tate, I was a freelance writer, which sounds to many like the last word in carefree independence. But freelancing actually comes with its own special form of bondage.

Working for a company or a corporation is no more secure than working for oneself.

In fact, as anyone who has ever been downsized out of a job during a recession will tell you, it can certainly be less secure. If you're self-employed, no matter how tough the times become, you're hardly likely to lay *yourself* off.

Still, to the freelancer, from the inside, it doesn't feel that way. At least it didn't to me.

I harbored—and I've spoken with enough freelancers to be certain this is a common condition—a sort of continual dread that whatever writing assignment I'd just received was certain to be my last, after which there'd be no alternative but to hand-letter a cardboard sign and stand next to a freeway exit.

So, to forestall this fate, I took every assignment I was offered, and the result that I often worked sixty-hour weeks, composing everything under the sun, from healthcare articles, to marketing pieces for aftermarket automotive industries, to corporate and political speeches, to feature stories for adventure-travel magazines, the occasional piece of short fiction and, of course, that first novel, on which the clock was tick-tick-ticking.

But despite the blessings provided by this surfeit of work, I realized I needed to concentrate on writing that would help make my fiction stronger. That would mean giving some other stuff up.

At the time for instance, I was writing a regular quarterly newsletter for a company that provided automotive finishes—paint. The readers were people who owned and operated body shops. And the money was good—a single issue brought in enough to cover the family's rent for three months.

But when I looked at that work in terms of my overall mission—becoming a stronger fiction writer—I couldn't justify the time I was spending on that newsletter. I couldn't justify *anything* that didn't feed my talents as a novelist.

Chucking it all and spending my days writing dialogue was the logical alternative, but not the practical one. Our family was financially secure, but we weren't *that* financially secure. So I had to keep working, but in areas that would contribute to my fiction writing, rather than standing alongside of it. And with this in mind, I analyzed what I was doing.

Immersion Training

It went without saying that I was going to continue to write fiction. That, after all, was the whole point of the exercise.

As for the travel writing, I could see a clear line between that and my fiction. The settings of my first novel—Florida's cave country, the island of Cozumel and Mexico's Yucatan Peninsula—were all places I'd visited initially as a travel writer. It was obvious to me that other settings I'd encountered in a similar manner would be useful for future novels.

So I wanted to keep that connection and that ability to visit new places and derive an income from those visits.

And there was one other type of writing that I wanted to keep doing because I could see a direct line between it and dialogue and voice: the two areas of my fiction in which I needed the most improvement.

As I already had settings lined up for my next novels, it was even more important to me than my travel pieces.

And that was speechwriting.

In Another Person

There are a couple of schools of thought on voice in speechwriting.

Michael Long, a professor at Georgetown who frequently lectures for Ragan Communications, an organization that trains corporate communicators, says that, while people often say they can hear in his writing the voice of his clients, he writes every speech in the same voice—his own.

Clarity and brevity, Long says, are the keys. As long as you have those, the inflections of the person delivering the speech will make the words his or her own.

I'm from the opposite school of thought. Possibly because I expanded my speechwriting specifically to work on voice, I gravitate to speechwriting clients with distinctive speaking mannerisms.

So I always write in the voice of my clients, and when I am asked to prepare a speech that is going to be delivered in multiple places by multiple speakers, I usually act only as a manager on that project, and job the actual composition out to another speechwriter.

I've seen that my method works. At least it does for the leaders I've had as clients.

One of those clients was, for instance, a very senior executive with a major automaker. She was also, at that time, that automaker's most senior woman, so the company wanted to see her do more public speaking.

But, despite sessions with speech coaches But, despite sessions with speech coaches, her delivery was wooden and subdued; she was unable to captivate an audience.

A member of that company's public affairs team knew me and brought me in as a consultant.

I asked for and read copies of her most recent speeches, and then I requested an hour with the executive, during which I asked her to tell me about her family, her pets, her hobbies and her life in general. And it was instantly obvious to me that not only did she have a subtle regional accent, but she spoke in a subtle regional dialect that was quite different from what she'd been reading in her scripts.

I jotted down sentences and phrases as she spoke. Later, I analyzed those sentences and phrases as if they were poetry, looking for meter and pacing, whether she gravitated to hard or soft consonants, how her sentences were inflected, and so forth.

Using this analysis as a guide, I wrote her next two speeches. Both were interrupted frequently by applause, and both received standing ovations.

After that, I met with the executive's regular speechwriters, gave them my style sheet, and explained how to use it. And from what I hear, that executive is still in great demand as a speaker.

That is still pretty much the way I work whenever I take on a new speechwriting client. These days, analysis has become so second-nature to me that I no longer have to create the style sheet; all I have to do is listen.

My method of importing that into my fiction is twofold. Some of my characters—virtually all of the racecar drivers and NASCAR officials in my novel, *Turn Four*, for instance—are based on real people, and they speak the way those real people speak. And for other characters and narrators, I invent a person, think long and hard about how that person would sound, and then try to work in that voice. Sheila McIntyre, the young Australian marine archaeologist in *Pirate Hunter*, is one example of such a character.

Zeroing In

Now, I'm not saying that you should drop what you are doing and run out and get a gig as a speechwriter. That's a fairly specialized area of writing, and breaking into it is well nigh as difficult as breaking into fiction writing.

But if voice is your area of greatest concern, you might find other ways of doing your own regular "cloud studies."

Does the head of a local charity have a distinctive voice? Maybe you can volunteer to help them with their correspondence. Or perhaps a local person wants to write a memoir to pass down to the grandchildren. Think creatively and you can probably find an outlet, right in your community, where you can write and step outside your own voice.

Or perhaps voice and dialogue aren't your areas of concern at all. Maybe you learn to think strategically to create stronger plots and better structure. Working as a writer in marketing or a political campaign could help there.

You're a creative person. Were you not, you wouldn't be interested in writing a novel. So identify your weaknesses and think creatively about ways that you can work that will require you to turn those weaknesses into strengths.

Or, if you aren't as mercenary as I am, you can do as John Constable did and simply practice specifically those areas of craft in which you are seeking improvement. If you want stronger dialogue, imagine a situation involving two characters and create a conversation between the two of them. If you need help creating characters, write a backstory for and describe a character from a specific time and place. If your fight scenes drag (and most do), write out a fight scene and then pare it down to its bare essentials so it moves.

And whatever you are working on, work on it at whatever time of day you usually feel freshest, and do it every day for at least three-and-a-half months. Behavioral psychologists tell us that 100 days is the threshold at which anything done regularly becomes ingrained as a habit, and you want to make a habit of writing well.

The Sound of Music

Another regular writing exercise has to do with the most essential nature of writing. It is, after all, not what most people think it is; it is not recorded *thought*. Writing is, instead, recorded *sound*.

Whether we're conscious of it or not, this has a lot to do with what we consider to be good or great writing. When you read—not skim, but really read—there's this little person in your head who's saying each word aloud as you encounter it. And when you read great writing, that little person stops talking and bursts, instead, into song.

To encourage that music, Ray Bradbury used to begin each writing day by working, not on the fantastic or speculative fiction for which he is best known, but on poetry. Rhymed verse, blank verse, free verse—he wrote in all of these forms; the object was to get the words moving and flowing in his head before he got to the day's work on whatever book he had in progress at the moment.

I also often begin my writing day by composing poetry although, unlike Ray Bradbury, I do not publish mine. The difference between us is that Bradbury wrote very good poetry while I write… well, the fact that it goes unpublished probably speaks for itself. Many times, I'll delete the day's poetry before beginning on the day's prose, but it serves the same primary purpose for my work that Bradbury's poetry did for him; it gets me thinking about the sound of the words, and how they work with one another, and so puts me in a mindset in which I am ready to work in earnest.

Ready to Write

Another great writing habit—one that seems obvious to every experience novelist that I know, but may not be so obvious to newcomers—is to always be ready to write.

For instance, in addition to being a bestselling novelist, Audrey Niffenegger is an artist and a professor at Columbia College Chicago and, in her studio at Columbia, she has a table which she keeps covered with a huge sheet of paper, where she can jot a note, make a quick sketch, scratch down a telephone number or simply record any stray thought or phrase that happens to pass through her head. Several years ago, one such stray thought was a phrase, "the time traveler's wife," and she jotted it down on her paper tablecover, and didn't give it a second thought until a few weeks later, when the paper had become so densely covered with sketches and scrawls that it was time to replace it with a fresh one.

Whenever she replaces that large sheet of paper, it's Audrey's habit to glance over the one that's filled up, to see if there's anything she'd like to keep and transfer to a more permanent location. And that phrase, "the time traveler's wife," gave her pause. She saved it and started thinking about it: what would it be like to be in a relationship which someone who continually traveled, not only physically, but temporally?

That curiosity got her writing, and the result was a debut bestseller that took its name from that fleeting, hastily scrawled phrase.

Lightning in a Bottle

Most novelists try to take this principle one step further by making sure they always have writing material available, wherever they are.

This can be as simple and ubiquitous as a note-taking application on a smart phone: a solution I used myself for a while, until I found myself slipping up and deleting the contents of the app while syncing the phone.

So now I'm back to using the method I've used for years, which is to carry a notebook and a writing instrument with me at all times.

Early on, I numbered these notebooks sequentially and tried keeping them in chronological order.

That's still probably a great way to do it for anyone who lives a regimented and orderly life, but I tend to leave my notebooks in random places, notice I don't have one in my pocket, and pull a fresh one out of the drawer and start using it, until I find the one that I misplaced and… well, you see where this is going. I might wind up with two or three notebooks all going at the same time.

When filled up, the notebooks get tossed into a drawer with the other dead soldiers, and one of these days I may catalog them, although I probably will not. To-do lists and the like get struck through as they are completed, so they don't have any archival value. Any drafts or scenes I've roughed out in the notebooks generally find their way into the work-in-progress on the computer the same day. And as for any stray phrases I've jotted down, I glance through the notebook before it goes into the drawer and enter those into a word-processing document that I keep for just such things.

A notebook is with me at practically all times; when I'm asleep, I have one sitting on the nightstand. Some writers do this so they can record their dreams when they are still fresh in their minds upon waking.

My dreams are all either scary, nonsensical or unrepeatable in mixed (or any) company, so I don't write them down. But if I wake up with an idea that I want to be sure to remember in the harsh, busy light of the day, then I write it down.

As long as it is convenient to carry, any notebook will work for this purpose. But as some people seem to be intensely interested in such things, I will share that there are two brands of notebooks to which I typically gravitate.

One is the Field Notes brand of pocket notebooks, modeled after the advertising notebooks that seed companies once handed out free to farmers all across the Midwest. These forty-eight-page, pocket-size notebooks are available in blank, squared or lined pages and, although I sometimes sketch in my notebooks, I use the lined paper nonetheless, because if I write on unlined paper, and particularly if I write on unlined paper in a moving vehicle, my lines tend to slump like snow getting ready to slough off a pitched roof.

After a couple of years of using Field Notes, I discovered that Pencils.com, the site where I buy—you guessed it—my pencils, offers a Palomino Small Flex Notebook that has the same physical dimensions as the Field Notes, but contains eighty pages, rather than forty-eight, and inside the Palomino's back cover there is a small pocket, open on two sides, but large enough to contain a business card, a bus ticket or a folded piece of currency. The Palomino comes in the same page-printing options as the Field Notes and (as of this writing) costs a dollar less per three-pack. Then again, Field Notes offers a very competitive discount as long as one buys twenty three-packs at a time—which I occasionally do—while Palomino (again, as of this writing) does not.

So the notebook I have at any given moment could be a Field Notes or it could be a Palomino. The one in my pocket as I write this is a Palomino. To help me find the current one in the disorganized pile atop my dresser, this notebook has the name of my current work-in-progress written in permanent marker on its front cover, and on the back number is my name and cell-phone number (did I mention that I tend to leave these everywhere?).

For a writing instrument, I prefer a pencil to a pen, as any rough draft I write in pen is apt to contain so many cross-outs and re-direct arrows as to be illegible. For a while my preferred brand was the Blackwing 602, a pencil equipped with a flat eraser that helps prevent the pencil from rolling off a desk or table. This pencil, while a skosh softer that a regular number two, was still a little too hard for my liking, and the alternative—a soft illustrator's pencil—broke too easily. I emailed Pencils.com complaining about this. Apparently legions of others had the same complaint, because they introduced a new product—the Blackwing Pearl—that glides nicely on the paper but is resistant to breakage.

For carrying the pencil in my pocket, I put a cap on it (you can get these at art-supply stores). And when I lose the cap—which happens with woeful regularity—I roll a strip of paper tightly around the pencil, pinch the end shut, secure the shape with Scotch tape, and use that for my pencil cap.

As I fill my notebook, I clip the tip of the corner off each filled page, using scissors if I have some handy, and by folding and tearing if I do not. This allows me to find instantly the section I am currently on in the notebook. It is a system I have used for years, and it works.

As the notebook currently in my pocket has only about three or four pages filled at the moment, it is still relatively pristine. It won't be for long; eventually I will wear a shirt without pockets, at which point the notebook will get shoved into a hip pocket, from which it will emerge concave and wrinkled.

But I don't care. It will still be legible, and that's all that matters. When lightning strikes, I need a bottle in which to store it. And for my fiction, that pocket notebook is my bottle.

Frequency

Some people claim novelists should write daily, and if you count jotting things down in notebooks, then I suppose I do.

But as for actual, disciplined writing—working on a book—unless I am in real danger of missing a deadline, I write only six days in any given week, using the seventh day as a "sabbath" when I rest and allow the writing battery to recharge.

My method is to read the previous day's work on the computer, correcting it as I go. Then I move onto the fresh stuff.

If I am trying for quantity as well as quality, I will write on my AlphaSmart Neo and, as I find myself running out of steam on one chapter I will—provided I have enough of an outline to allow me to do this—work on another chapter while waiting for the rest of the first to come to me.

At the moment, for instance, I have pieces of the book you are currently reading open in three different files on the Neo, and I am hopping between the three as the thoughts come to me.

Once I am pretty sure I have exhausted the creative juices for the day, I will take out my pocket notebook and pencil in some thoughts about what comes next.

Then I fire up the laptop, open the Word document, and stream the day's work into the appropriate openings. And after that I back everything up onto a backup drive or the cloud.

For quite some time, that was my work pattern, but lately I have added three more steps.

After saving my work as a Word file, I re-save it as an HTML file—a web page—complete with a hyperlinked table of contents, using the "save only viewable data" option, which produces a smaller file.

Then I upload this work to Kindle Direct Publishing where, even if I don't intend to self-publish that particular work as an e-book, I have it saved as an e-book in process.

Amazon is constantly streamlining and updating its process for creating a Kindle book, so I won't go into the details here. You're much better off looking for the most current information online. But the end result of the process is that I will end up with a .mobi file, which I can then download back to my computer.

My next step is to plug my Kindle into my computer and open its "Documents" folder. I then move my fresh .mobi file into the "Documents" folder, undock the Kindle, and—voila—I have a copy of my novel on my Kindle, looking for all the world like a book I've just purchased from the Amazon bookstore.

Like any computer document, a Kindle book is easily searchable. In addition, as I update my table of contents as I go, I can easily jump to any chapter in my work-in-progress and see what I have there, to refresh my memory or avoid repetitions.

Caveat

That is my process right now. It is subject to change, especially as technologies mature and evolve.

Even now, many of my novelist friends tell me I am missing the boat by not using Literature and Latte's Scrivener software, which automatically does several of the steps I am manually pursuing in the description above.

I have, in fact, purchased a copy of Scrivener. But, on the few occasions I've delved into it, I've found its process less than intuitive: a conclusion that mystifies my Scrivener-using novelist colleagues.

Eventually, I imagine that either I will set a week aside to learn Scrivener, or (more likely) Literature and Latte will upgrade it into a more approachable, more user-friendly form. And when that happens I will adopt it (and come back to revise most of the second half of this chapter).

Write!

It doesn't matter. The important thing is to write.

Write regularly and write frequently: six days a week, if you follow my example. If you do that, the novelty and scariness of that blank sheet of paper will begin to wear off, and you'll start amassing words: sentences at first, and then entire chapters.

And once you've begun to achieve that, a logical next step is to seek out a knowledgeable "test audience" with which to share them.

| EIGHT: The Company You Keep

It is not often that someone comes along who is a true friend and a good writer. — E.B. WHITE

BY ANY CRITERIA, Steve Berry is a educated man. As a boy, he was taught by nuns in parochial schools; as a young man, his studies culminated in a law degree from Mercer University. He also harbors a lifelong fascination with history, and is exceptionally well read in the subject.

But in 1990, when he decided to put that fascination to work by writing novels that used historical incidents as their catalysts, he knew he needed some guidance—some way to ground him in the craft of creating book-length fiction. So he did some research and found a well-respected writers' group.

Writers' groups, also known as writers' critique groups, or workshops, can be found in most urban areas. To find one, you used to scour the bulletin boards at bookshops and libraries; these days, most are listed on the Internet.

Some are very general groups, so you might find yourself sitting down at a big table with a poet, a biographer and a person writing a memoir. Other groups specialize in fiction, and some specialize in particular genres of fiction.

I'm not sure what sort of group Steve Berry attended, but I suspect it was a group of fiction writers who specialized in creating thrillers, because he was living in Georgia at the time, yet he drove—every week—across the state line to northeastern Florida to attend his workshop, and northeastern Florida is a part of the country that has an unusually large number of successful thriller writers.

Berry participated in that workshop every week for six years. It didn't turn him into a star immediately, but it did give him a very good base. And, twelve years after he started, when he finally did sell a novel, *The Amber Room* shot straight onto the *New York Times* bestseller list.

A Matter of Opinion

This is not to say that Steve Berry was taught to write by the writers' group he attended. Such groups are not fiction-writing classes—not customarily, at least. Rather, they are a means of making your writing stronger by pointing out what works well and what does not, so you can have more of the former and less of the latter.

A good workshop or critique group is, in essence, a small-scale method of crowd-sourcing opinions about your work. At the same time, participation in a group will require you to render opinions on other writers' work, and see first-hand what works well in fiction and what does not. And while it may not seem so initially, that second part is just as valuable as, if not more valuable than, the first.

Newer fiction writers are accustomed to seeing books as finished products: after the author has polished and revised the work, after a line editor has worked with the author to make sure the plot works well and the writing sings, after a copy editor has checked grammar, punctuation and style, and after a proofreader has gone through the files to make sure that all the changes requested have, indeed, been made.

Novels that have been polished by this process and then published are like the builder's models in a new subdivision: finished and furnished, they tell you a lot about what's possible, but little about how one gets there.

But first drafts and works in progress are like homes under construction. It's easier to see the framework, and how efficient design results in something that is easier to build. And critiquing the work of other writers gives you a better grasp of how to do that good and effective work yourself.

That, after all, is what happens in an ongoing workshop; writers critique the work of other writers. And this criticism can shave years off the time it would otherwise take to become an accomplished writer.

Of course, that's assuming you have found the right group.

Finding a Group

Again, particularly if you live in or near a major city, locating a writers' group is not difficult at all. A few minutes on Google or Meetup is all it should take to give you several to choose from.

But narrowing that field down to the groups that are right for you ... that's going to take a little research.

First, even if the group is billed as a fiction-writers' workshop, you need to find out if it is composed of your kind of fiction writers. If you write Christian mystery, and the group you are considering is composed primarily of people who specialize in erotica ... that is probably not going to work out very well. If romance writers predominate in a group, they may come with some surprisingly rigid expectations regarding the relationships in your novel—expectations that may or may not fit with your vision. And if you write speculative or fantasy fiction, but your group is neck-deep into crime novels or thrillers, then neither of you may "get it" when it comes to the other's genre.

Ideally, you want to find a group composed of people who love the sort of fiction you love.

By far the best way to do this is to know something about the group going in. If you have friends or colleagues who participate in writers' groups, you can ask them about their groups: what they like about them, and where they feel they might fall a little short. Or if you're the only writer in your circle of friends and family, you can do a little research; start with the reviews or comments online, look at the group's blog if it maintains one, and see if they maintain a calendar and, if so, what sort of activities they have. For instance, some groups will have published authors in from time to time to talk about their work and share their path to publication, and that's always a nice plus.

Look at the frequency of the meetings; anything less than weekly may not give you the consistent feedback you are looking for, while a group that meets several times a week will probably overwhelm you, if you are trying to both write and hold down a conventional job.

If the group has been running for a while, what success stories does it have? It's always good to know that several of the alumni—or even the current participants—have written saleable fiction and are producing work that is welcomed in the marketplace.

Check also to see if there is a cost. A nominal amount to cover the cost of meeting space and refreshments is not unreasonable. Some groups meet in bookstores or libraries or church breakout rooms, and so the space is free, but they ask members to chip in to cover incidentals. But if the cost seems steep, that's a red flag—the results you will see from a writers' group will not be instantaneous, and you want to be certain that whatever you are paying is something you can foot month after month for years.

And if you can't find this information online, phone up the contact person for the group and ask about it.

When you find a group (or two or three) that seems promising, reach out to the contact person and ask if you can sit in for a meeting or two and observe. Most workshops will be more than fine with this; they want people who are a good fit for their group just as much as you want to find a group that will work for you.

Taking the Pulse

As a working novelist and a frequent presenter at writers conferences, I have spoken to a number of writers' groups. And I often can tell whether the group I'm speaking with is viable, just by the attitudes of the people present. In fact, usually I can tell this before the meeting has formally begun.

Great groups have a palpable energy to them. They love reading and love writing, and they are excited by the opportunity to do both. They understand that publishers are still looking for great novels and that, if their work is spectacular in every regard, it is going to get noticed and make it into traditional print. Sometimes these groups have a natural leader, and sometimes that leader is a novelist whose work has published by conventional, nationally known, advance- and royalty-paying publishers. Sometimes the leaders are still somewhere on the path before publication as well, and that is fine, provided they are open to learning and new information, and still enthused about what they are doing.

At the other end of the spectrum are what I think of as the toxic writers' groups. These are groups that have become discouraged about the process, and rather than meeting to talk about how to make their writing better, they get together to commiserate and—I'll speak plainly here—bitch about the publishing industry. Rather than working to create manuscripts that can find a home in mainstream publishing, they get together to complain that it has no taste, and share their bitterness about the fact that it is not scooping up their manuscripts by the armful.

Oftentimes a toxic group will be dominated by a leader who has set himself or herself up as an expert in all things novel-related, despite a lack of personal success in the field.

I remember well one group that I spoke to in a major East Coast city several years back. I sensed a distant negative vibe almost immediately, but assumed that perhaps they did not get all that many outside speakers. Then, during the question-and-answer period following my remarks, the group leader raised her hand.

"You said that your novel, *Deep Blue*, had a different title originally."

"That's right," I said. "The working title, and the title I originally submitted the manuscript under, was *Halcyon Gold*."

"Yes." She was almost smirking as she said this. "Can you tell us about the process of coming up with the new title?"

"Well," I said, "my editor called me and said that they were getting push-back from both their marketing managers and their distributors on the working title. This novel and my next one would both feature the same protagonist, so technically it was a series, and to give it a better launch, they wanted something more descriptive. The editorial, marketing, advertising and distribution managers were meeting to discuss it and, as I lived only three hours away from my publisher at the time, I asked if I could attend the meeting."

At this point, I noticed several members of the group glancing at one another.

"We met and I asked what qualities they were looking for in the title," I continued. "They told me they were looking for something that suggested water or the sea, and that a book such as this would do well with a color in the title. I remember one of the marketing people giving *Blue Waters Run Red*, as an example. Then, after listening to everyone, I suggested *Deep Blue* as the alternate, they ran it against their database of current and upcoming titles in the marketplace, and it became the title under which the novel was published."

The group went silent. Then the leader spoke up again.

"No," she said. "That's not possible. A publisher would never allow an author into a meeting of that sort."

Needless to say, I was a bit stunned. Thankfully, the Q&A session didn't run much longer. And afterward, more than a few of the group members apologized to me for their leader's impertinence.

I brushed it aside, saying that I obviously had contradicted something she'd assumed to be true, and she'd probably just reacted without thinking about her response.

But inside, I felt sorry for that group and its prospects for success in the publishing industry, and—yes—I felt sorry for that group leader. She'd obviously become so hardened in her attitude that, when presented with facts that refuted what she believed, she simply rejected them.

Long story short: when presented with the opportunity to join a toxic group, politely decline. And if the group you are working with turns toxic, do everything you can to get it back on a positive path and then, if that does not work, leave the group and find another.

Backstory

At this point, in the interest of candor, I should add that I have never attended an informal writers' group, except as a presenter. In fact, in the pre-Internet years when I first began writing fiction—or trying to write fiction—I'm not even sure if I knew that there was such a thing as a writers' group. That is probably part of the reason it took me so excruciatingly long to get published.

This is not to say that I went it alone on my journey toward publication.

The critically acclaimed poet and novelist Howard McCord was director of the graduate program in creative writing at Bowling Green University when I interviewed him for a radio assignment and—mostly because he and I both loved the outdoors—we hit it off and he encouraged me to apply for his program, which I did. I was accepted (I assume Howard had more than a hand in this) and started the next fall.

At the time, I didn't have a clear idea of what one did in a graduate-level fine arts writing program. Naively, I assumed it would resemble the MA in literature program I was completing at the time I interviewed Howard. That is, I thought it would include courses on how to plot, how to create characters, how to write dialogue and the like. But it turned out to be none of that (such courses are, by the way, often offered in undergraduate creative writing programs).

I quickly learned during the orientation that my fellow creative-writing graduate students and I would mostly be teaching one another how to write better through the time-honored and reductive process of the workshop.

In that respect, it was almost exactly like the sort of regular writers' workshop you might sign up for at the local library, except everyone in the MFA workshops had been hand-selected out of hundreds of applicants for inclusion, the leader was a writer widely respected in literary circles, and if we wanted to get a master's degree out of the deal, we had to keep taking those workshops for two or three years, so there was very little chance that any of us were going to pick up our ball and go home.

Which was good because, under any other circumstances, picking up my ball and going home would probably have been my first inclination.

My classmates at Bowling Green were all good people: considerate, always ready to help load or unload a moving van, and good company over a pizza after class. But our ideas on literature were very, very different. Most of my classmates were aiming their efforts squarely at university presses and small literary magazines.

In principle, I saw nothing wrong with that. While at Bowling Green, I helped found *The Mid-American Review*, the university's own small literary magazine, which is still published today.

But as a practical matter, I already considered myself a professional writer, and I wanted to write for an audience considerably broader than a university library shelf. My focus was commercial fiction: fiction that was suitable for mainstream magazines and the larger trade publishing houses.

With that as my goal, I greatly admired writers such as Kurt Vonnegut, Jr. and Stephen King, whose bestselling novels were not held in high regard by my literati colleagues. The fine-arts view was that these bestsellers had "sold out" their art. But as far as I could see, bestselling novelists tended to be people who wrote extremely well and reached people at their emotional and visceral core, and I wanted to do that as well.

Fortunately, I was not the only one of that ilk in the group. The popular magazine writer Albert Lee started in the writing program at the same time as me, and John Calderazzo, who now straddles both the worlds of popular writing and creative-writing academia, was another of my classmates.

Al and I even developed a game of sorts. We would submit our short stories to our peers for critiques, allow our classmates to shoot our work full of holes, and then, a few weeks later, we would come back to that same workshop and show them the checks we'd received from popular magazines for the work they'd declared unsound.

We were, in short, general pains in the backsides.

But we must not have been so all of the time, because people appeared to tolerate and even like us. And in small ways, they allowed us to shape our mutual environment.

One requirement of the program, for instance, was to do a public reading of your work. To publicize these readings, the department had a small budget: you got a photo session with a university photographer, and the print shop would use that portrait to run off a small number of posters that would be displayed at the student union, the library and the local bookstores.

The poster images all tended to be very much the same: turtleneck sweaters or sport coats with patches on the elbows, maybe a pipe thrown in as a prop. The headline was usually your name and the words, "Reads from His/Her Work."

And so the readings tended to draw the same people all the time: the other MFA students, a smattering of MFA faculty, and perhaps some undergrads who were taking classes from whoever was reading.

When it came my turn to read, I was sharing the evening with another fiction writer and, rather than having separate posters made, we opted to have our picture taken together. Then, rather than going with tweed jackets and cable-knit turtlenecks, we put on leather jackets, antique flying helmets (actually the canvas cold-weather liners they make for hardhats) and long silk scarves, and we put goggles on our foreheads and strapped clipboards to our thighs. We were a reasonable facsimile of a couple of Battle-of-Britain-era fighter pilots.

The setting for our poster photo was not a library or a writer's desk, but the airport next door to the university; we each took a knee next to a World War II warbird on display there. And the resulting poster had our names, together with the line, "Any Reading You Can Walk Away From is a Good One."

In other words, rather than making it sound artsy, we made it sound fun.

On the night of our reading, the place was packed; people were standing along the back wall. In addition to more serious work, we'd each included a piece or two designed to get the crowd laughing, and they did laugh. It was reading, not as art, but as entertainment, and I like to think it added a new dimension to that degree requirement.

While I would probably not have readily admitted it at the time, I learned volumes during my MFA years, both from my classmates and from the incredibly generous and conscientious faculty. I even had time invested in me by university writers who were not formally part of the Creative Writing program (James Baldwin, whom I mention in the foreword to this book, was just one of them). And the process made me a better and more mature writer.

Some of us stayed in contact after we received our MFAs. Albert Lee was both my best friend and best man at my wedding, and we spoke daily until his sudden and early death from a heart attack. And I still hear every now and then from John Calderazzo. Mostly the three of us encouraged one another in our popular and commercial writing, and whenever one of us was working as an editor, we would call on the others for pieces in our magazines. So I would say that, although it was some seventeen years after I received my MFA that I first published a novel, my time at Bowling Green was very well spent.

Today

These days, I am an active member of an international group of nearly 300 novelists. It's an under-the-radar association that accepts new members by invitation only; just to be nominated for consideration, a writer must have three novels published (two at the time that I joined), and the acclamation of the current membership.

I am in contact with this group pretty much daily. We maintain a private website where we can post and respond to questions and comments, and as we each have our own areas of subject expertise (I am the go-to guy for scuba diving and certain types of firearms knowledge, while others are fonts of wisdom on everything from medical and legal matters to eighteenth-century English history and nineteenth-century American quilts). We also use one another as first readers (just what it sounds like: people to go to for a first read of a manuscript) and ways to take the temperature of the current state of the industry. We also meet once a year in an annual retreat, sort of a writers conference in which everyone—from the people presenting to the people taking the workshops—is a novelist published many times over.

We are an ethical group (we do not share competitive details of our contracts, such as the amounts of advances), and we are also highly confidential; if a subject is discussed on our loop, it is never discussed outside the group without the express approval of everyone that was a party to the discussion. Ever.

So while I do not currently belong to a writer's group in Florida, where I live, I am a member of a virtual group that I can talk with every day. And if I feel the need for a face-to-face chat, there are enough members of the group around the country that, even when traveling, I can always find someone to sit down with for a lunch if one of us feels the need.

About a year ago, while traveling on business in Hollywood, I did just that with legal-thriller writer and writing guru James Scott Bell, as well as bestselling storyteller Steven James. And back home in Florida, police novelist Mark Mynheir and I have been known to get together at a local gun club to shoot pistols.

Working with a Group

Regardless of which sort of group you wind up with, whether it's a local group of folks who get together at a church fellowship hall or a library, a formal creative-writing program at a university, or an association of published authors, there are three things you can do to make certain that you get as much as you can out of the association.

The first is to check your ego at the door. The reason you join a writers' critique group is to get criticized, so go in expecting that. Remember that, even when the person addressing you is saying things like, "Your dialogue sounds wooden…" they are not really criticizing *you*; they are just talking about a bunch of words you put on paper—words that you have shared so they can help you make them better.

So, even if it sounds personal, don't take it that way.

The second way to maximize your benefit from a writers' group is to resolve to give much, much more than you get from the relationship.

Like many things that sound counterintuitive at first hearing, this makes more sense the more you think about it.

After all, if everyone in a writers' group is concerned solely with receiving feedback on their own work, and either is not critiquing the work of others, or is simply "phoning it in" and offering a substandard critique, then pretty soon no one is getting what they wanted from the group.

If this happens, they are also short-changing themselves, because most of what you'll learn from a writers' group is what to look for, and how to critique, and after a while, whether you are conscious of it or not, you will begin to look at your own work with the same detached and critical eye that you bring to the work of others. You will, in short, become adept at self-criticism, and the ability to coolly and dispassionately critique your own work is an absolutely essential tool for any novelist and any writer who has dreams of becoming a novelist.

Above Average

And the third thing to do to get the most out of working with a critique group is to decide, going in, that you will not try to be all things to all people, no matter how vigorously those people may present their opinions.

Go to Amazon.com, select one of my novels (or any popular novel by any traditionally published, popular novelist), and you'll find plenty of five-star "Customer Reviews." In fact, as online booksellers usually let you sample a book beforehand (and thus weed out the customers who don't like the way the book begins), on most traditionally published novels, the five-star reviews will outnumber every other rating.

Then, if you keep on reading, you'll also find reviews that give the same work less than five stars, and possibly some reviews by readers who just plain hated the book and thought the way it was written was stupid, unbelievable, or just plain poorly done.

But here's the thing: oftentimes the things that the negative reviewers disliked intensely, and the things that the positive reviewers stood up and raved about … *are exactly the same thing.*

Take my novel, *Pirate Hunter*, for instance. That book tells two stories. One is that of a young African freed by pirates from a slave ship in the Caribbean in the early eighteenth century. And the other story is that of a modern-day marine archeologist in twenty-first-century Key West. The novel jumps back and forth between the two stories, never staying in either one longer than two or three chapters.

To some readers, this was a wonderful surprise and a delight, and they used words such as "intriguing" and "amazing" to describe it.

And to others, this was the dumbest way to write a novel that they had ever seen.

Many—most—readers also praised the relationships that evolved within the two stories, calling them credible and realistic and touching.

Other cited the book as evidence that this Morrisey guy just flat-out cannot write a romantic storyline.

So who's right?

No one.

Opinions are like bellybuttons: everyone's got one. And (again like bellybuttons, come to think of it) no two opinions are ever going to be precisely the same. Some will, in fact, be polar opposites. And because they are opinions, and a matter of taste, there is no right or wrong to it.

That being the case, if you present a work to a critique group, and you get responses telling you that your approach to comedy is the freshest and most novel thing that they have ever seen, but you also get responses telling you that your approach violates every basic writing principle known to man… the question is this: how do you react to such a conflicted and contrary set of mixed signals?

Filters

First, you need to understand that, in any writers' group, the opinions you receive are going to be influenced by the filters through which the other members are reading your work.

One filter is going to be the genres of literature with which the other writers in your group are most familiar. This is why it is not going to be extremely productive to present your historical romance to a critique group composed almost entirely of people who write contemporary thrillers: consciously or not, they will offer feedback aimed at turning your book into a modern-day thriller. And in a writers' group composed of writers representing a multitude of fiction genres, each critic's response is going to be colored to a certain extent by the particular variety of fiction to which they gravitate.

Another filter is the fact that, in a writers' group, virtually every member is going to be hard at work on his or her own novel, novella or short story, and so each member is going to view everything they read through the filter of their own work-in-progress.

Let's say that you are in a fairly substantial writers' group and you get input from twenty colleagues on your experimental work. Of the twenty, nineteen say that writing a nineteenth-century detective story from a second-person, future-tense point of view is just too much of a stretch for them. And the twentieth says that doing so is a stroke of genius and she totally gets what you are trying to do by adopting that point of view.

The very human thing to do in such a case is to dismiss the overwhelming majority of opinions as proof that the other folks in your critique group are not the sharpest tacks in the drawer, and cling to that single, minority opinion as proof that your approach *does* work.

And maybe it does.

Or maybe it only proves that there is one other person in your critique group who is trying to write a historical novel from a second-person, future-tense point of view, as well.

Either way, if your critique group usually delivers opinions that seem logical and correct to you, then I would accept that nineteen-to-one feedback as evidence that, no matter how much you admire the opinion of the single person who applauds what you have done, there is a ninety-five percent chance that most readers—and this includes most acquisitions editors and most agents—are going to see this particular approach as off-putting and weird.

Trends

This is why, particularly for newer and unpublished novelists—novelists who are still trying to create that first manuscript—I believe the collegiate environment of a writers' group is preferable to a one-on-one relationship with a book doctor.

A book doctor is a freelance editor—one hired by the writer rather than a publisher. The book doctor can help turn a mediocre manuscript into a good manuscript, or a good manuscript into a great manuscript, and this either increases the novel's chances of being placed with a publisher, or give the publisher's editor a substantially improved manuscript with which to work.

For established writers, a good book doctor can be a real blessing, particularly for a problem manuscript, because the freelance editor can read the writer's published work, get a sense of their style and voice, and then preserve that as they work with the novelist. The new book will have the voice and hallmarks of the books that made the writer popular in the first place.

But for a newer writer, a book doctor can be so much of an influence that they may smother the nascent originality, producing work that is not distinctively that writer's work, but more of a collaboration.

This is not to say that a book doctor will hijack your novel. But in the absence of information regarding your voice and your vision, the person helping you is probably going to resort to their own, or their best judgment of what you should sound like, and the real you may be lost in the process.

A writer's group, while it might take considerably longer than a book doctor, can eventually help you arrive at a book that is more readable, more engaging and more viable, without substituting its voice for your own.

Add to this the fact that a good freelance editor comes with a substantial price tag. Plus, most of the novelists I know did not get published with the very first novel that they wrote—and if you spend yourself into a hole paying someone to edit your manuscript and then it still does not sell, you are probably going to fall out of love with this whole novelist thing pretty quickly.

So save the book doctor until a time when—or if—you have specific areas of your fiction that you know need some expert help.

In the meantime, work with a group. Your writing will improve, and you'll make some new friends at the same time.

Then, months or years later, once you have a couple of manuscripts with which you are thoroughly satisfied, you can move on to the strange new world of finding someone to publish them.

| NINE: The Business Part

The trick is in what one emphasizes. We either make ourselves miserable or make ourselves strong. The amount of work is the same. — CARLOS CASTANEDA

THERE IS THIS CONVERSATION that I often have at writers' conferences. I'll be on my way to a workshop, or carrying a tray in the dining hall, when I'll meet a former student with a 100-watt look on his or her face; it will be obvious that person is just bursting to tell me something.

So I'll slow down to say hello and, after the preliminary pleasantries, I'll hear it:

"I've finally been accepted by a literary agent." Or...

"I've done it; I've landed an agent." Or even...

"I *sold my book* to an agent."

And I will say something complimentary and encouraging and validating, because this, after all, is what that person is looking for. But inside, what I'm really thinking is, "What on earth did you do *that* for?"

Uncommon Knowledge

It is common knowledge around the novelists' water cooler that you *need to* have an agent, you *have to* have an agent, you *must have* an agent... etcetera.

But like most common knowledge, this really needs to be questioned. And the answers, in my opinion, don't point in the must-have-an-agent direction—at least not for unpublished writers.

Now, I realize that this is very much a minority opinion; I have lost count of the number of author's websites I've seen that urge new writers to get an agent as soon as possible.

People who know me well might hear this and also raise an eyebrow or two, because they know for a fact that I have a literary agent of my own, and he has been with me for nearly a decade.

My agent is smart, he's connected, he asks knowledgeable questions and gives astute answers, he talks to me like I am the only writer in the world (even though he represents many other novelists, several of whom out-earn me by a factor of ... well ... *depressing*), he and his family have become good friends with my family and me, and I seriously believe he lies awake at night thinking about ways that he can extend my franchise and make me more successful. I owe a great deal to him and his agency, and there are opportunities that have been presented to me that never would have arisen, had it not been for his knowledge, acumen and expertise.

But here's the point. He was not my agent when I landed my first book contract.

Nobody was; I didn't *have* an agent.

And I didn't have one because I—quite deliberately—had not gone looking for one.

What's My Line?

Although many newer writers seem dead-certain that they need an agent, I have found that, when I speak with them, they are not all that certain of what they need an agent *for*. Either that, or they want an agent for the wrong reasons.

Many writers are of the mind that, once they find an agent, they'll have a wise and experienced industry professional who will review their book, give them advice on how to make it better, tutor them on how to better focus it, and maybe break out a blue pencil and give their manuscript a content edit, or even a line edit.

That's a lovely thought, but that's not an agent. That's not what an agent is supposed to be doing: not in (or for) my book, anyhow.

Writers looking for advisors, collaborators, copyeditors and hand-holders are in search of *mentors*, not agents, and the really great agents—ones who are truly and deeply respected in and by the publishing industry—are all *way* too busy to be mentors.

Great agents are, first and foremost, businesspeople.

Yes, they love books. And if their specialty is selling fiction, they love literature and eat, breathe and sleep novels. They are the kinds of folks who keep a stack of new releases on their nightstands (or their Kindles), and go through books the way regular human beings go through meals.

But it's important to understand that agents aren't reading all that stuff so they can sit down with budding novelists and tell them how to fix their work. They are reading it to stay current on the industry, to track trends and detect emerging themes.

Great agents also develop close relationships with acquisition editors and the people who sit on the publication boards at the major houses.

They don't do this so they can leverage sympathy and use it to make a sale for a new and possibly marginal writer; they do this to build a necessary trust, and to learn what publishers already have established in their product pipeline, what they are looking for, and what they need.

And while great agents realize that they have a fiduciary responsibility to advocate for the authors they represent, they also have a professional obligation to do so with integrity, to seek vigorously those publication deals that will be of tremendous benefit to both parties, and to comport themselves in a fashion that will leave both author and publisher eager to work with them again. Then, once agreements are reached, great agents make it their business to see that what has been agreed upon is delivered—by both parties.

Doing this is a fulltime job. It is *more* than a fulltime job. It doesn't leave time to be a book doctor or a teacher.

I know that there are people who will object to this, because they have—and may have enjoyed long relationships with—agents who *do* help them fix their manuscripts and advise them on their craft. But every time I hear about an agent doing this, I can't help but wonder: when do they find the time to stay current with their industry?

And, more importantly … when do they find the time to sell books?

Much Pain, No Gain

Add to this the fact that finding an agent is hard work. Very hard work.

First, you have to separate the wheat from the chaff, and come up with a list of agents who are both reputable and productive. There is no board test, bar exam or license required to be an agent; all you have to do is declare that you are one, and you can set up shop. This means that some self-identified literary agents may have no more contacts within the industry than you do. Some charge reading fees and make almost all of their money that way, rather than earning commissions on the royalties they negotiate. Others recommend an editorial service to virtually every writer who contacts them—and then get a commission from the editorial service. Still others may be semi-retired and no longer as in touch with their industry as they need to be.

Don't get me wrong. It's not completely the wild, wild West. Every year, in September, Writer's Digest Books publishes the next year's *Guide to Literary Agents*, which explains what agents do and how to work with one, as well as listing more than a thousand literary agents and providing access to an online agent database. There is also a professional organization called Association of Authors' Representatives; agents who belong to it either follow its extremely reasonable code of ethics, or they don't stay members for long. But there are also honest and reputable agents who do not belong to AAR, so to conduct a thorough and inclusive search, you will need to do some legwork.

Next, you have to put together an outstanding query.

It's common today for people to talk about queries and proposals as if they are two terms for the same thing, but they are not. A query is a letter (or an email—I know of no agents who insist that the query be ink-on-paper) that makes the business case for your book. Just as the name implies, it asks a question—essentially, "Is my book something you'd be interested in representing?"

To help answer that question, a query also provides the necessary essential details. It establishes your credentials and why you are the right and logical author for your novel, what genre your novel fits into (and if it is not a romance, a mystery, a thriller, etc., it's perfectly okay to say things such as "general" or "contemporary"), and what sets your novel apart from (and, hopefully, makes it preferable to) all the other novels it resembles.

A query is very brief—three or four paragraphs and one page or one screen. It does not contain sample chapters. But here's the thing—a query is written, and you wrote it, so it automatically becomes a writing sample. This is easy to understand, but once understood it is also easy to overdo it and run purple in your prose, which actually works against you. The important thing is to be clear and conversant, and demonstrate that you understand the basic principles of grammar and composition.

Then you need to get that query into the hands of the agents you are interested in. You can do this "cold" and just mail it in, in which case it may be read first by a pre-reader (known in the industry as a "slush reader")—a more junior person or intern who understands that his or her viability hinges on *not* selecting potential projects that waste the agent's time, and so is incented to reject out of hand the vast majority of queries submitted.

Once you tire of being a resident of the slush pile, you can do the extra work of going to a writers' conference, a seminar, or another gathering at which the agent is going to appear, make contact, and deliver a summary form of the query as a face-to-face "pitch."

We'll look at pitches in detail in a moment. But for right now, bear in mind that if you do the pitch well and your idea's good, you may get the go-ahead to move to the next step immediately. Or, if you mailed or emailed the query in, it might take anywhere from several days to several months to get a response—some agents are one-person shops, and so may not be able to get to a query immediately.

Either way, once you get the have green light to go to the next step, that next step will be a publishing proposal.

A proposal contains all of the information contained in a pitch, albeit in a slightly more regimented and navigable style, and this time it *does* contain sample chapters from the book you're proposing. Again, we'll look at this in detail in a moment. The idea is that, if you've done your job perfectly, the agent should be able to hand what you have written to a publisher, and that publisher will have all the information they need to decide whether or not your book is a good fit for them.

Now ... the chances are good that, even if you pique an agent's interest with your proposal, you are going to be asked to revise it at least once, and possibly many times, in order to make it something that, in the agent's mind, is more saleable.

Then, if you do that to the agent's satisfaction, you may get an offer or representation, which might entail further discussion.

And after that, you *may* sign with that agent.

But guess what?

You *still* haven't "sold" your book.

In fact, you are no nearer to a book deal than you were when you started.

All you've done is arrive at a place from which you can start trying. And in the meantime, you've invited a third party into the private world of you and your book, running the risk of diluting or even altering entirely your vision, in the hopes of arriving at something that might be more marketable ... although that's all a matter of opinion at this point.

This is not to say that, as you write and revise your novel manuscripts, you should turn a blind eye to literary agents. On the contrary, you should keep your antennae up.

When agents are being discussed on blogs you follow, pay attention. If an agent is speaking to a writer's group or at a conference near you, by all means, go. And if that agent seems to be of a similar mind to you on literature and business practices, try to introduce yourself, not to pitch a book, but simply to say that you might be in need of an agent in the near future. Get smart about the industry and the agencies that best understand it. If you can get a short list of four or five agents, any of whom you would not mind doing business with, then you're on the right track.

But were I an unpublished novelist, I wouldn't launch an all-out effort to place my manuscript with an agent. In my mind, that is wheel-spinning and wasted energy. Worse still, it's inviting an opinion into the process that you simply may not need right at the moment—not if you are truly talented and polished enough to merit publication.

The Horse's Mouth

So what makes more sense?

What if, instead of spinning your wheels trying to find a reputable agent to represent your initial and unpublished novel, you spent the same energy looking, instead, for an *acquisitions editor*—a person at a publishing house who can either make an offer on your novel outright, or take it to a publications board so they can make the offer?

This, to me, makes infinitely more sense. A good acquisitions editor is no more difficult to find than a great agent. In fact, unlike agents, it's fairly easy to tell a good acquisitions editor from a bad one; as long as the editor is with a publishing house that you recognize—preferably a publisher whose books you have enjoyed—and that publisher pays advances and royalties, then that's someone you want to talk to. And if the editor is with a publisher that expects you to pay money to it for the privilege of doing business with you, then—simply my opinion here—that's someone you want to avoid like the plague.

Now, it's true that some acquisitions editors will not look at queries at all unless they come from either an author they know of or an agent they know and trust. And if the only appropriate publishing house for your manuscript is one with such a policy, or if your heart is absolutely set on getting published by a house that will not look at unrepresented authors then, point taken, you need an agent. You can't get past that lock without a key.

But my experience has been that some editors, and I dare say most editors, will not consider an agent a prerequisite for a novelist who has a book that is truly worth reading. And there are enough approachable editors in the business to give you a broad range of great people to work with.

So how do you contact an acquisitions editor?

While some publishers list editors' names in *Writers Market* (a print and online resource with publishers' contact information, published—like the *Guide to Literary Agents*—by Writer's Digest Books), many do not, and a query letter sent "blind" to a publisher is almost guaranteed to be seen first, and perhaps solely, by (you guessed it) a slush reader.

There are, of course, ways to discover the names of specific editors. Novelists often thank their editors in the forewords, afterwords, or acknowledgement sections of their books. And if you Google a combination of the name of a well-known publisher together with the words "fiction" and "editor," you'll find specific names in industry news items, or notices concerning when they will be speaking at lectures series or writers conferences. In fact, many online guides and blogs mention these as a means of discovering specific names.

But even if you managed to Sherlock out the information that Jane Doe is the new fiction acquisitions editor at Desperation Press, merely addressing your query letter to her by no means guarantees that she will ever lay eyes on it. It may still go to the publisher's slush readers, routed there by the fiction department's administrative assistant.

And before you get the idea of labeling the envelope "Personal," a word of warning. If you do that, you will probably alienate that editor. Maybe for good. And in a world in which virtually all of the major imprints are owned by only four or five large publishing houses, you cannot afford to alienate an editor.

How, then, does one crack the code and get one's work in front of an actual gatekeeper?

There are a couple of ways, but both require work.

Of course, by now, you are probably thinking, "Enough with the generalities, bucko. Let's hear an actual case study. You've been published, which means you had to sell a first novel somewhere along the line, there. So enough with the coyness. Straight up now, tell us: how did *you* do it?"

Fair enough. I'll tell you. But be warned: it is by far the more difficult and time-consuming of the two ways.

True Story

I started working on my first novel when I was in graduate school, so long ago that I cannot even remember what I called it. I do remember that it was a Stephen-King-esque tale of a bunch of college archaeology students working on a dig in the American Midwest. A bunch of strange apparitions show up, and eventually the students realize that they have freed an ancient demon that was trapped centuries before in an Indian burial ground.

This book was hopelessly derivative, and did not deserve to be published. So it wasn't.

So next I tried my hand at a novel about the first woman to become a Navy SEAL, even though I have never been a Navy SEAL, or in the Navy, or any of the armed services (the whole write-what-you-know thing apparently escaped me at this early point). This one actually got some interest, but not enough, and it, too, died on the vine. And yes, I know that, several years later, Demi Moore made a movie with the same premise, and no, I don't think for a moment that anyone stole my idea.

In the meantime, I'd been succeeding at other types of writing, so much so that the whole idea of writing novels began fading as a prospect. It never faded entirely, and I made some false starts at a couple of other manuscripts and published a few short stories, but the truth is that I got to the point where I could support myself through other types of writing—advertising copy, marketing writing and magazine articles.

In other words, I got busy. The magazine work led to magazine editorships, eventually I became an executive at first one small magazine publisher and then another, and then later I made enough contacts in the auto industry that I left publishing and concentrated on marketing and executive speechwriting.

I didn't even stop to take a cathartic caesura and burn those two novel manuscripts; I just lost them somewhere along the way over the course of several moves. Besides, although I had never published a novel under my own name, I did have a book out with my name on it: a travelogue of American mountaineering that I'd sold on the strength of my reputation as an adventure-travel writer while I was still back in grad school. Plus I'd ghosted a couple of books, and one of them was a novelized biography of a financier, so I figured I'd gotten the whole book-length-fiction thing out of my system.

But I had been working slowly on a book of travel and adventure essays and, toward the end of the 1990s, I opened up the current edition of *Writer's Market*, found four publishers with editors' names listed, and—banking on the hope that my name recognition as an adventure travel writer would get my foot in the door—emailed all four a very brief note with two sentences. The first established who I was, and the other explained what sort of book I was proposing. And attached to that note was my publishing proposal.

True, I was jumping the gun a bit by going straight to a proposal, but I was trusting that my reputation would get me in. And I felt that examples would be needed for the sort of nonfiction book I was proposing.

Did that e-mail and its attachment get read by slush editors? Perhaps. But if it did, it passed muster, because three of the four publishers expressed interest (based largely on my following of adventure-travel magazine readers). And one of those, publishers—Baker Books—eventually brought it out as my 2001 hardcover, *Wild by Nature*.

The fourth publisher—the Zondervan imprint of Harper-Collins—passed on the book of essays. But in his rejection e-mail, the acquisitions editor, who was also responsible for his house's fiction line, noted, "You do have a nice writing touch. Have you ever considered writing a novel?"

Silly question.

I responded immediately. We initiated an ongoing email conversation. I'm truncating and simplifying immensely here to shorten an already too-long story, but eventually, at this editor's invitation, I drove up to Zondervan's headquarters (only about two hours from where I then lived, in Michigan) and met with him. He introduced me to the staff there, then we had lunch and I pitched him an idea, describing to him the opening scene and premise of the book that would become my first novel, *Yucatan Deep.*

He liked the idea. He told me they'd buy it if I wrote up a formal proposal, so I did and, about two weeks later, I signed a two-book contract.

Hold the Tomatoes

Now, in the times I've delivered keynotes at writers conferences, I have never told that story onstage, because I can imagine the outrage: "What? The publisher *asked you* to pitch an idea? And agreed to *buy it* before you'd written so much as the first word?"

I can see it now. I'd be dodging rotten produce all the way to the wings of the stage.

But that editor asked me to pitch an idea because he knew that, while I was certainly not a Jon Krakauer or a Sebastian Junger, I was nonetheless known in the world of adventure-travel writing; there were people who followed my work. He knew that I had contracted for books before (I'd told him about the ghost work, as well as the travelogue) and delivered them in good faith and on time. He didn't need to see writing samples because he'd already seen samples of my writing in the book of essays that he'd passed on, plus he'd read some of my magazine work to make sure the quality was consistent.

During our lunch, we spoke about the literary market and he'd seen that I was conversant in what was doing well and why, and that I was well read in thrillers and suspense, which was where my intended novel leaned. He also knew some of the people I'd studied under when I earned my MFA in creative writing. And, most importantly, he knew that I made my living as a fulltime writer, and that I'd been writing professionally for better than two decades, so I knew what I'd be signing up for.

Ironically enough, by more or less giving up on the idea of ever becoming a novelist, I'd provided myself with the room to create the kind of pedigree that told publishers I was worth looking at.

And that is why I say that my way was by far the more difficult and time-consuming of the two ways of getting a book in front of a decision maker. It may sound like I fell into it and it happened virtually overnight, but in actuality, the process took better than twenty years.

Now, if you have already established your name as a writer in some other area, and if you have people who follow your work, then I don't see why you can't follow the same course. In fact, if you are that kind of writer, and you're reading this because you want to give the novel one more try, then I encourage you to go for it. Try a more straightforward variation of what I did, by putting all that experience to work. If what you've been writing is *sympatico* with where you want to go in your fiction, then send the editor samples of your nationally published, well-known nonfiction work, along with the query for your novel. It can open doors for you.

But if you are not already well established as a nonfiction writer, and you don't have two decades (and change) to spare before you break in to book-length fiction, then you might want to consider the easier and less twisted path.

Let's take a look at what that is.

The Wind-up and the …

We saw earlier that you can often learn the name of an acquisitions editor by Googling the name of the publisher and the words, "fiction editor," and that oftentimes the results will include faculty listings for upcoming writers conferences. Or you can simply search for writers conferences that are easy to get to from wherever you live, and check to see which editors are going to be on the faculty, and will be participating in manuscript critiques and "pitch sessions" at the conference.

Do that. And then spend a few of your vacation days attending that conference.

Let's back up a bit. Spend a few of your vacation days ... *after* you have *prepared* to attend the conference.

Many newer writers assume that "preparation" means you write up a query for your proposed novel, print up a dozen copies or so, and hand them out to decision-makers at the conference.

Actually, it's fine to have a query ready ... in fact, you *should* have both the query and the next step—a proposal—ready. But unless you are specifically asked to do so, handing those things out at a writers conference is wrong, for several reasons.

First, anything you give to the editor is going to be something that he or she will have to carry home. In an age in which airlines often charge, not only to check a bag, but to allow a person to bring aboard a carry-on bag, you are not going to make a new friend by giving the editor extra sheaves of paper to schlep through the airport.

Second, the editor's not going to have time to read a query at the conference.

Having attended numerous conferences as a presenter, I can tell you that virtually every waking minute is taken up by presentations, panel discussions and conversations. At mealtimes, I can count on having three or four (or more) people ask to sit and talk with me as I eat. If I want to take half an hour to catch up with an old friend who is also attending the conference, we will need to break out our calendars and schedule something; it's that busy a time for me. Unless it is absolutely necessary for something that is taking place at the conference, I will have no time to read. I will barely have time to think.

Editors are human and, in that sort of environment, your query could quite possibly go astray and never make it back to the editor's office.

And third, breaking out the proposal at the beginning of a pitch is jumping a gun and declaring that you're new to this and don't understand how the process works.

A pitch is the publishing-industry equivalent of having coffee with someone to decide if you want to go to the next stage and have dinner and a movie.

And the proposal is the dinner and the movie.

If all of this makes you frightfully nervous, go ahead and bring some copies of your query and proposal to the conference, but leave them in your satchel unless you are asked for them. Bear in mind that most publishers have a method of logging proposals and manuscripts in and out of their review process. By just handing paper to an editor, you are circumventing that process. You are far better off mailing your proposal to the office (or emailing, whichever is requested).

So, as the query and proposal are staying in your satchel, just what *do* you bring up at a pitch?

The first and by far the most important item is the certain knowledge that you have written a complete manuscript that is ready for successful publication. Actually, if you're following my advice completely (and human nature being what it is, I assume that few people will), you will have the certain knowledge that you have written *two* complete manuscripts that are ready for successful publication, although, unless what you're proposing is a series, or a set of novels with a recurring character, you're not going to discuss that second novel this time around.

The second thing you need to bring to the pitch session is—you guessed it—a brief, polished pitch.

Most people think that the pitch for a novel is a description of the story, but we already know that trying to describe a novel in one brief conversation is an exercise in futility. If a novel can be easily described, then it probably doesn't need to be a novel.

So, in a pitch, rather than describing the novel in its entirety, what you want to present is its *premise*. And—here's the really important part—you want to present that premise with a "hook:" a distinction that sets this novel apart from the hundreds of others that the editor is going to hear about this year, and a reason that readers are going to clamor for that novel and not want to set it down.

For instance, I'm not certain how, exactly, Audrey Niffinegger pitched *The Time Traveler's Wife*, or if she ever did a sit-down pitch at all.

But if I were pitching it, here's how I'd do it:

I'm here this morning to talk to you about a book in which time travel is an essential element. But it's not a science fiction story; it's a love story. And it doesn't concern itself with relativity and physics; it concerns itself with relationships. It does this by asking three questions.

The first question is this: What if time travel was not only possible, but *unavoidable*? What if it was an extremely rare and virtually unknown convulsive disorder; one that could strike the afflicted person at any time, without warning?

The second question is this: What would it be like to be such a person—to know that at any moment you might be snatched out of the present and deposited, naked and disoriented, at some point in your past or your future?

And the third question, and the question that is really at the crux of this book, is this:

What would it be like to be that person's *wife*?

That's the pitch—the entire thing. In this form, it's only 160 words long. And if I absolutely needed to, I could reduce it to a single sentence:

What would it be like to be in love with a person who, at any moment, and without notice, could be transported away from you in time?

That's just twenty-seven words. In fact, that's only 133 characters—brief enough to fit in a Tweet.

Both the long and the short forms of this pitch contain that essential, distinguishing hook. The book is not about time travel; it's about the ramifications of time travel on a relationship. And particularly for an unknown and unpublished novelist, the hook is the most important part of the pitch.

Here's why ... .

Paying it Forward

Let's say the editor loves your pitch and asks you to go to the next step and submit a proposal with sample chapters. And let's say the editor loves the writing and believes the book would make an amazing addition to the publishing house's fiction line.

If that's true, then a whole bunch of people are going to have to be convinced of the same thing.

The editor typically has to take the proposal in front of a publications board, also known as a "pub board"—a panel of leaders representing all the major stakeholders in the publishing house. It's not just the executives in charge of the fiction line—for a book to work, the marketing department, the advertising department and the sales department also need to be convinced that it's a great idea. The acquisitions editor's first step in convincing them of this is pitching them the book, and—especially if they have never heard of the author—that pitch is going to need a compelling hook.

Once the pub board is in agreement, there are others who are going to need to be sold on the idea. Most publishers have distributors—third parties who actually work with bookstores to get books on the shelves. And distributors have salespeople who call on those stores and make the case for stocking particular titles. In the course of their work, all of these people are getting excited by, and exciting others with, a well-crafted pitch.

So if the editor knows that your book is not only well written and an engrossing read, but eminently pitch-able, then you have just managed to distinguish your novel from the dozens of others that editor is likely to see at the same conference.

Dialogue, Not Monologue

By now, you have probably noticed that I'm talking quite a bit about crafting pitches here, while I've said virtually nothing about what goes into a query letter, or how one writes one.

And again, this is entirely intentional because I have never written a query to a fiction editor.

I know this also goes against the "common knowledge" you'll find on the Internet. But this, too, has been a deliberate decision on my part, based on the decided limitations of the query format.

After all, think about it: in a pitch, you are there, face to face with the person who is your potential gatekeeper at a publishing company. And sharing your idea, real-time and face to face, offers two significant advantages over the passive, written format of the query.

The first is that a pitch is the opening of a dialogue. If the editor has a question, you can answer it. If your idea is close-but-no-cigar, and the editor says why, then perhaps the ensuing dialogue will take your idea to a new level that you both find exciting.

If the editor has the same question or the same hesitation when looking at a query, it might take days or weeks of email exchanges to arrive at a point that can be reached in thirty seconds of conversation. And that's assuming that the editor takes the time to write back with a question or a comment; in the world of the query, when presented with an idea that does not ignite the fireworks immediately, the editor's shortest and simplest course is simply to "pass" on the idea and move on to the next query in the file.

The second significant advantage of the pitch is that the editor gets to meet *you*, and sense your energy and your passion for the project.

Energy and passion are difficult to show in a query letter. Unless done exactly right, passion on paper sounds like someone who has come unhinged, and editors have a natural and understandable aversion to entering into contracts with the deranged.

By meeting you in person, the editor also gets a sense of how likeable you are—an important consideration in a world in which author interviews and appearances make up a very big part of a book's promotion.

A Brief Digression on Appearance

Speaking of meetings, let's side-track a bit to talk about how to dress for a pitch.

It's worth making the side-track, because your appearance conveys volumes about who you are: a business suit or suit and tie says that you are eager but probably quite new at this, while the opposite extreme—say, torn jeans and a faded concert T-shirt— makes it look as if you don't take the whole thing very seriously.

I always suggest dressing for a pitch the way you would dress for a media interview about your book: for both men and women, a seasonable jacket over an open-collar shirt and subtle designer jeans is usually a very safe choice.

Publishers realize that, when they buy a book, they are also buying the author. And if the editor can go back and tell a publications board, "I've met them and they are personable and sharp…" then a lot of the open questions are taken off the table.

If a query letter is your only possible means of opening communication with a publisher, then by all means query—web and print resources abound on how to write the letter. But I consider the query to be the communication of last resort, which is why none of my books have been the result of one.

Another Scenario

All of the above assumes that your meeting with the editor takes place during a pitch session, which oftentimes looks like a speed-dating event, with writers moving from editor to editor or editor to agent, etc., at regular intervals.

Some conferences offer a more time-intensive opportunity to meet with faculty (including editors presenting at the conference), and allow you to pre-submit a writing sample for that editor to read before you meet.

If this is the case, then the conference will give you specific instructions concerning the format and length of the writing sample you should provide, and you need to follow those instructions. A word limit of 1,000 or even 500 words is not unusual.

If you are trying to sell a novel, then that brief sample should probably be the opening paragraphs of that book.

Your aim, in either case, is to intrigue the editor enough to say, "I'm interested in this; please send me a proposal."

Again—unless the editor asks for it (he or she *may* be FedEx-ing proposals from the conference, so they can be properly logged into the system back at the office) don't hand over your proposal at this point.

Assuming you're sending the proposal to the editor at the publishing house's home office, the right thing to do at the end of your pitch is to get the editor's business card (so you have an address to ship the proposal to) and leave the editor one of your cards.

Author! Author!

Now, about that card….

Lately, I've seen a lot of business cards from budding novelists that have the word, "Author" appended after the name or—worse still—use the word like a formal rank or title: "Author Melissa Wannabe."

I guess that's supposed to be validating. But to me, it just proclaims, "Guess what? I am a total newb at this whole novelist thing."

After all, if the guy fixing your leaky faucet handed you a card that said, "Plumber Joe Caulkit"—wouldn't that just strike you as odd: using a job description as a title?

If you are a newspaper columnist or a magazine writer or a broadcast personality, or have some other job in which you have already built a following, or if your day job establishes your credentials for the book you have written, leave the card for that role. For instance, my friend and sometimes collaborator, Jerry Boykin, can legitimately show his name as "Lt. General William G.

Boykin—USA (Retired)"—and that adds tons of cred when he and I are pitching a military novel.

If you don't have that sort of occupation, then just make up some nicely engraved cards on heavy stock with your name (no "author"), addresses (street and email, both) and telephone numbers.

Either way, flip the card over and, in front of the editor (so he or she does not think you have pre-written several dozen of these for the morning's pitch session), write on the back: *Sending fiction proposal for* (and put your book's working title here).

Then, after your meeting, send in the proposal.

Personally, I'd FedEx the proposal to the editor just as soon as the pitch session ends, from the conference hotel.

Now, let's talk about what that proposal should look like and what it should contain.

Pieces of the Proposal

This is one of those places where newer novelists tend to obsess: "Double-spaced? Space-and-a-half? How large should my margins be? What font and what point size? And if I hand in a printed version, should it be on linen paper? What paper weight and brightness should I use?"

The answer to all of these is: As long as it's easy to read and navigate, it doesn't matter. In fact, there is not even really a set format for a publishing proposal. You can look at two or three proposals that were successful—proposals that sold novels—and, outside of the fact that all will contain sample chapters and contact information, there may be few similarities among them.

That said, over the years, my agent and I have developed a general format we use. I say "general" because even I do not follow it slavishly or religiously; when a particular novel suggests a departure from it, I will modify it accordingly.

But this format usually works well because it takes into account the way publishing houses look at a book proposal. Each stakeholder—each entity involved in the publication of your book—needs to find specific information in your proposal. It is not uncommon at all for publishing proposals to get pulled apart and photocopied at a publishing house, with certain parties looking only at certain sections; the proposal template I use was created with that sort of environment in mind.

Publishers have told us how much they like this style of proposal. And when you are asking an organization to make a decision that might possibly change your life for the better, it only makes sense to give them tools they prefer.

So here, piece by piece, is a successful proposal—one that resulted in the publication of my 2009 novel, *Pirate Hunter*. With each piece, I've included a small image of that actual page from the proposal. These images are only there so you can get a general idea of what the page looks like. I'm not really expecting you to read them:

The Cover Page

F I C T I O N   P R O P O S A L

WORKING *PIRATE HUNTER*
TITLE: *A NOVEL*

AUTHOR: Tom Morrisey

CONTENT: In the early decades of the 18th century, 15-year-old Theodore
Bascombe – an African orphan raised by a Scottish merchant couple
– is captured by slavers and then freed by Henry Thatch, a pirate who
takes his ship. Bonding with his rescuer, young Ted is eager to
embrace the lawless, free life of a Caribbean pirate. But he soon
learns that this pirate has much to teach Ted about values and right.

Three centuries later, Greg Rhode – a preacher's kid who has
become a marine archaeologist – hires on to participate in Phil
Rackham's well-established treasure-hunting operation in the Florida
Keys. He is hoping that Rackham will make him rich, but he little
suspects that he is going to be the one doing the enriching.

These two parallel stories intersect and combine to deliver a timeless
message – that where your treasure is, there will your heart be also.

AUDIENCE: General readership; this novel explores relationships in two very
diverse settings. Approaching its questions in a natural and
uncontrived manner, it is a promising crossover candidate.

MANUSCRIPT: 80,000 to 100,000 words; manuscript ready October 1, 2008.

AUTHOR BIO: Tom Morrisey has one of the most sharply defined brands in
Christian fiction. In *PIRATEHUNTER*, he blends elements of the action-
contemporary novel and the classic historical, creating parallel tales
that deliver an epoch-crossing message of Christian values.

INCLUDED: Overview, marketing premise, character sketches, initial four
chapters, author biographical summary, and bibliography.

CONTACT: ▮▮▮▮
Alive Communications, Inc.
7680 Goddard Street, Suite 200
Colorado Springs, CO 80920
PH: 719-260-7080
▮▮▮▮▮▮

This is the "executive summary" of the proposal; one could read just this page and still grasp of what the book is all about.

If a pub board is considering several books, this might be the only page of the proposal handed out at the meeting—the assumption being that each party has read what they needed to read ahead of time. So the cover page is also a memory jogger.

One page long, the cover page has nine parts:

- **Headline**

  Atop my proposals for my novels, I put two words: "Fiction Proposal." This is simply to make sure that it ends up with the right department at the publishing house, and in the right section of the pub-board meeting.

- **Working Title**

  This is the proposed title for the novel. By calling it a "working title," I make it clear that I do not consider this a hill to die for—an important distinction, because publishers like to tweak titles to arrive at something they believe will achieve maximum sell-through.

- **Author**

  My name, as I prefer it to appear on the book. If I used a pen name (and I do not), I would add, in parentheses: "(pen name for Thomas Morrisey)." As this proposal was to a publisher at which several of the principals had not yet met me, we included a thumbnail mugshot on this cover page. The photograph is an entirely optional element, and it is as much of a picture of myself as I will include with a proposal. Models and actors send out 8 x 10 glossies; authors do not.

- **Content**

  Essentially, this is the copy that would show up on the back cover of the book. As such, it bears a decided resemblance to the contents of a pitch. And like a pitch, it contains a hook.

- **Audience**

  This describes the potential audience for the novel. Many authors, and most agents, like to see the word, "women" in here somewhere, because several studies have established that women account for eighty percent of fiction sales. But don't claim it's a women's book unless it truly is. General fiction does sell, and even men's fiction can do extremely well if an author can capture most of the men out there who read fiction. Remember, Scholastic, which publishes the *Harry Potter* books in the United States, reports that most of the readers for that series are male.

- **Manuscript**
  How long will the manuscript be, and when can the publisher expect a finished first draft? Length should be appropriate to genre: a good romance can be as little as 40,000 words, while a good thriller may be five times that long. And if the promised date for the finished manuscript is more than a year out, the proposal will probably be regarded as premature. Even if you've finished your first draft, I don't suggest putting "ready now" or ""available immediately" here. It's better to give yourself room to tweak, and say, "ready ninety days after signing," or words to that effect. That way, when you turn the manuscript in less than a month after signing, you begin a reputation as a novelist who under-promises and over-delivers—precisely the reputation you want to have.

- **Author Bio**
  Not your life story. This is, instead, two or three sentences on your background, indicating why you are the perfect author for this particular work.

- **Included**
  As proposals can be pulled apart and passed around, this is simply a sentence that details the various sections that are included in your proposal.

- **Contact**
  Just as the name implies, this is the point of contact for your proposal. If you do not have a literary agent, your name and

contact information go here. If you have an agent, it's their information that goes here. My literary agent and I are on very good speaking terms so, to keep things that way, I have blacked out his name and email address in the images of this sample proposal.

~ ~ ~

Overview

Overview – *PIRATEHUNTER* (working title)

Situation and Conflict: Tortola, the Virgin Islands, early 1700s

Fifteen-year-old Ted is on the cusp of embracing a wild and dangerous life. Rescued from slavery by pirates, he is on a ship being pursued by the navies of three nations, and if captured, will surely hang.

His rescuer, a gentleman privateer turned pirate, has the means and the charisma to convince Ted to follow him into his outlawed profession. But will the pirate do that? Or will he find in the vestiges of a gentler nature the wherewithal to point young Ted at a role model truly worth following?

Situation and Conflict: Key West, today

Clean-cut, intelligent and voluble, Greg Rhode seems like the ideal new hire for Phil Rackham's successful treasure-hunting operation – a trained marine archaeologist with an obvious drive to succeed. But as Rackham becomes more and more of a father figure to Greg, the truth emerges that Greg and his real father have not so much as spoken in years.

Rackham gently tries to help heal the rift in his young employee's life. But when he does, he little realizes that he is opening the door and exposing the great and gaping breach in his own.

The story:

Tom Morrisey's brand hallmarks are suspense and adventure in hyper-realistic, exotic settings. That's certainly true with *PIRATEHUNTER* — but in this book he goes one further, telling the parallel stories of two lives in flux and conflict ... 300 years apart.

Captured and sold into slavery, young Ted Bascombe slowly comes to the realization that his adoptive family moved to Africa to grow wealthy supporting the very institution that so very nearly destroyed his life. His inclination is to rebel against it all. But is he also rebelling against the only individual in the universe who can possibly save his soul?

At the same time Ted's story is unfolding, we are in the midst of another life, nearly three centuries removed. Greg Rhode is embarking on a new career, and possibly a new life with a girl so perfectly matched to him that she could very well be his soul-mate. But when a bitterness emerges from beneath Greg's guy-next-door exterior, he becomes a dangerous to even the closest members of his newfound community. A mentor steps in to save him ... and soon discovers that he needs saving himself.

This, the second page of the proposal, presents the principal conflict of the novel (or in this case, *conflicts*, as *Pirate Hunter* is a novel composed of paired plotlines).

The overview page also presents the story, not as an encapsulation of the plot (plot without supporting detail will always seem threadbare), but as a summary of the principal action of the novel—in this case, how the two separate storylines play against one another.

~ ~ ~

Marketing Premise

PIRATE*HUNTER* (working title)   Fiction Proposal
by Tom Morrisey   Contemporary/Suspense

MARKETING PREMISE

Tom Morrisey's fiction is known for high-adventure plots set in exotic and aspirational settings, and PIRATE*HUNTER* is no exception. While pulsing with the command of language and deep characterization that won such critical acclaim for *IN HIGH PLACES*, PIRATE*HUNTER* takes readers from the blue waters of the Caribbean and the Florida Keys to the wind-swept wilds of the Outer Banks, and links the stories of diverse characters three centuries distant from one another. In doing so, Tom follows the trend that has continued to widen his platform with each book – keeping the elements that readers crave, but raising the stakes and adding yet another twist to his writing and his craft.

Telling parallel stories set in the early 18th century – the Golden Age of Piracy – and in modern times, PIRATE*HUNTER* combines the romantic popularity of a pirate tale with an aspirational story of modern-day treasure hunters.

Pirate tales have captured reader and audience interest since 1883, when Robert Louis Stevenson's **Treasure Island** was first published in book form. Today, the immense popularity of the **Pirates of the Caribbean** movies shows that 125 years have done absolutely nothing to diminish the public's embrace of the pirate tale. And the popularity of Michael Crichton, Tom Clancy and others show that there is a definite appetite for novels that offer detailed and high-fidelity glimpses into world not accessible to the everyday person. Set these types of stories in the sorts of locales that people will gladly pay to visit, and you have multiple paths to success in one highly entertaining package.

In PIRATE*HUNTER* Tom Morrisey re-enters the worlds of underwater exploration and scuba diving for the first time in three novels – a step often requested in his reader mail. Known to millions of readers worldwide as an expert in dive travel, diving equipment and diving technique, Tom comes with a built-in platform in this arena – a platform that has expanded in recent years thanks to his fame within the dive industry and his high-profile position with SPORT DIVER – the world's largest and leading dive-travel magazine.

3

In a publishing house, two questions predominate when a manuscript is under consideration. The first, of course, is, "Is this a great book?"

If the answer to that is in the affirmative, then the second question comes up: "How well will it sell?"

This, the third page of the proposal, provides guidance with which the publisher can consider that question.

Publishers know that the popularity and attractiveness of a title really hinge on three things:

1. *Subject matter*—this is the trendiness and/or durability of the focus of the novel. In this marketing premise, I emphasize the timeless fascination the public has with pirate stories, from Robert Louis Stevenson's *Treasure Island*, to Johnny Depp's *Pirates of the Caribbean* films.

2. *Author brand and platform*—a "platform" is, in its simplest terms, the body of people who will be attracted to a work simply because it has the author's name on it. An author can form a platform through fame tied to something entirely unrelated to fiction (President Jimmy Carter, for instance, had a ready-made platform when he published his 2004 novel, *The Hornet's Nest*) or an author can maintain a platform simply because people know that writer's work and will gravitate to anything with the writer's name on it (Stephen King or Dean Koontz). In this particular marketing premise, I talk about the platform I enjoy both as an established novelist and as a notable figure in the world of scuba diving. Were I unpublished, I would concentrate here on those aspects of my career that would draw people interested in the setting and action of my novel.

3. *Word of mouth*—a novel will sell well when people are talking about it. The Harry Potter books sold almost exclusively because of the phenomenal word of mouth they enjoyed when first released. If your book has a natural hook that will trigger such word-of-mouth publicity, be sure to note it here. In this marketing premise I mention that, although I am known as a writer

who focuses on the worlds of divers and diving, my previous two books did not concentrate in that world, so *Pirate Hunter* is a return to that popular subject for me.

4. The object of the marketing-premise section of the proposal is to let the publisher's advertising, marketing and distribution departments know that they have several viable planks on which to build a campaign supporting this book.

~ ~ ~

Character Profiles

CHARACTER PROFILES

Theodore Bascombe ("Bold Ted" to his shipmates) is a bright and articulate 15-year-old who was taken in as an infant by Europeans when his African village was destroyed in a feudal war. Although he looks almost exactly like the slaves who are being taken to the 18th-century New World by the boatload, he is educated, inquisitive and brave. But his world takes a decided tilt when he discovers that the family he loved was making their money from the very institution that sought to make him a captive and a laborer for life.

Henry Thatch is a wealthy planter's son who has gone to sea and, within three years, become one of the most successful and feared pirates in the Caribbean West Indies. Once determined simply to amass enough riches to buy a sugar plantation for himself and his young wife, he has become so consumed by his new rogue lifestyle that he is given to wonder if he will ever be able to leave it behind – or if he will simply pursue it until he is inevitably captured and killed.

Meg Thatch, Henry Thatch's wife, is the daughter of an Irish indentured servant, discovered and whisked away by the pirate when she was still in her teens, and kept in silk-and-velvet luxury by her pirate husband. She is, ostensibly, the reason that Thatch continues to plunder and amass wealth. But as Meg tells Ted, "A wee house on the side of a hill? With a view of the sea and a garden to keep? That would be heaven enough for me."

Anna Rowle is a slave from the Carolina Colony when Ted Bascombe encounters her on a ship that he and his mates have taken. He steals her, hoping to falsify papers of emancipation for her and persuade her to be his bride.

Greg Rhode was raised in the church by his preacher father, but has a falling out with him shortly before Greg leaves home to get a master's degree in Marine Archaeology at Duke. Now Greg is on his own and signing on with Phil Rackham Treasure Hunters Inc. in hopes of starting a life of his own – and at least putting a dent in his looming student loans. Clean-cut, respectful and bright, Greg does not appear to be what he is – a tormented young man, distant from his family and distant from God.

4

We've already established that it is very difficult to talk in a pitch, a query, or a proposal about the plot and resolution of a novel. Without the thousands of words of development that the story will enjoy in book form, it will seem thin and insubstantial.

Characters are a different story. It's relatively easy to talk about a character and what he or she is seeking, and in just one brief paragraph, it is possible to depict a character with a surprising amount of depth.

So in this, the fourth element of my proposal, I offer profiles on each of my main characters.

Because *Pirate Hunter* consists of two parallel stories, each separated by nearly 300 years from the other, it has an unusually high number of main characters.

There are eight in all, taking up two pages of my proposal (for brevity, I am only showing the first page in the illustration). Each character is described in a single concise paragraph.

A quick note here: sharp-eyed readers familiar with *Pirate Hunter* will notice that this proposal includes one character, Anna Rowle, who appears nowhere in the published novel.

She was there in an early draft, but the section introducing her seemed to slow the story down to me, so I cut her out and replaced her with another character (Sally Emmons) who could be introduced and retained in the story in a more organic fashion.

This is perfectly legitimate. The proposal is a snapshot of the novel as it appeared when it was proposed; if the author changes something to make it better, the publisher will usually be fine with that, as long as it does not alter the central thrust of the novel.

Now, if I'd proposed a pirate yarn and replaced it with a space opera, my publisher probably would have balked.

But the essential story proposed is the one I delivered. I simply changed one of the characters on the path to my final draft.

~ ~ ~

Sample Chapters: Title Page

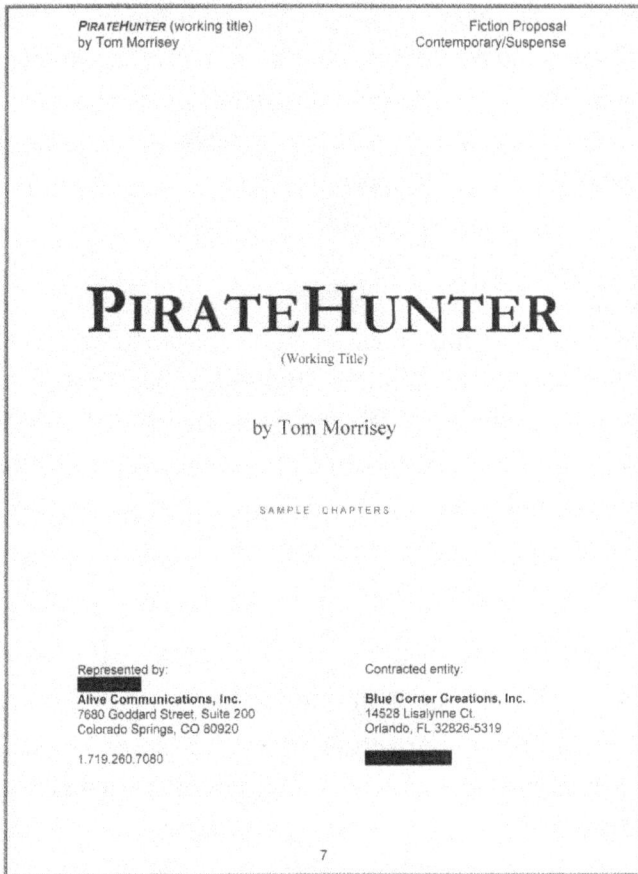

PIRATEHUNTER

(Working Title)

by Tom Morrisey

SAMPLE CHAPTERS

Represented by:

Alive Communications, Inc.
7680 Goddard Street, Suite 200
Colorado Springs, CO 80920

1.719.260.7080

Contracted entity:

Blue Corner Creations, Inc.
14528 Lisalynne Ct.
Orlando, FL 32826-5319

7

The title page opens the most essential element of the proposal: the sample chapters.

While there is no rule that the sample chapters must be the opening chapters of the novel, there are many compelling reasons for beginning at the beginning. The opening chapters demonstrate the writer's ability to immediately grab the reader's attention. The opening chapters are also the ones most likely to get browsed by the potential buyer in the bookstore, and they are always the chapters that are going to show up in an ebook sample. And for these reasons, the opening chapters are *always* the ones I showcase in a proposal.

That being the case, I open with a title page, and I expend a little effort to give that title page a "book" look and feel.

If you choose to do the same, consider how you will be sharing your proposal with potential publishers.

If you are sending out printed copies of your proposal, your font and layout choices are up to you. What comes out of your printer is what the recipient is going to see.

But if you are submitting by emailing a Word document, the appearance of your proposal is going to be dictated by the defaults of the printer attached to the recipient's computer and, if the font you select is not available on that printer, or varies in leading and kerning from the font of that same name on that printer, the resulting document may look decidedly different from what you intended; it may look like a disorganized mess.

There are a couple of solutions to this.

One is to send the proposal as a PDF file. This turns the pages into images of themselves, so they will print properly even if the recipient's printer does not contain your selected fonts.

The downside to PDF files is that they can be quite large, which can fill up your acquisition editor's mailbox (not a way to make friends), or take an extremely long time to download, open, and print.

A preferable option—one that I mention here because people tend to go font-crazy on title pages—is to limit yourself to fonts that every printer contains: Arial and Times New Roman in conventional font sizes are usually very safe choices.

While I usually e-mailed proposals when I represented myself, my agent prefers to FedEx printed proposals. This means that, as long as I select fonts that work well on the agency's printers, what we see is what the publisher will get.

~ ~ ~

Sample Chapters: Front Matter

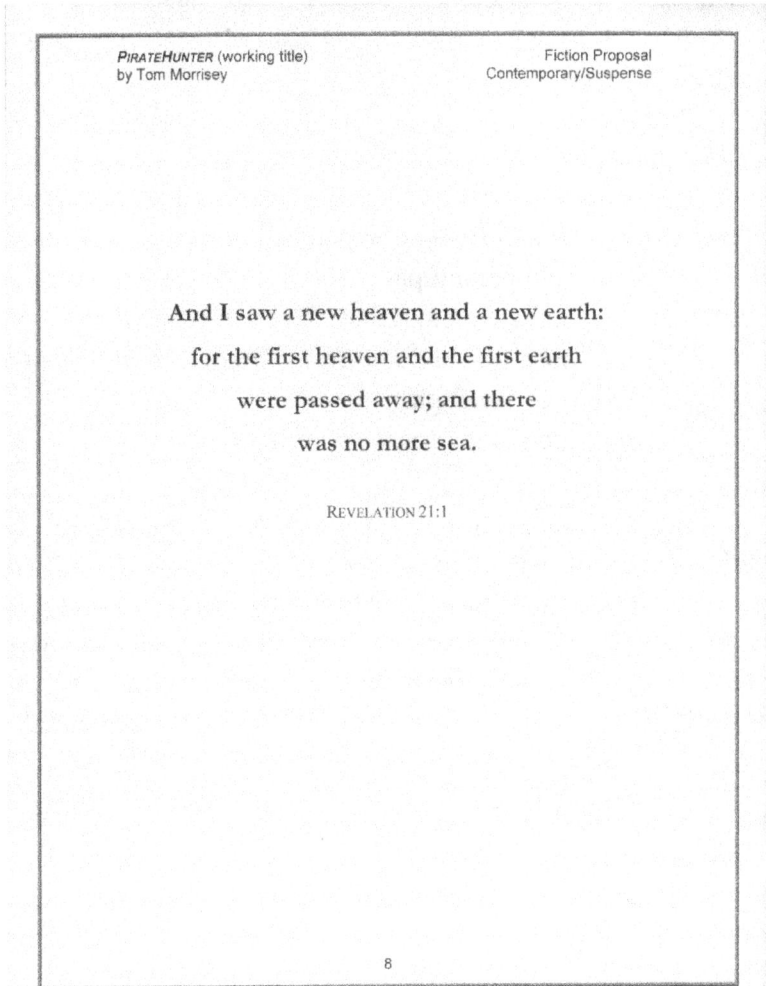

<table>
<tr><td>*PirateHunter* (working title)
by Tom Morrisey</td><td align="right">Fiction Proposal
Contemporary/Suspense</td></tr>
</table>

And I saw a new heaven and a new earth:

for the first heaven and the first earth

were passed away; and there

was no more sea.

REVELATION 21:1

8

Not everyone includes front matter (the stuff in a printed book that goes between the title page and the first page of Chapter One). But I include one page of it—it might be a tone-setting quotation (as I have here in this sample proposal), or a map or other image. If my setting is a three-masted sailing ship, for instance, I might open with an image of that ship under sail.

I do this for two reasons.

The first is that it continues to give a book-like feel to the sample, which I feel contributes to a reasonable suspension of disbelief on the parts of the readers who are reviewing my sample.

The second is that, if I do send my sample electronically, and if the publishing company prints it out in duplex mode (two-sided printing, a practice becoming more and more common in environmentally conscious companies), it assures that both my title page and my opening page of the first chapter appear on the right-hand page, the way that they would in a book.

If you choose to include front matter, don't overdo it, though. One page is enough.

And *don't* make the sample front-matter page your copyright page.

Copyright information is superfluous in a proposal. Under U.S. Copyright law, any original work is protected by copyright the moment it's written down. Every publisher knows and respects this, and if you put copyright information on your proposal, you imply that they do not (which insults their intelligence). Besides, it makes you look amateurish and paranoid; not your best foot forward.

So… a quote is fine. So is an image. And so is nothing at all.

~ ~ ~

Sample Chapters: Text

PIRATEHUNTER (working title)   Fiction Proposal
by Tom Morrisey   Contemporary/Suspense

CHAPTER ONE

"I favor the red ribbons because they look like blood."

The pirate worked as he spoke, plaiting thin, woven lengths of silk into the raven hair of a wig on its table-top stand. His own hair was almost exactly the same color of black, but closely cropped, the short growth even, suggesting that he had shaved his head a fortnight or two back. His beard, on the other hand, was thick and long, the ends of it bleached to a lighter brown by salt air and sun. Every strand had been combed and lightly dampened with sperm-whale oil, the scent of it warm and very nearly spicy in the small, close cabin.

The pirate stepped back a bit to look at his work, leaning naturally to keep his footing as the sloop canted over onto a fresh heel. Above their heads, the ship groaned and creaked with the turn, and the mate's commands came through the wooden bulkheads as a series of curt, muffled shouts.

The pirate gazed down his nose at the barefoot and bare-chested fifteen-year-old on the other side of the table. The younger man's skin was a deep, chocolate brown, very nearly as dark as his jet-black hair, a fact that made his eyes appear larger than they were, giving him the appearance of an innocent.

"Why do you think that is, boy?"

The young man startled and stood a little straighter. "Sir?"

"The ribbons, boy." The man's voice was a calm baritone. "Why would I favor ribbons that resembled blood?"

The younger man kept his eyes fixed on those of the pirate, but canted his head slightly down and to his right, a mannerism he had when he knew the answer to something, but was thinking it through one more time, just to be certain. Lips still closed, he took a quick dart of breath through his nose.

"Because a fierce man, streaming blood but on the attack, would frighten the average person, captain. Because a person so startled would hesitate in his own defense, and a moment of hesitation is an opportunity in which to attack. At very least that is how I see it, sir."

9

The actual chapters that you include are the basis on which your writing and, essentially, your proposal will be judged. The object here is to include writing that shines, but has not been overworked.

The chapters to include here are your opening chapters (including any prologue).

These should grab the reader immediately (and if they do not, then you may wish to re-think your opening chapters).

How much should you include? I only show one page in my illustration, but the sample I included in this proposal was actually a little more than 5,600 words long (sixteen pages in manuscript form), and covered all of the initial three chapters, plus a significant section of the fourth. I stopped the fourth chapter at a point where I knew the reader would want to see what happens next.

The sample you include can be a bit shorter or a bit longer. The more you include, the more likely the reader is to reach for an editing pencil, so I don't believe that I have ever shown a publisher a proposal sample that was more than twenty pages in length.

~ ~ ~

Author Biography

PirateHunter (working title)
by Tom Morrisey

Fiction Proposal
Contemporary/Suspense

TOM MORRISEY
Biographical Summary

Twice a finalist for Christian fiction's prestigious Christy Award, Tom Morrisey is the
author of six novels and short stories, and a world-renowned adventure-travel writer
whose work has appeared in *Outside, Sport Diver* (where he serves as Editor at Large)
and other leading magazines.

He holds an MA in English Language and Literature from the University of Toledo and
an MFA in Creative Writing from Bowling Green State University, and has taught
creative writing at the university level.

His ministries have ranged from lay-preaching in correctional institutions and teaching at
Christian writers' conferences to volunteering to sound "Taps" at military and veterans'
funerals.

Tom lives with his wife and daughter in Orlando, Florida. His Web site can be found at
www.tommorrisey.com

26

You'll recall that we included an author bionote on the cover
page of the proposal. This second "biographical summary" is
still not a biography in the classic sense; it doesn't say when I
was born, or where, but it does include a bit more detail,
especially in terms of my writing experience and my education.

As such, this biography is very similar to the "about the author" section that you typically see on the inside back flyleaf of a hardcover book. And for those who want further information, I have included my website address.

The object here is to think of what the publisher wants to hear, and present yourself in the best light possible, without crossing over into hyperbole. Try to impress, but remember that a little humility goes a long way.

~ ~ ~

Author Bibliography

PirateHunter (working title)
by Tom Morrisey

Fiction Proposal
Contemporary/Suspense

SELECTED BOOKS BY TOM MORRISEY

In High Places (**novel**) – Hardcover published by Bethany House Publishers in March, 2007. Paperback edition published April, 2008. One of Christian Fiction Review's ten "Best of 2007."

Dark Fathom (**novel**) – Published by Zondervan in January, 2006. A successful "prequel" to **Deep Blue**.

Deep Blue (**novel**) – Published by Zondervan in January, 2005. Selected for sale at 440 of the nation's 570 Sam's Clubs, where it quickly saw a 50% sell-through.

Turn Four: A Novel of the Superspeedways – Published by Zondervan in March, 2004. Marketed through a program that included ministry presence at NASCAR Nextel Cup venues and media mentions by NASCAR superstars Kyle Petty, Jimmie Johnson, and others. In multiple printings.

Yucatan Deep (**novel**) – Published by Zondervan in September, 2002. Listed on the CBA Bestseller list in November, 2002. A finalist for the 2003 Christy Award in the First Novel category.

Wild by Nature (**nonfiction**) – Published March, 2001, in hardcover by Baker Books.

27

This selected bibliography lists my books, but it does not list all of my books. I am, for instance, the editor of an extremely well-received anthology of golf stories, and I am also the author of a travelogue of American mountaineering; neither of those are included here, because neither is germane to the discussion at hand.

The bibliography does list all of the novels that I had in print at the time of the proposal. And it also includes a book of essays with which I assume the publisher will be familiar. The intention here is to show that it ain't my first rodeo.

Of course, for everyone, there is one time at which it *will* be your first rodeo. If that is the case with you, it's perfectly acceptable to list here those short stories and/or magazine feature stories that you feel best showcase your work. Or, if you don't have any of those that seem appropriate to promote your fiction writing, you can leave the bibliography off entirely. As I said, proposals can and do take every form under the sun, and the one I include here is just a single example.

Besides, there is no shame in being new. In fact, publishers enjoy discovering great first novelists. So, for an extremely strong and talented writer, being new at the game can actually be an advantage.

~ ~ ~

Now What?

Several things can happen with your proposal.

The sad statistical likelihood is that it will get rejected by the publisher. In its most ignominious fashion, this may come as a form letter, something along the lines of "we regret that this does not fit our current editorial needs."

True, you have lowered the odds of this happening by taking the time to seek out and pitch the editor, and thus get the manuscript past the nose of the more junior editorial staff, who are pretty much paid to say "no." But work does get rejected even beyond that point. It happens more often than not.

Sometimes manuscripts are rejected simply because they are insufficiently polished, unoriginal, or just plain badly written or fundamentally flawed. My first two novels—the ones I can no longer even recall the names of—went down in flames because they were, for one reason or another, really lousy books.

At other times, though, a novel will get rejected simply because it just doesn't sync with its times.

A Confederacy of Dunces, by John Kennedy Toole, is one such book. Published in 1980, this picaresque novel about a Southern Luddite won the 1981 Pulitzer Prize for Fiction—a dozen years after its author took his own life, largely because of his inability to find anyone interested in publishing his work. Toole's mother found a carbon copy of his manuscript after his death, persuaded literary giant Walker Percy to take a look at it, and Percy convinced Louisiana State University Press that it was worth publishing.

So, while a publisher's rejections may come your way because you are writing crap, there is also a slight chance that you are getting them because you are an unrecognized genius.

If your writing is getting praised by people who have neither given birth to you nor shared your bed, there is a (likewise slight) chance that you fall into the latter category.

So if, during the cold light of day, you firmly believe you have created something worth publishing, then don't let the rejections bother you.

Press on because, as trite as it sounds, it only takes a single "yes" to change your life.

Non-Form Rejections

Because you took the time to pitch an editor before sending in your proposal, you may receive responses other than the standard rejection form letter.

You may receive a personal letter from the acquisitions editor, explaining why the publishing house has decided against publishing your work.

If you do, you may naturally feel moved to phone the editor up and offer to change things: "You said that you didn't want my book because the market is overcrowded with zombie novels right now, so what if I changed it to a vampire story, instead?"

Resist this urge.

Once a publisher has rejected a novel, it is dead in their eyes, and any offer to amend it is tantamount to trying to reanimate a corpse. Besides, it is hard to make an offer to change things post-decision without sounding whiney or desperate: two things you never want to seem like to a publisher.

If the editor has rejected your work but sounds positive about your writing and urges you to try again with other ideas, then you might want to pitch that second manuscript that you've finished.

And if you get several rejections, all of which cite the same issues, then you may wish to revise the manuscript accordingly and try again—just not with the publishing houses that have already rejected it.

One further thought on being rejected: J.K. Rowling's *Harry Potter* novels comprise the best-selling series of books in English history, yet the first novel in the series, *Harry Potter and the Philosopher's Stone*, was rejected by the first twelve publishers who looked at it. And even when it was published, the initial publisher's run was only a thousand copies, 500 of which were sold to libraries. So rejection might mean your book's no good—or it might mean that the market sense of those who rejected it is no good.

Great novels will get published. The only question is when.

All right. That covers rejection letters. Let's move on to happier responses.

The Maybes

It's possible to get letters, or emails or even phone calls from the publishing house that are neither rejections nor acceptances.

The acquisitions editor may contact you, for instance, and ask if you would consider changing the plot, the setting, one or more characters—or any other element that the editor feels is keeping the manuscript from being publishable.

There are three ways to respond to this.

One, the writer may decide that the editor's suggestion violates the artistic integrity of the novel, and refuse to make the requested changes.

Two, the writer may not give a hoot about artistic integrity. The writer may be completely willing to make the literary equivalent of the Faustian compact in return for a book with his or her name on the cover.

Or three, the writer may see wisdom in the editor's suggestions, agree that the proposed changes would result in a better, more solid and more sales-worthy book, and happily make the proposed revisions.

And on those three possibilities, I have two thoughts.

Count Ten...

The first is that, when an editor suggests a revision—particularly a major revision—the initial inclination of most writers might be to see it as an attempt to ruin the book. This is natural; that manuscript is your baby, and nobody wants to hear that their baby *might* become handsome, but only with a little plastic surgery.

That's why I don't recommend responding with an immediate "no" to a request for revisions. Give it a day. For that matter, give it a week. Give yourself time to reflect coolly and calmly and consider whether the baby just might be more attractive with a bit of cosmetic work. Then respond thoughtfully, rather than emotionally. What the editor is suggesting just might be the foundation for a wonderful career and if, upon reflection, you agree, then you just might be off to the races.

The operative words here, though, are "just might."

Robert Gottlieb, the legendary Simon and Schuster editor who worked with such household names as John Cheever, Ray Bradbury, Michael Crichton and Toni Morrison, before moving on to edit *The New Yorker*, was also one of the few major editors to take an interest in *A Confederacy of Dunces* while John Kennedy Toole was still alive. Toole corresponded with Gottlieb and made several revisions to his manuscript as a result of those conversations. Yet in the end, Gottlieb passed on the manuscript. And in Toole's case, Gottlieb passed, not on the proposal and some sample chapters, but on a revised and finished manuscript.

To a newer or unpublished writer, this may seem like a betrayal. After all, the editor asked for changes, and the changes were made, so why was the manuscript not then accepted?

But there is no *quid pro quo* in novel acquisition. In asking for revisions, an editor is going above and beyond. The editor is doing the writer a favor. Guidance is being provided and wisdom is being shared, and this wise guidance might—just might—help that novel see the light of day.

So, regardless of whether the novel is accepted or rejected in the end, the novelist's reaction to that act of kindness should never be bitterness. It should always be gratitude. And if you show that to an editor who tried to help you, even if in the end that editor did not make an offer on your book, then your mature grasp of the situation will long be remembered.

Integrity? What Integrity?

My second thought is aimed at writers who are at the opposite end of the spectrum—writers who will do *anything* to get published.

And that thought is a reminder that copies of the Gutenberg Bible are still around. The scary, modern-day corollary to this is that, in an age of digital memory, anything published with your name on it is likely to live pretty close to forever.

So, enticing as the idea of a published novel may seem, I would agree to make only those revisions that I would be thrilled to see published under my name.

For an unpublished novelist, this could be an uncomfortably high road to take, but try to look at the proposition the way you would when you are five, ten or twenty published novels down the road: will the revised book be something that you will be proud to have in your canon, or will it be something that you will want desperately to buy all the copies of, so you can burn them?

If your name is going on the cover, publish only those books of which you will be proud.

Movin' on Up

In that editorial purgatory between rejection and acceptance, there is one other piece of information you might receive from an editor, and that is the news that your proposal is being presented to the pub board.

Granted, this is rarely information that is shared by an editor with an unpublished novelist. Few unpublished novelists even know what a pub board is, and editors know that. And besides, the editor usually won't want to get a newcomer's hopes up, as a book's odds of getting approval by a publications board, while statistically much better than those of making the first cut, are still far from a sure thing.

The Golden Message

The other possible outcome of submitting a proposal (or, in some cases, the complete manuscript) is that the publisher will make an offer on the novel.

Happy days: the novel is going to be published.

So what next?

Well, if I were starting anew, and had never published a novel before, and I knew then what I know now, my first reaction upon getting an offer on my novel—or even upon hearing that my book was going before a publications board—would not be to sign on the dotted line of whatever contract it was that may have arrived with the letter of acceptance.

My first reaction would be to go through that short list of literary agents I'd compiled, and look for representation.

What? An Agent? Now?

I realize this sounds about as logical as shopping for a midwife after the baby is already born. But trust me—it makes perfect sense.

It makes sense, first, because now that you have an offer on a novel, finding an agent is going to be easy. Agents who may have seemed distant before will now suddenly be interested in you. You have already done the hardest part—you have made the sale and a publisher wants your novel—so the agent knows that this is not going to be an exercise in futility: that he or she is going to make a commission on this sale.

And if you have not yet signed anything (not even a letter of intent or a summary deal), then the agent knows that the offer you've received is a "floor"—the minimum that is going to be made on this book. A good agent might be able to use professional insight and negotiating skills to push that number upward.

It is a situation that, for the agent, has no downside.

For you, the situation has a minimal downside; the amount the publisher is offering you is going to be lightened by fifteen percent (as of this writing, the usual commission earned by an agent on a newly signed author). But getting a publishing professional to represent you from this point forward may sweeten the deal on the book you're getting the offer on, will probably save you money in the long run, and will almost definitely save you some heartache both now and in the future.

And to explain how that works, probably the best thing for me to do now is to share with you the story of my experience in the book business, and how I came to be represented by a literary agent.

Just Enough to be Dangerous

Although I published my first nonfiction book when I was still in my twenties, by the time I sold my first novel, I'd had decades of experience working in the publishing industry. The difference was that I'd been working for years as a magazine writer and editor and, outside of that one nonfiction book, a couple of books that I'd ghosted for others, and the occasional anthology produced by the magazines I edited, I knew very little about book publishing.

That said, I knew enough to understand that, except for advertising copywriting and other specific sorts of what is known as "work for hire" writing, most writing is never "sold" in the conventional sense of the term. Generally a writer—and especially a fiction writer—will continue to own the work that he or she creates. The copyright belongs to the author; what the publisher purchases is not the work, but the right to publish and profit from the work.

As a magazine editor, I understood this because it was part of my daily work. If a writer sent me a piece that I wanted to publish, or if I commissioned a piece to be written for the magazine, I would generally contract with that writer to acquire "First North American Serial Rights"—that is, the right to be first to publish that work in a serial publication (a newspaper, newsletter or magazine) in North America. The contract I made with the author would stipulate that I would publish the piece within a given period of time (customarily a year), and that the writer would agree not to re-publish the work for a set period of time after it appeared in my magazine (usually six months to a year).

From this experience, I knew that, while many publishers would seek first to gain World Rights (the right to publish anywhere in the world) for the length of the copyright (the lifetime of the author, plus seventy years), it was relatively routine to negotiate a more geographically restrictive right, such as the right to publish in the United States, its territories, and Canada. And by insisting on an Out of Print clause in the contract, I could limit the publisher's rights to that book to only the period during which the book would be available from the publisher's warehouse to booksellers. At the time, less than a decade and a half ago, this meant that either the publisher had to be willing to initiate new print runs whenever warehouse stock fell below a certain level, or the book would be deemed to be "OOP," and I could legally ask for the rights to be reverted back to me.

I also understood that while, as a magazine editor, I would pay a writer a certain set amount and then be allowed to keep all of the revenue generated by the issue in which the article appeared, books worked differently.

Advances Explained

In most novel contracts, the author is entitled to what is known as a "royalty"—a percentage of what the publisher makes in sales of the book. This is usually calculated per copy at the time that the novel is shipped to the distributors (and later, this amount will be adjusted to account for the returns of unsold copies).

As it takes many months for an accepted manuscript to be edited, formatted, advertised in the publisher's catalogue and then finally released, book contracts usually stipulate an advance against royalties to be paid to the author.

"Advance" makes this sound like a payday advance: the advance one might request against a future paycheck. To a certain extent this is accurate. Customarily, an author receives a percentage of the advance upon signing the contract, then another percentage upon either delivery or acceptance of the manuscript. At the time I sold my first novel, half on signing and half on acceptance was fairly customary throughout the North American publishing industry. Today some publishers pay their advances in thirds.

The advance is, in effect, a loan. And the loan gets paid back, not directly out of the author's pocket, but through debits from the royalties owed to the publisher. Essentially, everything the book makes goes into paying back this advance.

Then, once the advance is repaid, the author begins to receive royalties, usually issued in quarterly checks. And if sales of the book are insufficient to pay back the advance during the time that the publisher holds the rights, then the remainder of the advance is written off, and the author owes nothing.

As this is the way the system works, newer writers and literary agents usually want the highest advance possible. This gives the publisher extra incentive to market, advertise and publicize the book aggressively, and it has the additional merit of putting extra money in the writer's pocket (and the agency's coffers) up front.

Publishers, on the other hand, usually want to be frugal with the advance, because it is an expense paid out against income that has not yet been received.

Publishers also have extremely long memories when it comes to how quickly an advance is repaid. If a writer's books sell briskly, generating sufficient royalties to pay off the advance in a few months (or, better still, a few weeks), then that is an author to whom the publisher is likely to extend larger advances in the future. And if you are a writer known for those kinds of sales, you agent may even work additional advances into your contracts—for instance, if your first advance is fully paid in the first quarter, a second advance will be due against future royalties—*if* this advance was negotiated *before* the contract was signed.

If, on the other hand, a writer has the reputation for selling slowly but steadily—taking years to pay off an advance—or for generating insufficient sales to pay back the full advance... then publishers will note this and be very hesitant to extend themselves on future advances. And the industry trend in recent years has been toward smaller and smaller advances, regardless of sales.

It's smart to be aware of this upfront. By demanding an exorbitant advance, you and your agent could easily bargain yourselves right out of a book deal. And even if the publisher seems amicable to a whopper of an advance, it might be smarter not to ask for it, and to take a smaller advance that you know you can zero out quickly.

As I said before, you want to be known as an author who under-promises and over-delivers.

Gone Rogue

Back when I began, I had at least a rudimentary grasp of all of this and, insofar as I was accustomed to dealing with contracts from my magazine work, did not feel that I needed an industry professional to handle my business affairs with my publisher.

Indeed, the contract that my first publisher offered only confirmed that. It restricted the publisher to publication within the U.S. and Canada, it offered what I considered a very fair advance, and the entire contract, as I recall, what fewer than four pages in length, including the space for signatures. So I signed and was happy to act as my own agent.

Then, over the next few years, several things happened to change my mind on that.

Rube Meets World

The first thing that happened took place at a trade show for the publishing industry. The second novel in my first contract was coming out, and I was signing copies for booksellers who were attending the show.

One lady with what I first mistook as a British accent was overjoyed to meet me.

"This is such an honor," she told me. "At my shop in Capetown, your novels just fly off the shelves. You are the best-selling author in your genre in South Africa."

"Well," I said with a smile, "I'm delighted to hear that."

But inside, what I was thinking was, *When on earth did I sell the rights to publish this book in South Africa?*

And after I got home, one of the first things I did was to go to my office, open my safe and pull out that contract.

At first I felt vindicated. Right there in the rights section, the contract stipulated that the publisher was acquiring the right to publish the book in the United States, Canada and territories thereof.

Then I read a little further, and found the clause concerning distribution, which stipulated that the publisher could distribute the book anywhere in the world, provided the copies were printed in the

United States or Canada.

I had, by that time, signed a further contract for two additional titles and, sure enough, the language in it was identical.

Now, let's be clear here. The publisher in no way had set out to pull one over on me. Everything was there in black and white, and the contract was brief enough that I should have caught the distribution language. But I had made the rookie mistake of reading just one section of the contract and deciding that I had restricted international distribution, when I should only have come to my conclusion after reading the contract as a whole.

So I started to feel that perhaps I needed to hook up with someone who read book contracts every day.

Out of This World

The next moment that gave me pause came one day when, out of the blue, the subsidiary rights manager at my publisher called me up. She told me that she had a Canadian film producer on the line who wanted to option my first novel for development as a feature film. Would I mind if she brought him into the call so the three of us could discuss the deal together?

I agreed, but this time, in the back of my mind, I was thinking, *Option? What the heck's an option?*

And for the next half hour, I chatted with this producer and the subsidiary rights manager, and throughout the call, I imagined a little demon perched on my shoulder, chanting into my ear, "You don't know what you're talking about… Nah, nah, nah, nah-nah…."

Now I was really starting to think that I needed an agent—or, rather, an *agency* that had on its staff people well versed in film rights.

And, come to think of it, *contracts*.

The End of the World as We Know It

Three other things were going on about this same time.

One was the consolidation of the publishing world. Smaller specialty publishers were being bought up by national, or even international, conglomerates. This meant that, even with smaller presses where the author was on a first-name basis with everybody, contract terms might have been dictated by legal departments half a continent away. Publishing contracts were becoming multi-page behemoths in which rights granted on one page could very possibly be rescinded on another.

The second was that, for folks like me who had signed simple, letter-length publishing contracts years before, publishers were often sending out letters of amendment.

I know some novelists, not represented by agents, who thought that signing the letters of amendment was a requirement, so they did it. Others read only the letters of amendment, and did not read what the letters amended, which was the book contract they'd originally signed. Still others only read the cover letters that came with the legal forms, which told the authors what a great deal this was and how it was to their advantage, so they signed them and sent them back.

The truth, of course, was that the only reason a publisher would want to send out a letter of amendment in the first place would be to get out of having to live by the terms of the contract they'd originally signed. So it was—and is—rarely in an author's best interest to sign such a thing.

Some people, understanding this, signed anyhow because they didn't want to alienate their publisher.

There were other things. E-books, which were barely a blip on the radar when I signed my first novel contract, were coming on in a big way.

So was print-on-demand technology, which created a contractual conundrum: if a publisher could produce books one at a time to satisfy demand from bookshops, it could conceivably keep a novel "in print" forever, decades after the initial print runs, effectively preventing the book from ever going out of print and allowing the rights to revert back to the author.

A good agent could negotiate a minimum number of sales required for a book to be considered "in print," but I did not believe that I, as an individual author (and provably inept in legalese), could do that.

An Intermediary

And the last straw, the final thing that made me decide that I needed an agent, may sound silly, but it was literally the tipping point: social awkwardness.

I was finishing *In High Places*, the novel I talked about so much earlier in this book.

As I mentioned, *In High Places* took me bits and pieces of seven years to write, and it was no secret that I was writing it. My novelist friends knew, and so did several editors. Some of those editors had left their original jobs and moved on to roles with other publishing houses, so the word got around that I had this multi-year project nearing completion, and it was unsold. Some editors had even read bits and pieces of it—I'd shared it to get a reaction, always stipulating that I would entertain no offers, no book deals or even the possibility of a book deal, until I'd finished the novel and taken it through one revision, on my own.

In the end, I had four editors to whom I'd promised to show the manuscript upon completion. All had abided by my terms; none had jumped the gun to propose a deal.

And all were more than my colleagues. They were my friends, folks I loved to grab a coffee with at conferences. All were interested in the same book and, as I finished my work, it became more and more apparent to me that I was going to have to tell three of these good friends that they could not have it.

The prospect of transferring that uncomfortable duty to a professional intermediary—a literary agent—became more attractive with each passing day.

I finished the book. I sent it off, as I promised, to four editors with four different publishing houses.

Then I began reviewing the notes I'd made on the literary agents I'd met over the years.

Matchmaking

Now, I readily admit that my situation at the time was different from that of a first-time novelist. I had four novels and two nonfiction books in print by that time and many people knew that I was working without representation, so for quite a while I'd had agents calling and writing me, offering their services.

So I not only had a short list; I had already spoken at one time or another with all of the agencies I was considering. I'd also spoken with authors these agents represented, to get an idea of what they were like to work with, and from those conversations, as I thought about the book I'd just sent out, plus the ones I was planning to write next, I'd narrowed the list down to two agencies.

As I was narrowing the field, two of the editors I'd sent the manuscript to sent me emails, telling me that they were very interested in the book, that they were discussing it with their leadership, and expected to be contacting me with and offer very soon.

Thinking back, I may be mistaken, but I don't ever recall writing a proposal for *In High Places.* The editors I was sharing it with had all had their appetites whetted already, so I just mailed them the complete first-draft manuscript. Which I realize is a violation of my own advice, but this was a book that I had finished in pretty much the form in which I wanted to see it published, so I wanted its potential editors to have a good grasp of the overall picture. And as that is what the editors were looking at, that is what I sent to the two agencies I was considering, as well.

Both agencies knew that I had potential offers on the line, so both got back to me within the week.

One, a well-respected East Coast agent, called to let me know that he thought the book was amazing, and that he believed I had written something significant. Then he dropped the bomb.

"As you know, at least eighty percent of the fiction market is women," he told me. "I think we can get a much better deal if we change the story from one about a teenage boy and his father to one about a teenage girl and her mother."

My heart sank. Several novelists had sung this agent's praises, but here I had a novel that was all but sold, and he wanted to wade into the very essence of the creative process and change it. Certainly his intentions were good, but this wasn't what I wanted for this book. Nor did I want to have this sort of conversation on every project I proposed in the future.

So I was frank. I told him that I needed an agent to represent me, not to shape me, and I believed that going into business together would only create friction for us both, so while I respected his opinion (and admitted that his idea might actually move more books), I felt that the work produced by following it would not be a Tom Morrisey novel. So I didn't feel we should work together.

And he, to his great credit, agreed.

Naturally, when the other agency called, I was leery: all my eggs had ended up in this one basket.

But the conversation I had with them was quite different.

They asked what I was looking for in an agency. I told them I wanted someone to manage the business end of my fiction work—negotiating rights, handling subsidiary rights, looking for opportunities in the marketplace. I also made it clear that I was not looking for a creative sounding board or a book doctor.

All terms to which they happily agreed.

By this time, all four editors were calling me on the book. One wanted the exact same change that the first agent had suggested. Another loved the book, but didn't think the mention of suicide would strike a favorable chord with its intended market, so wanted me to take that out. A third called with an offer that was uncompetitively low. Only Bethany House indicated that they liked the book as it was, and would make a reasonable offer on it.

So, as it turned out, I didn't have to break the news to three of my friends that I would not be asking them to the prom. Three of them were offering terms that I could not entertain, and only the fourth was viable. But all my other reasons for seeking an agent—the growing complexity of the market and my lack of familiarity with subsidiary rights—were still there.

My new agency handled the contract for *In High Places* and the two other titles that I would publish with Bethany House. In good faith, they even did this before I had formally signed with them; as I recall, I signed my agency contract at pretty much the same time that I signed my book contract.

A Marriage Made in Heaven

Over the years, my literary agent has stayed true to the promise his agency made when I signed with them. He has never offered me unsolicited creative advice, yet when I have asked for his opinion on creative matters, he has responded with pensive insight and (I hate the fact that he is going to read this) brilliance.

Nor has he been a literary short-order cook, simply handling the contracts on books I'd conceived and written.

A few years ago, for instance, he learned that a publisher was creating a new line of men's fiction, based around the military world. Upon hearing that, he immediately thought of two of his clients: General Jerry Boykin (the agency had recently published his memoir) and me. He thought that the two of us, together, could produce something formidable in this genre.

He floated the idea in one-on-one conversations with each of us… and we were both skeptical about a collaboration, especially a collaboration with someone we'd never met. So he made us an offer.

At the time, both Jerry and I had more frequent-flyer miles than we'd ever know what to do with. So our mutual agent suggested that we each cash some in and fly out the following Friday to Colorado Springs, where the agency was. Jerry had friends in Colorado Springs that he could bunk with, and our agent told me I'd be staying in his home.

We flew out, met at the literary agency, and had dinner together to break the ice. Then, the next morning, the three of us met in our agent's family room, with its spectacular view of Pikes Peak.

"Alright," he told us. "My wife and I are going shopping. Why don't you two talk and see if you feel as if you could work together? I'll be back at noon with lunch."

Jerry and I talked. We shared ideas for a story. We liked the ideas we were coming up with. I opened my laptop and began writing as he and I tossed lines back and forth.

Shortly after noon, our agent came back with deli sacks and soft drinks.

"So," he asked us, "what do you think?"

I looked at the bottom toolbar on my Microsoft Word document.

"I think," I said, "that we have almost four thousand words of a novel written."

Changes

So that's my story. It's how I got published and found and have worked with an agent in the publishing world that was there when I published my first novel.

But if you are unpublished right now, you are coming into an entirely different world.

I had to get by gatekeepers. You have to as well, if you choose to follow a traditional publishing route.

But as you probably know, there are now alternatives to that route. You can publish your work without selling it to a traditional, advance- and royalty-paying publisher.

You can, if you so desire, publish it yourself.

Rolling Your Own

Shortcuts to publication have always existed for those who wanted to pay for the privilege. Derisively referred to as "vanity presses" and "publishers of last resort," there have been (and still are) publishing houses that employed no editorial screening process whatsoever, and would publish any book for which the author was willing to pay their fee (in 1990, anywhere from $3,000 to $20,000, according to *The New York Times*... and it's gone up considerably since then).

Famous for advertising that authors ranging from Mark Twain and Zane Grey to Lewis Carroll had paid to have their work published (all true, although none of these writers hired a vanity press—they simply paid printers to print and bind their books and acted as their own publishers … and Mark Twain went bankrupt doing so), vanity presses have long advertised their abilities to copyedit, typeset, print, bind, advertise, market and distribute an author's work, all for a fee.

One of the most longstanding of these, Vantage Press, stayed in business for sixty-three years, although it never completely recovered from a 1990 class-action lawsuit, in which a New York jury ruled that the publisher had systematically defrauded its clients. Vantage ultimately closed its doors in 2012.

Not that this mattered.

By 2012, far more affordable paths to publication had already appeared. For about $500, Abbott Press could turn your Word-document manuscript into an e-book. Double the price, and you could get it made into a paperback: they'd even provide you with five complimentary copies. And Abbott, last I checked, is still in business and doing fine.

Don't have even that amount of spare cash lying around? Not a problem. Kindle, Nook and iBooks all have free online apps that will allow you to generate an e-book from your word-processing document. If you formatted your document so it would work with a digital publication program (big hint here: do *not* use manual paragraph indentations), the process takes all of about five minutes; even I can do it. And all three services come with distribution—with the Kindle, the distribution engine is Amazon, the King Kong of online bookstores.

For a few more minutes of your time and no upfront investment of cash, CreateSpace will allow you to create an actual, you-can-hold-it-in-your-hands, paperback book. You'll only keep a small percentage of the sales price, but again one of the sales outlets they include is Amazon (Amazon *owns* CreateSpace). And for a nominal fee, they'll include it in a listing so brick-and-mortar bookstores can order it.

Moreover, self-publishing is no longer the sole domain of little old ladies writing memoirs about their cats.

J.K. Rowling is a self-publisher of a sort, in that her Pottermore.com website is the sole source for the Harry Potter series in e-book form (yes, you can find it listed on Amazon, but—as of this writing, at least—clicking the "Buy" button redirects you to Pottermore). Judge Judy is published on CreateSpace. And I personally know dozens of highly regarded novelists who are reviving their out-of-print titles as self-published e-books and print-on-demand paperbacks. Some are even writing fresh material and bringing those new novels out as e-books, conventional books and audiobooks that they have created on their own, without the assistance of a traditional publisher.

These books are selling very well and making money—serious money—for their authors.

So… should you self-publish as well?

Probably not.

The Catch

Not yet, at least.

It turns out that all those gatekeepers in traditional publishing serve a purpose.

A publisher looks for a novel that will fill a void in the marketplace, and can add to the aggregate sales of a house's line, without cannibalizing its sales from any of the house's existing catalogue. A distributor understands that shelf space in a book store is precious, and shelf space in newsstands and airport gift shops is even more so, so a distributor is looking for a title that will not linger on that shelf for long; one that will sell rapidly and repeatedly. The publisher's marketing department is looking for a story and a voice that will lend itself to the creation of a brand, and a novel that will be worthy of the extra money they might spend to, say, place an end-cap—a freestanding display at the end of an aisle—in a bookstore, or get the title on the store's "new releases" table. The advertising department wants a novel with a definite hook; something that can be use to start a word-of-mouth buzz, and the publicity department wants the same thing. And at the beginning of it all, the acquisitions editor is looking for great, strong, tight and confident writing and a fresh and original story.

Self-publishing, for the most part, employs none of these screens. There are no filters in place. And the result is an enormous field filled with books that are repetitive, derivative, uninteresting, bland, undistinguished, stale and—worst of all—very badly written.

Most self-published novels fall into one or more of these categories. Some observers place the number of just plain awful self-pubbed novels at ninety-nine percent, and some say it is higher.

Even if you have written the novel of the century, getting it discovered by readers amongst the hundreds of thousands of self-published novels that come out each year is like asking potential readers to go looking for a pearl in a cesspool. The odds are enormously against you.

Now, at this point, you are supposed to tap me on the shoulder and say, "Excuse me, Mr. Negativity, but didn't you say that there are well-known writers who are publishing their own novels. And didn't you say that they are selling well?"

I did, on both counts. But there is a difference between those well-known writers and the undiscovered and as-yet unpublished novelist: the fact that those well-known writers *are* well known. They have what is known as *brand*.

About Brand

"Brand" is one of the most illusive and ill-defined terms in marketing in general and in publishing in particular. Writers—even deeply experienced writers who should know better—often confuse it with slogans and taglines. They look for workshops on how to build a brand and seek out ways to make their own brand, but the truth of the matter is that brand is not built by, and does not belong to, a writer.

Brand is a quality that belongs to that author's *readership*; they are the ones who truly create it. The only thing an author can do to help it along is provide enough material—in the form of published novels—to help those readers form an opinion.

The essences of brand are trust and expectation. When you look at a bookshelf and see "Stephen King" or "John Irving" or "Anne Rice" or "Nora Roberts" on the spine of a book, you have an instant image, a feeling for the type and quality of story that is going to be inside.

If that expectation matches well with your taste, and you have not yet read that book, then you'll probably want it, even if you were not previously aware it existed. If you have the money in your pocket and the rent's not due, you are probably going to buy it. In marketing speak, you are part of that author's "platform;" you have an affinity to his or her brand.

How important is brand? Consider this…

Not all that long ago, Jo Rowling wrote a crime novel. She sent it off to publishers, not under the "J.K. Rowling" pen name for which she has become world-renowned (the initials were something her publishers originally suggested to obfuscate the fact that she was a woman), but a pseudonym, "Robert Galbraith." She even concocted a fiction behind her fiction, and provided her alter ego with a fake CV, complete with a military background.

That novel, *The Cuckoo's Calling*, had the strong and confident writing and interesting storyline one would expect from J.K. Rowling, but because it lacked her identity and her brand, it was rejected by at least one publisher. Finally it was brought out in April of 2013 by Sphere Books, an imprint of Little, Brown and Company.

One assumes that this publisher was brought in on the subterfuge, in that Rowling's previous non-Harry novel, *The Casual Vacancy*, was likewise published by Little, Brown and Company. But if they were, they kept mum about the book's true author, and stuck to the story that it was written by a relatively unknown ex-military man with a background in the security industry.

The first ninety days that a novel is on sale are the equivalent of "the golden hour" in publishing. If a title is going to catch fire, it will usually do so during this window. And if it is not, it will likewise expire with a whimper during this time.

The initial performance of *The Cuckoo's Calling* would best be described as a fairly robust whimper. During its first ninety days in print, it sold 1,500 copies—about what a Harry Potter book would do in the first minute or so that it was on sale. But *The Cuckoo's Calling* was stronger in ebook, audiobook and library editions, selling a grand total of 7,000 copies amongst those.

Still, 8,500 total copies barely qualifies as a strong midlist showing, and is about 1,500 copies shy of what most publishers would consider a successful debut. Bear in mind that this is for a novel that was professionally edited, and then brought out, marketed, advertised and publicized by one of the strongest publishing conglomerates in the world (not to mention written by the best-selling author in the English language).

The review's for "Galbraith's debut novel" were likewise mixed, although they leaned heavily to the favorable side. And toward the end of June, *The Cuckoo's Calling* was pretty much the apparent loss-leader one would expect from an unknown novelist—a nicely reviewed book that didn't start fireworks with its sales, from a writer who showed hope of possibly amounting to something in the future.

Then in July of 2013, word leaked that Rowling was the book's true author (although Rowling swore that neither she, her publishers, her publicist nor her agent were the source of the leak). And the book took about one day to surge from number 4,709 on Amazon's bestseller list to the very top.

That's how important brand is.

Known Versus Unknown

It takes quite a few people to make a workable platform. Your mother and your best friend are not nearly enough—unless one of them is Oprah Winfrey.

And if you do have a workable platform, you can probably get a decent response in the marketplace, even if you have never written a novel before.

James Franco, who seems constantly to be in production on one film or another, somehow found time to write *Actors Anonymous*, the print edition of which was published under the New Harvest pseudonym of Amazon Publishing in the fall of 2013... to mostly negative reviews.

New novelist, lousy reviews, but still Franco's book managed to hit number-one in category in two separate categories in the Amazon Kindle bestseller list. And it danced around in respectable numbers in the general Kindle bestseller list as well.

That's because while Franco may not enjoy a solid brand in the literary world, he does in film, and that brand aura crosses over, bringing with it fans who are all potential readers. That's enough of a potential reader base to make it worth his (and Amazon's) while to publish a book.

One supposed exception to the need for brand is E.L. James, whose *Fifty Shades of Grey* trilogy, or at least the first book of it, was initially published by an Australian print-on-demand service, and rocketed in popularity, supposedly powered entirely by blog-driven viral messaging.

But James first established a nascent readership through participation in a fanfiction site (her characters were initially based on those in the *Twilight* series).

Then she moved to a dedicated website to build a following, and those two avenues apparently created enough of a readership to achieve critical mass as a platform—that, plus devotees of bondage-and-domination mommy porn seem to be really, really good at operating a search engine.

Both of those provided the initial inertia for the novel's print-on-demand paperback launch. And the book's popularity moved Vintage to pick James up a year later as a traditionally published novelist.

Novelists who are neither cinema stars nor Internet celebrities will have to earn brand the old fashioned way, which is by creating books that get noticed both by legitimate reviewers and by readers.

That's the case with all those known novelists who are now enjoying success publishing their own books. They began by publishing through traditional publishers, and then moved their titles into self-publication when they went out of print with the original publishers.

And those who have gone a step further and are now self-publishing original work are not doing it because they could not initially sell their work to traditional publishers. To the contrary, *all* got their start with traditional and conventional advance- and royalty-paying publishers. While a few have moved away from traditional publishing entirely, preferring to publish and market their own work, most are still publishing traditionally as well, reserving the self-publication route for a revival of out-of-print work, or for boutique titles that they do not feel would result in a good deal with a conventional publisher.

When they self-publish, most of these known authors will contract with well-respected copy editors (and, in many cases, line editors) to get their work show-ready before bringing it to market. Many commission original cover work, and purchase ISBNs (international standard book numbers) and, for printed work, corresponding bar codes so the books can be tracked, ordered and sold by third-party retailers.

An important point: while some successful writers are doing these things through services that are initially free (such as the self-publishing apps offered by Kindle, Nook and iBooks, or print-on-demand services such as CreateSpace), and while some are making investments that may run into the thousands for their editing and their cover art, *none* of them are paying vanity-press packagers for these services. They know that they can get better prices, and far better services, by contracting with the same professionals that are used by the traditional publishing industry.

So, if you are tempted to go to a book packager to get your novel published, know this: there is a world of difference between a book self-published by a brand-name author who can publish and has published traditionally, and a book self-published out of desperation, because no one in traditional publishing would accept it. The former may be a commercial success, while the latter almost never will be.

Bucket Listing

If, on the other hand, you want to get your novel published because you want to give it to friends and family for Christmas, or you want to have it out there before you or a loved one passes on to the great beyond, or you simply want to have a book on the shelf with your name on it, and you don't care if it ever makes a dime, then go ahead and self-publish.

But please... don't pay tens of thousands (or even thousands) to a packager to do it. Those companies prey upon the gullible, the deluded and the desperate, and if you've read this book to this point, you are obviously none of those things.

What to Do

In summary, my business advice is to write the very best book you can, then write another, and create good, solid publishing proposals for each of them. Then start attending writer's conference and book fairs so you can pitch the first of those two books to editors and learn which agents you might eventually want to do business with. Once you find an editor who likes the pitch, send that editor your proposal. And when you get offered a deal, find an agent to take the business part forward from there.

This will save you headache and heartache.

And it will allow you to move forward with the other part of authorship, which is living with the fact that you are now a published novelist.

| TEN: Living with the Craft

Writing a book is a horrible, exhausting struggle, like a long bout of some painful illness. One would never undertake such a thing if one were not driven on by some demon whom one can neither resist or understand.
— GEORGE ORWELL

WHEN I AM IN THE MIDDLE of writing a novel, I tend to sit for long hours and at odd hours, sometimes at a desk, or other times in a comfortable chair on the lanai, with a laptop or pencil and notepad before me. I do not move, I do not talk, I tend not to hear it when spoken to, and when I do hear it, often as not I resent the interruption.

This makes me extremely poor company.

In fact, the only friend or family member that ever liked me this way was the dog.

And earlier this year, the dog died.

I am little better company away from the keyboard.

When I surface from one of those marathon writing sessions, being with me is like attending someone else's high-school reunion. Here I am, obsessed with stories, characters and details that those around me cannot possibly know about, because I am still in the middle of making it all up.

Welcome to the Funhouse

Now, on the surface there seems to be an obvious solution to the situation; just share your book with your loved ones as you write it.

This rarely works.

Ernest Hemingway is reputed to have proclaimed, "All first drafts are … " Well, I won't finish the sentence, but use your imagination. After all, it was Hemingway.

And the essence of that sentence is true.

Your book, as you write it, is at best a diamond in the rough.

273

But chances are your family is accustomed to seeing that diamond as a highly polished, brilliant cut, mounted in a white-gold Tiffany setting. And if they are not personally familiar with the creative process, that is probably what they are expecting.

So when you read the morning's draft to them (probably pausing or backing up as you go to put in the words you forgot to include, or correct the typos), their reaction is likely to be less than enthusiastic. They might even look dismayed.

You, on the other hand, are probably looking for validation. You want to know those four hours of work produced something wonderful, something laudable. "Dismayed" is not anywhere near the reaction you are seeking.

So sharing first drafts with the family tends to leave everyone dissatisfied.

All in the Family

It works a little better for novelists who are married to other novelists. They know, and agree with, what Hemingway said about first drafts, and so they can picture that diamond-in-the-rough with fifty percent of its weight cut away, and all the facets polished.

But, being novelists, they very probably want to help with the cutting and the polishing. As it is being read to them. Before you have even finished reading the first paragraph. This means that they are no longer simply listeners; they are collaborators.

Which may not be what you wanted.

In fact, if you read first drafts often enough to anyone, they are probably going to feel inclined to help you, and if they do, it's your fault because, after all, you're the one who opened the door.

This assumes that your loved ones are even remotely interested in what you write.

That might not be the case. Opposites do, after all, attract, and as you are reading that touching scene in which the dashing seventeenth-century English colonist first meets the beautiful Powhatan maiden, your spouse may be wishing you'd throw in a scene or two where a helicopter blows up.

My wife's first acquaintance with my personal brand of fiction came when she settled down on the chaise lounge next to our pool, a fresh iced tea at her elbow, to enjoy an ARC (advance reader's copy) of *Deep Blue*, the first Beck Easton novel. The Easton books always open with backstory—a historical prologue in which someone dies—and in this case, that someone was a freed slave, an eminently likeable, middle-aged gentleman, who suffers death by drowning in agonizing, Technicolor detail.

Linda (my wife) read the prologue, stopped, and came back into the house, ARC in hand.

"Is *this* what you spend all your time thinking about?" Her eyes, as I recall, were pretty wide as she asked this. "Why on earth would someone want to even *imagine* something like that?"

Linda couldn't sleep that night, and the experience got her wondering who, exactly, she had married—something that I imagine she still ponders from time to time.

If this is sounding like, until such time as *if* is published and released, you should not share your work except with industry peers … then you are catching my drift. In *Byline Ernest Hemingway*, no less an authority than Papa put it this way:

You must be prepared to work always without applause. When you are excited about something is when the first draft is done. But no one can see it until you have gone over it again and again until you have communicated the emotion, the sights and the sounds to the reader, and by the time you have completed this, the words, sometimes, will not make sense to you as you read them, so many times have you re-read them.

So while the essence of relationships is sharing, it will rarely profit either your relationships or your writing if you share the work before it is baked. And as you cannot do that, you'll have to find another way to be present with those you love.

... And Accounted For

Perhaps we should make that present *and engaged.*

Several years ago my wife, was battling cancer. She is fine now, but at the time, she was having weekly chemotherapy to shrink the tumor to a size that could safely be removed.

These chemotherapy sessions would last for hours at a time, and I was determined that I would not force her to endure them alone. So I went out and bought a laptop computer, the first I'd ever owned, loaded it with word-processing software and my work-in-progress, and took it along to the hospital for her first session.

The nurse rigged and started the IV, Linda opened a magazine and began to read, and I opened the laptop and commenced on a fresh chapter. I felt like the good and noble husband, there at my wife's side in her moment of need.

All seemed right with the world ... for about five minutes.

Then Linda took off her reading glasses, set aside the magazine, and said, "Tap-tap-tap-tap-tap-tap-*tap.* Would you *please* go do that someplace else?"

This is not to say I never write around my wife. As I'm working on this chapter, we are sitting together on the screened lanai behind our home in Florida. She is working on a sudoku puzzle, and I am writing (on a device that has a much quieter keyboard than that old Windows laptop). Then again, we have reached a state in our marriage in which we can sit quietly together and simply enjoy the nearness.

But earlier, especially when our daughter was small, nearness was not enough. And if there was ever any doubt, that experience in the hospital taught me that being in the same place does not necessarily constitute time spent together.

Chewing Baseball

I've also learned that trying to do two things at once usually means doing neither one well.

My good friend, the poet and essayist John Calderazzo, shared this story with me:

Along about 1992, I attended a retreat for environmentalists with the Vietnamese Buddhist monk, peace activist, and well-known author Thich Nhat Hahn. While sitting cross-legged with about forty other adults, I heard him tell a story about a friend of his who was eating string beans, but simultaneously talking with great enthusiasm about the baseball game he was going to watch that evening on TV. Thich Nhat Hahn found it troubling, though in an amusing way, that his friend was therefore not living in the present moment of enjoying the string beans. Even as he crunched away, he had been swept forward into the future by his desire to watch baseball (forsaking "desire" is a very big Buddhist concept). In Thich Nhat Hahn's opinion, his friend wasn't really living in the moment, wasn't really chewing string beans; he was "chewing baseball."

I like that story because, having lived for years now in a world in which we expect our computers to download videos, play music, track incoming email and run an office program, plus keep a game open in a separate window—all at the same time—we believe that *we* can multitask as well. But we cannot, because human multitasking—that is, multitasking as a conscious, rather than a subconscious effort—is a myth.

Behavioral psychologists have solidly established that people who *think* they are multitasking are actually dividing their conscious streams of thought into tiny windows, some as miniscule as a tenth of a second or less. So while people might think they can send a text while they drive, they actually give the text all of their attention as they enter it, which explains why most people killed while texting never see the curve they drive off of or the other vehicle that they run into.

Now, I'll trust that you are far too smart to try texting while driving. But if you decide to try sitting off in a corner and drafting a chapter while you attend your niece's graduation party, or take the notebook to your kid's Little League game, both the activity and your writing will suffer. Do one thing or another, not both.

Episodes

The thing that has worked best for me is to arrange my life in episodes: time when I write, time I spend with family and friends, business time for calls with editors, time to do any non-writing chores that I have not been able to postpone, time for phone interviews, doctor appointments and the like, time to eat and sleep and—one day a week—time when nothing is scheduled and the only thing I don't do is write.

I say "write" euphemistically, because I recognize that, for me at least, the grunt work of composition—imagining settings, determining plot points, even coming up with dialogue—usually takes place subconsciously, away from the keyboard. It's the time when the bulk of the work is being done by what Stephen King refers to as "the boys in the back room." And I have found that, because this background level of creation is primarily a subconscious process, it takes place most effectively while I am busy doing other things.

Mowing the lawn, for instance—the white noise of the lawn mower just seems to help me mull things over. My wife loves it; when I am on deadline, I have been known to cut the grass seven or eight times in a single week.

As for the part that looks like writing—the time spent sitting at a desk or before a keyboard—that is the part where I become the antisocial guy at the desk (or in my chair on the patio, or hunched silently off to the side of the family room), because that is conscious action. And, being conscious, that action requires my attention and turns me into what my wife refers to as "the bear."

Working in episodes helps me keep the bear largely invisible. Essentially, I spend time at the keyboard when the rest of the family is not around.

Occasionally, this is when they are out shopping, or gone to the beach, or at a theme park (we live in Florida). But mostly this happens when the rest of the family is asleep. And as I have been a lifelong early riser (and my wife and my daughter are, by nature, night people), I am usually awake long and at the desk long before sunrise each day. The rest of the house is still asleep and, unless someone is dead, I am relatively certain that the phone is not going to ring. It's a good time to concentrate on craft.

But the thing about the actual words-on-paper element of writing is that it is time-consuming. Word choice comes into play here. This is the part where I am listening to the music—the phrasing and sound of the words—and it may take me several tries to get it right. I have novelist friends who regularly put 5,000 words on paper in a single day, but a thousand words is more than enough to make me feel as if I've accomplished something epic. I write more slowly than some novelists, but my first drafts are much nearer to what I'll eventually publish.

Or at least I like to think that's the case.

And if it is not, I would rather not know.

As my novels are usually right around 100,000 words in length, this means I should be able to crank one out in a little over three months. But I don't write at all one day a week, so that adds a little more than fourteen days to the process.

Add to this the fact that my first drafts are not 100,000 words long. They could be 150,000 words; that adds nearly two months to the process. Some days—many days—I am not able to write 1,000 words. If there are repairmen in the house, or I'm traveling, there are days when I do not get anything written at all. Nor do I write when I am teaching writers' workshops; the student work is rarely harmonious with my own, and I find I lose the sound of my narrative voice when I am reading the shorter pieces involved in a workshop.

And until I know what the ending is, I generally don't write much more than notes, anyhow. That preparatory thinking, alone, could eat up several months.

So the bottom line is that the twelve months most contracts allot for completion of the first draft of a novel is a bit of a reach for me. More than a bit of a reach.

Even if I follow my own advice and try to at least occasionally write a novel without a contract attached to it, I usually do so with a planned end date in mind. And when my deadline—real or self-imposed—is fast approaching, my regular writing time in the early morning is often not enough to get the job done.

Hiding the Bear

This is how it used to happen: the family would have an activity planned, and I would not be able to go along because I needed to write. Or, if I bit the bullet and went along, I would be miserable company.

Human memory being what it is, even if I was like this only one month of the year, to my family, I was writing "all of the time." Which made me seem like a drag to be around ... or not be around as the case may be.

Now, this was a few years ago, when laptop computers were still fairly heavy, with only a few hours of battery time, and, even if carried in a case, could be put out of commission with a smart knock against a doorframe. So, for writing on airplanes, I'd acquired an AlphaSmart Neo. This was (unfortunately, they are no longer produced) a two-pound, self-contained word processor—a keyboard with a rudimentary character-display screen. Designed for use by middle-school students, the Neo will hold upwards of 70,000 words of text in storage; when one gets back to a computer, the Neo is connected to it via a USB cord, and the text can be sent into a Word document (or any other application that accepts textual input). The device runs for 700 hours on a set of three AA batteries and, while it lacks a backlight for writing in the dark, I quickly figured out how to overcome that with a booklight and two strips of Velcro tape.

And even though I got my first Neo to use it on airplanes, it was what I thought of when, as I was racing to complete the final chapters on a novel, Linda told me that she'd like to spend the next day with Carly (our daughter) at Greenfield Village.

This was when we lived in Michigan. Greenfield Village, in Dearborn, is the outdoor display section of The Henry Ford, a museum and educational complex constructed in the first half of the twentieth century by the automotive industrialist. Most of it is composed of homes once owned by famous Americans, dismantled board by board and then reconstructed by curators in Dearborn.

We had an annual pass to The Henry Ford, so my wife and daughter liked to visit often; their favorite activity was to walk through the historic homes and pick out details they had never noticed before.

I, on the other hand, would customarily take a walk through a home, reflect on the fact that I was looking at the room where Noah Webster wrote his dictionary, and then fidget—usually passing time by people-watching—until Linda and Carly were ready to move on. But on our numerous earlier trips I had noticed that most of those old houses had a front porch, or at least a broad stoop, where a person could grab a seat or a step. And I had the Neo, and a small messenger bag it could fit in.

Needless to say, Linda was a little surprised when I told her, "Sure. I can go."

So, the next morning, after everyone was up and I had already completed my usual early morning writing, we made the one-hour trip to Dearborn. I even drove. And I encouraged my family to spend all the time they wanted. I walked with them and stopped into every historic home. And in each home, I spent my usual two to five minutes walking through.

Then, while the ladies of the family stayed inside to memorize the wallpaper, I would step outside, find a seat, fire up the Neo (start-up time—about three seconds), and write. Ten or fifteen minutes later, when the family came out, I would turn the Neo off with a single keystroke, put it back into the messenger bag, and we would continue on to the next house. We even had a leisurely dinner in Greenfield Village at the end of the day.

The point here is that I was not working on my novel while I walked around with my wife and daughter, Instead, I was inserting small novel-writing episodes in between those times when my family and I were visiting the houses and they had my full attention. It is a fine distinction, but an important one.

My daughter was in grade school then, and as we tucked her into bed, my wife whispered how much she appreciated the fact that, even though I was on deadline, I had sacrificed an entire day to make memories and have fun with the family. And then, when I went down to my office to transfer my work to the computer, I discovered that, between my early morning hours and my "porch time" at Greenfield Village, I had written nearly 2,500 words—better than twice my usual daily output.

Since then, whenever time is of the essence, I have become an expert at finding stolen moments in which—without being antisocial or ignoring those I am with—I can write, no matter where I am. I have written at tables outside the ice cream parlor at Walt Disney World, in the waiting rooms at body shops and dentists' offices, and while sitting in the "daddy chair" outside ladies' wear dressing rooms.

Laptop computers are much better today, and oftentimes I do the work on my MacBook Pro, which weighs less than six pounds, and offers battery life upwards of seven hours. But often as not I still do that writing, and much of my regular-hours writing, on the old AlphaSmart Neo. I have owned two Neos over the years, and my current model is a "Frankeneo," cobbled together from bits and pieces of both of them. The negligible weight, long battery life, nice full-size keyboard and simplicity still make it my favorite go-to device for first drafts.

When I'm approaching deadline, I use the Neo to write when the moments present themselves. By writing in those episodes and stolen moments, I've saved my family from becoming a writing widow and a novel orphan.

And that is how it should be.

A Legend in Your Own Mind

There is another very important element to one's social demeanor as a novelist, and that is how one acts when one succeeds.

Certainly, there are few things in life as exciting and validating as the first time you have your novel accepted by a legitimate, honest-to-goodness, advance-and-royalty-paying publisher. When that happens, it's understandable if you go a little crazy. It's even expected.

F. Scott Fitzgerald was living in a brownstone on Summit Avenue in St. Paul when it first happened to him. In 1919, when he received word that *This Side of Paradise* was going to be published by Scribner's, he reacted by running out the front door and dashing up and down the street, stopping traffic so he could tell startled drivers the news.

This happens to everyone—maybe not the stopping-traffic part, but certainly the elation. And it's understandable.

It's what happens later that you need to be concerned about.

After all, having any book accepted by a traditional publisher is a long shot. In terms of probability, it ranks somewhere between winning a small prize in the lottery and being elected President. It's a rare accomplishment. And being a rare accomplishment, it can make you feel special.

Maybe a little too special.

The first time you have a novel accepted for publication, it's tempting to feel that you have cracked the code—that you hold the key to an accomplishment most people only dream about. I know that I did; I felt like Frodo with the ring. And my initial elation quickly transitioned to conceit; I went from being full of joy to being full of myself.

I am not alone. I've seen the same thing time and time again in other writers: the feeling that they have fully arrived and are now licensed to deliver all manner of insight and advice on every nook, cranny and intricacy of writing and publication.

To make matters worse, new novelists usually find an audience for their pontification.

And in retrospect … it's embarrassing.

Getting the Black Belt

It reminds me of when I decided to study karate. I was working as editorial director at a magazine publisher at the time, and a dojo opened up on my drive home. It sounded like a good way to get some exercise.

Besides, I was excited at the thought of eventually earning a black belt—what I saw at the time as an ancient symbol of mastery of an equally ancient martial art. So I signed up and began taking classes, six days a week.

In less than a month, I earned my yellow *obi*, or karate belt, the first colored belt ranking in the style that I studied. I received it in a ceremony along with a certificate personally signed and presented to me by my sensei, a former All-Japan/Asia karate champion who had grown up on a small farm just outside of Tokyo. I still remember getting it and celebrating the fact that I was no longer a mere white-belt novice.

I worked my way up through the other belts: orange, purple, and several levels of green and brown—some earned through examination, and others awarded after I took first place in my age- weight- and skill-classes at major competitions.

But *sho-dan*—the senior rank indicated by the first level of black belt—had to be earned through literally years of classes, and an extensive formal testing process.

On the Saturday that I tested, I first performed an exhaustive repertoire of *kata*—the traditional forms used to integrate karate's long roster of blocks, kicks, punches and take-downs into a fluid and seamless system. Then, winded by what had been more than an hour of continuous exercise, I moved on to three rounds of scored *kumite* (sparring) with my sensei, in which I was expected to punch and kick hard enough and swiftly enough that my strikes would sound clearly against the heavy canvas *do-gi* that he wore, but with enough control that no blow ever landed on him.

Finally, my examination ended with three rounds of *bōjutsu,* or staff-fighting, using the *rokushakubō,* a heavy hardwood staff just under six feet long. In this, the final part of the examination, we did not pull our strikes, and I vividly remember how my *bō* rang in my hands as I blocked blows that would otherwise have cracked my skull.

I passed. I received my first *kuro obi,* or black belt. I became a *sempai*—one of the senior students of my *sensei,* and students of lower belt rankings were expected to address me as "sensei" as well.

I had achieved what I, when I first stepped into the dojo, had thought of as completion. But along the way, my sensei had opened my eyes to several things.

The first was that the system of belt rankings was not nearly as ancient as I'd assumed. The first Japanese martial art to use colored belts to indicate rank was judo, and its system was not adopted until just before the turn of the twentieth century.

As for karate, while it is a martial art with roots more than 700 years old, its institution as a formal course of organized group study dates back to only 1901, and my sensei taught me that, originally, in many styles, only two belts were used: the white belt (actually the second belt ranking in judo), and the black. The use of colored belts to indicate intermediate levels was only adopted on a wider scale later, when American servicemen began studying the Okinawan fighting style, and desired the gratification of additional belt ranks.

The real shocker came, though, in the third revelation. In traditional *bu-do,* or Japanese martial arts, a black belt is the designation, not of a master of the art, but of someone who has amassed enough practice and knowledge to be considered a serious student.

So my black belt, which I had at first thought of as an indication that I had completed my education in karate, was in fact an indication that I was finally ready to begin it.

Attitude Adjustment

My sensei, in other words, had understood intuitively my preconceptions about the art that he practiced, and so had done me the favor of gradually teaching me the true nature of what I was studying. He grounded me in a manner that circumvented any eventual need to take me down a notch.

In this business of novel-writing, I got taken down a notch. I do not believe that it was intentional, but it still worked out that way.

It happened a few months before the publication of my first novel, *Yucatan Deep*. Early readers of my edited manuscript had nothing but praise for it, and even before I'd completed the second book called for in my two-book contract, my publisher had contracted with me for two more books—assuring that I would stay busy as a novelist for at least three more years.

I had been writing professionally for more than twenty years at this point. That experience, plus the validation provided by my contracts and my early critical reception, had me convinced that I had arrived. I'd done it. And that, in my mind, made me an expert.

Then my publisher at the time—which was Zondervan, an imprint of Harper-Collins—held a novelists' retreat. More than a dozen of us converged on their headquarters city, where we were treated to a very exclusive conference designed specifically for our small, select group, with workshops and seminars presented by the heads of Zondervan's editorial, marketing and advertising departments, as well as several of the authors attending.

The attendees included household names: James Scott Bell, author of legal thrillers and multiple guides for writers; Terri Blackstock, author of more than forty novels, with more than twelve million volumes in print; T. Davis Bunn, a writer in residence at Oxford; Brandilyn Collins, whose two dozen books include a classic on character construction; Alton Gansky, now director of the prestigious Blue Ridge Mountains Christian Writers Conference; and Robin Lee Hatcher, whose more than seventy novels and novellas have won her pages full of awards.

These well-known novelists treated me as an equal, which at first only fueled my hubris. But then, as the week progressed and the extent of my colleagues' accomplishments began to truly sink in with me, I compared them to my own, which amounted literally to nothing; I'd written just one publishable novel, and it wasn't even in print yet.

This comeuppance was nothing intentional on the part of my publishers. They were just holding a bonding week for their stable of writers; their intention was not to set me in my place.

But I found it, nonetheless.

I would like to say that I learned my lesson, but it turns out that, in this respect at least, I am a multiple-lesson kind of person.

I still find it far too easy to get re-full of myself. Which is crazy, because the world is packed with people who write as well as and better than me. Some of them are still trying to find publishers, and the difference between them and me is that I have readers who know me.

I'm serious. And every time I start thinking that I have something special going for myself, I try to stop and remind myself of one key fact—that the difference between an unknown novelist and a successful novelist is readership.

Once you realize this, it's crazy to think that you are on anything other than the same level as the people who read your work and make you successful. Realistically, you're a step below, because they are the ones who control your professional destiny, and not the other way around.

Learning to Listen

I share this thought about attitude because it seems to be a chronic issue with writers and novelists. Not with all writers and novelists: I know some who are nothing less than saints. But I see it, and I see it especially in newer writers.

In fact, when newer writers phone me up and ask if we can have coffee so they can ask my advice or hear about my journey, the same thing has happened so often that I have come to expect it:

First we exchange pleasantries, then they begin to talk about themselves, their path in writing, why they think there is a market for what they do, what people have said about their work... and I cannot get a word in edgewise. And when I try to turn the conversation around to my thoughts on what they should try, and what has worked for me—which, ostensibly was the reason we met in the first place—they seem eager to leave. It is almost as if no one has ever taught them how to listen.

I come away with the feeling that I've been pitched—that somehow they feel that I have the power to get their book published (which I do not), or that I am going to make a call to an editor and recommend them (which I will not—not unless I have read lots of their fiction and am thoroughly familiar with their fiction, their dependability and their work ethic). Either that, or they are simply in love with themselves, their work and what they see as its potential... which gets high marks in the "confidence" department, but does not carry you far in an industry that hinges almost entirely on the extent to which readers like you.

The Bottom Line

Ultimately, if you work as a novelist long enough and pay attention to what works and what does not, you'll come to the conclusion that it is not about you.

The bottom line is that, if you want to be happy in your work, you'll need to learn how to do that work in a way that still makes you available—fully available—to family and friends. All great novels are about relationships, and if you want to write about them intelligently, you need to nurture the ones you have.

And all successful novelists have one thing in common—a readership that loves them and loves their work—and this, too, is something that needs to be cultivated. I understand that, for a long time—long after his book sales climbed into the millions—Stephen King tried to answer every piece of reader correspondence that he received. Obviously, he no longer does this; there are simply not enough hours in the day. But the fact that he did so for so long illustrates that he knows where his livelihood comes from.

I guess, then, that my parting advice is to write as well as you can and be the best person you can be. Those seem to be the keys.

And now for the last word....

Earlier in this chapter, we quoted a paragraph from *Byline Ernest Hemingway*. Let's close with how he finished that thought:

Finally, in some other place, some other time, when you can't work and feel like hell you will pick up the book and look in it and start to read and go on and in a little while say to your wife, "Why this stuff is bloody marvelous."

And she will say, "Darling, I always told you it was."
Or maybe she doesn't hear you and says, "What did you say?" and you do not repeat the remark.

* * *

Appendices

| THANKS

A thousand thanks to John Calderazzo, Alton Gansky, Robin Lee Hatcher, DiAnn Mills, Anna Patrick, Roxanne Rustand, Chuck Snearly and Brad Whittington, extraordinarily talented writers who were gracious enough to pre-read this book either in part or in its entirety, and offer feedback that was both constructive and kind. They also pointed out—most gently, I must add—an exceptional number of typos, wordos, bad formatting and other bonehead mistakes. Any errors that remain are solely the result of the ignorance and/or stubbornness of the author.

Thanks also to James Scott Bell, Athol Dickson and several other novelists who shared their knowledge on how to produce this book in its electronic format (all while managing to hide their amazement at my extraordinary ignorance of the process).

And finally—this will sound gratuitous, but I assure you it was not—my thanks go out to you: my reader. You, and thousands of others like you, are the people who make the difference between me being an author and me being a guy with a bunch of ratty manuscripts stuffed in the furthest corner of the closet.

I do not take that for granted for a single second, and I hope I never will.

—TM

| Glossary

advance—short for "advance against royalties." This is money paid in advance to a writer (customarily half when the contract is signed for a book and half when the initial draft is accepted) in anticipation of the royalties that the book will earn. Usually, the publisher keeps royalties earned by a work until the advance has been repaid in full, and if this does not happen, then the remainder of the advance is written off by the publisher and needn't be repaid.

antagonist—the character who is working to keep the protagonist from reaching his or her goal.

anticipation—the reader's expectation of an event.

arc (or **"narrative arc"**) - the classic curve of storyline, generally considered to be composed of *exposition, rising action, climax, falling action* and *resolution.*

ARC—"advance reader's copy," a pre-release version of the book that generally represents the first content edit and the copy edit, but may not represent the book as published. The ARC is usually furnished to individuals providing endorsements and to long-lead media so they can review the book in a timely fashion.

Bildungsroman—a type of coming-of-age novel in which the main character usually suffers a loss and then grows and prevails despite (or because of) that loss; *Great Expectations* is often cited as a classic example of a Bildungsroman, and a more modern example is *Harry Potter and the Philosopher's Stone.*

climax—in a narrative arc, that part of the work that comes at the peak of action; the climax is what most of the book build up to.

conflict—the state or action that exists in a story when two characters or elements desire different outcomes; conflict is a necessary element for a narrative to be considered a story.

contagonist—a character that shares the protagonist role.

contract with the reader, the—in nonfiction, the understanding that everything written in the piece is true and can be believed.

e-book—a book published in a format designed to be read on an electronic device.

e-reader—a dedicated device for reading e-books; alternatively, an app that allows a tablet, smartphone or computer to perform the same function. As of this edition, the world's most popular dedicated e-reader is Amazon's Kindle.

exotic setting—a setting with which most readers are apt to be unfamiliar.

exposition—background information necessary to understand the story, usually given near the beginning, often as reminiscence or dialogue.

falling action - in a narrative arc, that portion of the work that comes after the climax, or peak of action.

flat adverb—an adverb that does not end in "ly" ("tight" rather than "tightly" in "sleep tight" is a classic example).

Kindle—the Amazon family of e-book readers (and, as of this writing, the most popular dedicated e-book reader in the world).

major characters—those characters without which the narrative could not proceed.

narrative - the story as told.

narrative tension—the hint (or more than a hint) of anxiety that keeps the reader reading.

narrator—the ostensible storyteller of the work.

Nook—the Barnes & Noble family of e-book readers.

novel—a longer book-length work of fiction (35,000-40,000 words is usually considered the minimum); the novel also usually has numerous subplots and may be told from more than one point of view—two additional attributes that distinguish it from the novella.

novella—a book that is longer than a short story (at least 20,000 words) and shorter than a novel, and lacks the subplot complexity of the novel.

pastiche—a derivative work that imitates and celebrates the work or form of another (usually well-known) writer.

picara - the protagonist in a picaresque novel, if that character is a woman or a girl.

picaresque—an episodic type of novel that is narrated by its roguish protagonist, who is often swept along through the book by forces outside his or her control; *The Adventures of Huckleberry Finn* is a picaresque novel.

picaro - the protagonist in a picaresque novel, if that character is a man or a boy.

plot—the sequence of events that make up the story.

POD - print-on-demand.

point of view (abbr. **POV**)—phrase used to describe who narrates the story, and the amount of awareness that narrator has about the thoughts and actions of the characters in the story.

protagonist—the character encountering the principal conflict in a story: usually the central character, often called the "hero" or "heroine."

royalties– monies paid to the creator of a work, usually as a percentage of the unit price.

reasonable suspension of disbelief—the reader's agreement to enter fully the world of the story—that is, to set aside the fact that he or she is reading something that has been invented, and to follow that story as if it is fact ... provided the writer does nothing to interrupt that state.

resolution—that sort of solution to conflict that readers, by and large, prefer; the puzzle, in effect, is worked out.

rising action—in a narrative arc, that portion of the work that comes before the climax, or peak of action.

Scrivener—British writer Keith Blount's fiction-writing software, available through his company, Literature and Latte.

setting—the place, era and focal "world" of a work of fiction.

short story—a work of fiction less than 20,000 words in length, usually without subplots, and told from a single point of view.

slush reader—the person in an acquisitions department who reads unsolicited manuscripts in order to determine which ones should be read by someone with the authority to act on them.

solution—the action that concludes the conflict; it may be resolution, or it may be dissolution, but either way the conflict is over.

story—generalized term for the subject of a narrative in fiction.

style sheet—a document submitted by a writer along with a manuscript, the purpose of which is to clarify spellings and unusual usages employed in the work.

subplot—the events that make up the story that is secondary to the main plot.

voice—the style in which the narrative is delivered, or in which a writer naturally writes; while "narrative voice" is often used as a synonym for "point of view," most traditional writers distinguish between the two.

Word—Microsoft Word, the world's most popular word-processing application; its .doc or .docx files are the formats in which most editors are accustomed to receiving a manuscript.

| Bibliography

Berry, Steve. *The Amber Room*. New York: Ballentine Books, 2003.

----------.*The Templar Legacy*. New York: Ballentine Books, 2006.

Boykin, William G., and Morrisey, Tom. *Danger Close*. Nashville: Fidelis, 2010.

----------. *Kiloton Threat*. Nashville: Fidelis, 2011.

Brown, Dan. *The Da Vinci Code*. New York: Doubleday, 2003.

Burroughs, Edgar Rice. *A Princess of Mars*. Chicago: A.C. McClurg, 1917.

Carter, Jimmy. *The Hornet's Nest*. New York: Simon & Schuster, 2004

Catton. Bruce. Mr. Lincoln's Army. New York: Doubleday & Company, 1951

Chercover, Sean. *The Trinity Game*. Las Vegas: Thomas & Mercer, 2012.

Dickens, Charles. *A Christmas Carol*. Mineola, New York: Dover Thrift Editions, 1991. Originally published in 1843.

----------, *Great Expectations*. Mineola, New York: Dover Thrift Editions, 2001. Originally published in 1860.

----------, *Oliver Twist*. Mineola, New York: Dover Thrift Editions, 2002. Originally published in 1838.

Doyle, Arthur Conan. *The Adventures of Sherlock Holmes*. New York: Harper, 1892.

Eco, Umberto (translated by William Weaver). *The Name of the Rose*. New York: Houghton Mifflin Harcourt, 1983.

Fitzgerald, F. Scott. *This Side of Paradise*. New York: Charles Scribner's Sons, 1920.

----------. *The Great Gatsby*. New York: Charles Scribner's Sons, 1925.

Fleming, Ian. *Casino Royale*. London: Jonathan Cape, 1953.

----------. *Dr. No*. London: Jonathan Cape, 1958.

----------. *Goldfinger*. London: Jonathan Cape, 1959.

----------. *On Her Majesty's Secret Service*. London: Jonathan Cape, 1963

Fforde, Jasper. *The Eyre Affair*. London: Hodder and Stoughton, 2001.

Franco, James. *Actors Anonymous*. New York: New Harvest (Amazon Publishing), 2013

Harrison, Jim. *Legends of the Fall*. New York: Delta (Random House), 1980.

----------. *The Great Leader*. New York: Grove Press, 2011.

Hemingway, Ernest. *Men Without Women*. New York: Charles Scribner's Sons, 1927.

----------. *The Old Man and the Sea*. New York: Charles Scribner & Sons, 1952.

---------- (edited by William White). *Byline Ernest Hemingway*. New York: Charles Scribner's Sons, 1967.

Henry, O.. *The Gift of the Magic and Other Short Stories*. Mineola, New York: Dover Publications, 1992 (Originally published 1906).

Hiassen, Carl. *Skinny Dip*. New York: Alfred A. Knopf, 2004.

Hugo, Victor (translated by Walter J. Cobb). *The Hunchback of Notre Dame*. New York: Signet Classics, 2010 (Originally published 1831).

Irving, John. *The Cider House Rules*. New York: William Morrow & Co., 1985.

----------. *A Prayer for Owen Meany*. New York: William Morrow & Co., 1989.

----------. *A Widow for One Year*. New York: Random House, 1998.

James, E.L.. *Fifty Shades of Gray*. New York: Vintage Books, 2011.

King, Stephen. *11-22-63*. New York: Scribner, 2011.

Koontz, Dean. *Fear Nothing*. Forest Hill, Maryland: Cemetery Dance Publications, 1997.

Larrson, Stieg (translated by Reg Keeland). *The Girl Who Kicked the Hornets' Nest*. New York: Vintage Books (Random House), 2010.

----------. *The Girl Who Played with Fire*. New York: Vintage Books (Random House), 2009.

----------. *The Girl with the Dragon Tattoo*. New York: Vintage Books (Random House), 2008.

Lehane, Dennis. *Live by Night*. New York: William Morrow, 2012.

London, Jack. *The Call of the Wild, White Fang & to Build a Fire*. New York: Modern Library, 2002. "To Build a Fire" (second version) originally published in 1908.

Martel, Yann. *Life of Pi*. Toronto: Random House of Canada, 2001.

McInerney, Jay. *Bright Lights, Big City*. New York: Vintage Books, 1984.

McLarty, Ron. *The Memory of Running*. New York: Penguin Books, 2005.

Melville, Herman. *Moby-Dick; or, The Whale*. New York: Harper & Bros., 1851.

Michener, James. *Hawaii*. New York: Random House, 1959.

----------. *The Source*. New York: Random House, 1965.

Mitchell, Margaret. *Gone with the Wind*. New York: MacMillan Publishing, 1936.

Morrisey, Tom. *20 American Peaks & Crags*. Chicago: Contemporary Books, 1978.

----------. *Dark Fathom*. Grand Rapids: Zondervan (Harper-Collins), 2005.

----------. *Deep Blue*. Grand Rapids: Zondervan (Harper-Collins), 2004.

----------. *In High Places*. Minneapolis: Bethany House, 2007.

----------. *Pirate Hunter*. Minneapolis, Bethany House, 2009.

----------. *Turn Four*. Grand Rapids: Zondervan (Harper-Collins), 2004.

----------. *Wild by Nature*. Ada, Michigan: Baker Books, 2001

----------. *Wind River*. Minneapolis: Bethany House, 2008.

----------. *Yucatan Deep*. Grand Rapids: Zondervan (Harper-Collins), 2002.

Niffenegger, Audrey. *Her Fearful Symmetry*. New York: Simon & Schuster, 2009.

----------, *The Time Traveler's Wife*. San Francisco: MacAdam/Cage, 2003.

Oxford English Dictionary, The (2nd Edition), Oxford: Oxford University Press, 1989.

Phillips, Larry W. (Ed.). *Ernest Hemingway on Writing*. New York: Touchstone, 1984.

Plimpton, George. "Ernest Hemingway, The Art of Fiction No. 21." *The Paris Review* Spring 1958. Online

Rowling, J.K.. *Harry Potter and the Philosopher's Stone*. London: Bloomsbury, 1997.

Salinger, J.D.. *The Catcher in the Rye*. New York: Little, Brown & Company, 1951.

Süskind, Patrick (translated by John E. Woods). *Perfume: The Story of a Murderer*. New York: Alfred A. Knopf, 1985.

Tolstoy, Leo (translated by Richard Peaver). *Anna Karenina*. New York: Penguin Classics, 2004 (Originally published, 1978).

Toole, John Kennedy. *A Confederacy of Dunces*. Baton Rouge: Louisiana State University Press, 1980.

Twain, Mark. *The Adventures of Tom Sawyer*. Chicago: American Publishing Company, 1876.

| BOOKS by Tom Morrisey

Novels

Yucatan Deep

Turn Four

Deep Blue

Dark Fathom

In High Places

Wind River

Pirate Hunter

Novels with Lt. Gen. William G Boykin (USA-Ret.)

Danger Close

Kiloton Threat

Nonfiction

20 American Peaks and Crags

Wild by Nature

| ABOUT Tom Morrisey

TOM MORRISEY is the author or co-author of nine novels, all published by conventional, advance- and royalty-paying publishing houses, as well as two books of nonfiction and a variety of short stories. He is also an award-winning and world-renowned adventure-travel writer whose work has appeared in *Outside*, *Off Belay*, *Scuba Times* (where he was editor of the *Advanced Diving Journal* section), *Skin Diver*, *Sport Diver* (where he served as Executive Editor) and other leading national and international magazines.

Tom lectures widely on the craft of fiction and is a frequent workshop leader at writing conferences throughout North America.

He earned his MA in English from the University of Toledo, and his MFA in Creative Writing from Bowling Green State University. Tom lives with his wife, their daughter and an exceptionally spoiled dog (successor to the one mentioned in Chapter Ten) in Belle Isle, Florida.

Website: http://www.tommorrisey.com
Blog: http://tinyurl.com/novelandnovelist
Facebook: Tom Morrisey Novels
Twitter: @MorriseyWriting

THANK YOU for Reading

I deeply appreciate,
and never take for granted,
the time you have invested
in reading my work;
I hope that it has been
not only useful to you,
but enjoyable.

If you'd care to write,
my email address is
tom@tommorrisey.com.

While my work schedule
often precludes replies,
rest assured that I read
every piece of reader mail
that I receive.

Blessings abundant
on you and yours,

Tom Morrisey

TOM MORRISEY Novels Quoted in this Work

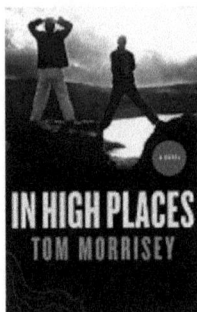

In High Places

"*In High Places* is my personal pick for best book of the year."
—*Christian Review of Books*

A finalist for the 2007 Christy Award.

Pirate Hunter

"The novel is well researched, and the characters are believable. This is not your rip-snorting, bodice-ripping pirate story, but a well-written tale of sin and forgiveness. Highly recommended."
—*Historical Novels Review*

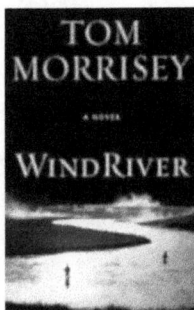

Wind River

"The unspoiled landscapes really come alive with cinematic clarity as Morrisey creates beautiful motion-picture scenes with his words." —Mary Fairchild, *About.com*

All titles available through booksellers or on all major ebook platforms.

www.ingramcontent.com/pod-product-compliance
Lightning Source LLC
Chambersburg PA
CBHW061817040426
42447CB00012B/2692